A History of the British Army

Sir John William Fortescue

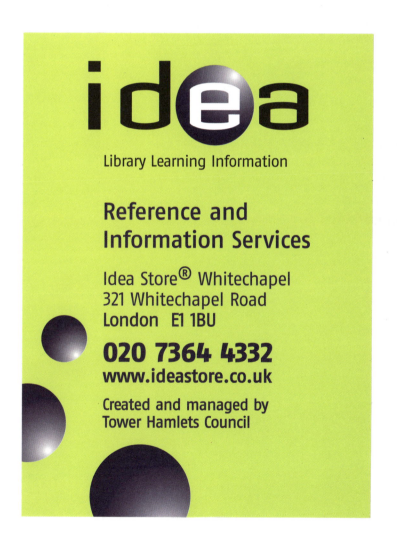

History of

A History of
The British Army

BY

THE HON. J. W. FORTESCUE

*SECOND PART CONTINUED—FROM THE FALL OF THE BASTILLE
TO THE PEACE OF AMIENS*

VOL. IV—PART II

1789–1801

Quæ caret ora cruore nostro

London

MACMILLAN AND CO., LIMITED

NEW YORK: THE MACMILLAN COMPANY

1906

Printed by R. & R. CLARK, LIMITED, *Edinburgh.*

CONTENTS

BOOK XII

CHAPTER XXII

THE MEDITERRANEAN

v

CHAPTER XXIII

The Expedition to North Holland

CHAPTER XXIV

THE EXPEDITION TO NORTH HOLLAND

CHAPTER XXV

THE EAST INDIES

CONTENTS

ix

CHAPTER XXVI

THE EAST INDIES

CHAPTER XXVIII

The Mediterranean

THE EXPEDITION TO EGYPT

CHAPTER XXIX

THE CAMPAIGN IN EGYPT

CHAPTER XXX

REVIEW OF THE PROGRESS OF THE ARMY FROM 1793-1802

CONTENTS

APPENDICES

MAPS AND PLANS

(In a Separate Case)

CAMPAIGN OF THE NETHERLANDS, 1793-1795

CAMPAIGN OF THE MEDITERRANEAN, 1793-1795

CAMPAIGNS OF THE WEST INDIES,[1] 1793-1798

Leeward Sphere

Windward Sphere

---

[1] For general map of the West Indies see Volume III.

ABBREVIATIONS USED IN REFERENCE TO THE ARCHIVES PRESERVED IN THE RECORD OFFICE

B.G.O. = Minutes of the Board of General Officers.
C.C.L.B. = Commander-in-chief's Letter Books.
H.O.M.E.B. = Home Office Military Entry Books.
S.C.L.B. = The Letter Books of the Secretary at War, known as the
    "Secretary's Common Letter Books."

CHAPTER XXII

THE chief interest of our history during the years 1798.
that lie before us, until the Peace of Amiens, centres
wholly in the Mediterranean. We have done with
the false and mistaken offensive operations in the
West Indies ; we have done with seizure of Dutch
Colonies ; we have done, at any rate for the present,
with Irish rebellions and with French projects of
invasion, of which last the battle of Camperdown
and Bonaparte's expedition to Egypt had been made a
final end.

The fleet had been moved from the Irish coast
to the Mediterranean in the full belief that Bonaparte's
armament at Toulon was designed for an attack upon
the British Isles ; and its object was therefore in
strictness defensive. Ireland in 1797 and 1798 might
be regarded as a city besieged by the British land-
forces, and the British fleet as the covering army
which kept the French at a distance while the siege
progressed. As has already been seen in Flanders,
a covering army may take the offensive temporarily
to parry a blow which is designed to interrupt a
siege ; and such counter-attacks, as, for instance, that
of Villers-en-Cauchies, may be brilliantly successful.
None the less, their success must as a rule be limited,
because they cannot be followed up ; a covering army
being, in its essence, a stationary army. But the
British Government contemplated no such limited
offensive mission as this for Nelson's squadron ; for,
as Portland wrote to Camden, the reappearance of

1798. the British fleet in the Mediterranean offered the only chance of rescuing Italy and bringing about a durable peace. Now, for such an object, it is clear that a fleet in itself was insufficient. It might meet Bonaparte's armament at sea and destroy it, or drive it back to port and hold it blockaded ; or, as actually happened, it might overtake it after its land-forces had been disembarked at their appointed destination, destroy the ships upon which depended their communication with France, and leave the troops stranded. In either of these cases the sea would be cleared of the French fleet, and this, apart from the moral effect of a victory, would be a great point gained ; but in itself it could do nothing, though it might pave the way for much, towards the salvation of Italy and the establishment of a lasting peace. It is useless for artillery to batter a breach unless there is infantry ready to rush into it ; and equally it is useless for a fleet to clear the sea for an offensive movement unless an army is ready to follow it.

Now, even if the Ministers had reflected upon this matter, which I think it certain that they had not, they possessed no army of their own to second Nelson's fleet. It was the nemesis for their wasteful squandering of troops upon secondary objects that, when a primary object at last commended itself to them, they could not find a battalion to their hand. The army had been destroyed by the end of 1794, and had never been reconstructed. Recruits had indeed been gathered from all sides, grouped together under the numbers of the old regiments, and hurried out to the West Indies to be buried ; but that was all, and it was worse than nothing. The English Militia was really the only sound force left. The gross mismanagement of 1794, and the awful sacrifice of life in the Caribbean Islands, had dried up the ordinary sources of recruits. In April 1798 when Camden, at Dublin, was crying out for reinforcements, Portland could only answer that none

could be sent from Great Britain, owing to great 1798.
disappointments in the recruiting service. In Ireland
the case was the same. Eight skeleton regiments
were there kept permanently open, in order to
collect men and draft them into the older corps,
but the whole of the eight did not possess above
sixteen hundred men between them.[1] Voluntary
service, even when propped by levies from parish to
parish, had broken down completely. The Government was just able, with great difficulty, to maintain
its garrisons over sea ; but it was absolutely beyond
its power to produce a striking force.

One small body of men, however, which has been
for some time withdrawn from our ken, must now
be recalled to notice. It will be remembered that
it was the declaration of war by Spain against England that had caused Pitt to withdraw the fleet
from the Mediterranean, and to evacuate Corsica
in the autumn of 1796. Immediately afterwards
Spain, under the influence of the French Directory,
threatened Portugal with invasion in order to compel
her to close her ports to the British ; and Portugal
appealed to England for help. Thereupon, the Government decided to send at once five thousand men to
Lisbon under General Charles Stuart, with instructions
to place himself under the command of the Portuguese
Commander-in-chief, and to act in concert with him
whether for the offensive or the defensive.[2] Dundas's
idea appears to have been to transfer the garrison,
which had lately been removed from Corsica to
Elba, at once to Lisbon; but it has already been
explained how, through the blunders of the War
Office, the troops were kept at Porto Ferrajo until
April 1797. However, in due time they arrived at
Gibraltar, and after a month's delay reached the 1797.
Tagus on the 21st of June, where Stuart was waiting June 21.
to receive them. The British regiments, namely,

[1] Portland to Camden, 4th April 1798.
[2] Dundas to C. Stuart, 3rd December 1796.

1797. the second battalion of the Royal Scots, the Fiftieth, and Fifty-first Foot and the Twelfth Light Dragoons, had been with him in Corsica, where the three first had served him brilliantly at Calvi ; but since that time they had received few recruits from England to fill the gaps made by active service, and were consequently very weak. The remainder of the force was made up of foreign regiments, of which the Duke of Mortemar's, the Duke of Castries's, the Loyal Emigrants, and some artillery were composed chiefly of French refugees ; two battalions of Dillon's regiment, which should have been Irish, seem also to have been French ; another regiment, De Roll's, was Swiss, and another detachment of artillery was Maltese. The numbers of the whole were approximately two thousand British and four thousand foreigners.

Stuart's first impression of this motley assemblage was not favourable. " I never in the course of my service saw two regiments more disgraceful to the British name than Roll and Dillon," he wrote ; and they did not improve on acquaintance. The French regiments had been encouraged by Ministers in the first enthusiasm of compassion for the Emigrants ; but in this case, as in so many others, the outcast French noble showed himself absolutely unworthy of pity or confidence. The officers seemed to regard it as an honour to England that they should receive her money and give her no service for it. They were to the last degree lazy and insubordinate. They corresponded secretly with their friends in France to make their peace with the Directory, no matter at what prejudice to the British, whom they professed to serve ; and they corresponded with their friends in England to gain favours, procure the perpetration of jobs, and generally to obtain for themselves ease, comfort, and independence in defiance of the General. Nor did they lack the support which they craved in Downing Street. The capitulations, upon which the corps had been raised, being vague, various, and founded

upon no uniform system, gave an excellent oppor- 1797.
tunity for every kind of abuse; and there seems to
have been no agreement among the British Ministers
as to the department which was in charge of foreign
regiments. The officers, as Stuart complained, were
promoted on one day and reduced on the next.
If he suspended any of them for misconduct, the
next mail brought an intimation from the Duke of
Portland's office that the Government would relieve
them of their punishment; and this although Dundas
had declared that all matters of discipline were in
the province of the Commander-in-chief. Nevertheless, despite all these impediments, Stuart contrived by a mixture of sternness and tact to train these
regiments to efficiency, and to make them live in
harmony with the British. He had no mercy on
the French officers who strove to make the drawing
of their pay their only military function, nor with
certain exalted privates called the *Chasseurs Nobles*
of Castries's corps, who refused either to wear their
uniform or do their duty; and his methodical administration, his vigilance in checking malpractices, and
his careful economy of public money were a lesson
to the careless unintelligence of the departments in
England.

In other respects besides discipline Stuart's difficulties were very great. His instructions bade him
place himself under the orders of the Portuguese
Commander-in-chief; but in the chaotic state of
Portugal there were at least three, if not more,
commanders-in-chief, namely, the Prince of Waldeck,
who had been called in from abroad to take up the
appointment; the Duke de la Foens, a Portuguese
Field-Marshal who refused to yield it up to him,
and the Marquis de la Rozière, a Frenchman, who
worked independently of both. A further complication was that it was doubtful whether the
Portuguese would fight or yield, whether the Spaniards
would attack them or refrain, whether the Court

1797. of Lisbon would give way to the French, and, if so, upon what terms the French would accept its submission.

Bewildered by the constant changes in the situation in Portugal, and being really very far from clear as to the duty which Stuart's force was actually expected to fulfil, Dundas wrote instruction after instruction, until he entangled himself in a maze of contradictory orders. Stuart, who always addressed him as if he and not the Minister were master, lost all patience. "I am determined to be guided by your instructions so long as they are within the reach of my comprehension," was the caustic prelude to one of his letters ; but, in truth, he was very well able to take care of himself. Without any instructions whatever, he had from the first made his dispositions so as to turn his troops into efficient soldiers, defend Lisbon, command the Tagus, and keep his communications open for an immediate embarkation if necessary. At the same time he carefully cultivated the friendship of the people, though he was fully determined, if the Portuguese should turn against him, not to repeat the disastrous experiment of Toulon. He knew better than to try to hold a single point in a foreign country against the armed force of a whole nation ; and he warned the Government by the examples both of Toulon and of America not again to embark on so fatal a policy. Meanwhile, his relations with Lord St. Vincent were perfectly harmonious, for the great Admiral recognised a good soldier when he met one, and was not a little impressed by Stuart's ability. It would not be too much to say that these two men possessed the highest strategic talent then to be found in the British Isles.[1]

Thus matters dragged on for a whole year ; and, notwithstanding frequent alarms of French and Spanish

[1] See Stuart's correspondence with Dundas in *W.O. Original Correspondence*. Portugal. 2nd July 1797 to 13th June 1798.

invasion and of the closing of Portuguese ports to 1798.
British ships, this little body of troops still remained
round Lisbon, and the harbour still lay open to the
British Navy. On the 13th of June 1798 Stuart left
Lisbon for England ; and in a letter of the 5th
Dundas ordered his successor, Major-general Fraser,
to maintain his predecessor's arrangements for embarkation at a moment's notice, in case the troops
should be required at home (whereby he really meant
in Ireland) or elsewhere. On the 26th Stuart arrived June 26.
in London, bringing with him a return of his force ;
and on the same day Dundas wrote to Fraser to hold
his three British battalions in readiness to embark for
India. News had come from Calcutta that two powerful native princes intended to combine with the French
in attacking the British East Indian possessions ; and
the rebellion in Ireland forbade any troops to be spared
for India except those in Portugal. Here therefore
was the main strength of the little force at Lisbon
engaged to service in the East, and lost to the
Mediterranean.[1]

This news from India gave something of a clue to
the destination of Bonaparte, which, owing to Grenville's
mistrust of his intelligence, was still a mystery to the
British ; but it is extremely doubtful whether that clue
was grasped in London. Nevertheless, since the danger
of an invasion of Portugal seemed to have passed away,
Dundas at that very moment proposed a supplementary
measure of aggression by inquiring of St. Vincent
whether the British forces in Lisbon and Gibraltar
were adequate for the capture of Minorca and the
destruction of Carthagena. At first sight it might
seem as though the Ministry had begun to com-
prehend the wide opportunities offered by a vigorous
offensive in the Mediterranean ; but this would, I
think, be an erroneous conclusion. The seizure of
Minorca, which meant really the mastery of Port

[1] Stuart to Dundas, 26th June ; Dundas to Fraser, 5th and 26th
June 1798.

1798. Mahon, was simply the first indication of a new policy of raids upon Spanish ports, whereon a vast deal of useless energy was to be expended during the next three years ; and Carthagena was designated as the first of those ports because it was that from which any expedition for the recapture of Minorca would certainly be fitted out. But the object of such raids could only be greater security for the British isles against invasion, and better assured supremacy of the British on the sea. In fact they were purely negative and defensive measures, which could have no decisive effect towards the conclusion of the war unless followed up by offensive operations on land.

St. Vincent answered without hesitation that the capture of Minorca would be a simple matter, and added, rather boldly, that the force proposed would be sufficient for the destruction of Carthagena. Moreover, he opined that the attack upon Minorca might proceed at once, without waiting for the result of Nelson's search for the French fleet ; though he warned Dundas that the island, however easily taken, could only be maintained by the constant presence of a squadron. But, above all, he pressed for the return of Stuart to take command of the troops, with an earnestness which amounted almost to refusal to undertake the enterprise on any other terms. "The loss of General Charles Stuart, whom I believe to be the best General that you have, is not to be repaired," he wrote. . . . "The more I reflect on the services expected of the troops, the more important I think it for him to be at their head. No one can manage Frenchmen as well as him, and the British will go to hell for him." The great Admiral's grammar was faulty ; but his meaning was sufficiently plain. Minorca in Stuart's hands might be turned to great purpose ; in the hands of any other it would probably be only an encumbrance to the fleet. We can only marvel that, since Stuart was actually in London, Dundas should not have con-

sulted him, particularly concerning the attack on Cartha-   1798.
gena, before writing to St. Vincent.[1]

Meanwhile Nelson's cruise in search of the French
fleet had been strangely unlucky. Bonaparte after
leaving Toulon on the 19th of May had been joined May 19.
at sea on the 26th and 28th by the convoys from
Corsica and Civita Vecchia. On the 9th of June he June 9.
reached Malta, which, after a faint show of resistance,
capitulated on the 12th. Leaving a garrison of four June 12.
thousand men to hold it, he sailed again on the 19th June 19.
for Egypt by the circuitous route of the coast of Crete;
and thus it was that Nelson, who could only guess at
his destination, arrived off Alexandria before him on
the 28th. The impetuous sailor finding, as was June 28.
natural, neither sign nor intelligence of the French,
sailed away somewhat hastily on the 29th to seek them June 29.
elsewhere. Three days later the entire French arma- July 1.
ment arrived likewise before Alexandria; and Bonaparte, who had already learned that Nelson was in
pursuit of him, began at once to disembark his troops
with all possible haste. With his subsequent operations we are not concerned. It must suffice to say
that after a brief campaign, similar to many fought by
the British in India, he entered Cairo on the 25th of
July, and left it again on the 7th of August to complete the conquest of Lower Egypt. But meanwhile
Nelson had returned to Syracuse on the 19th of July,
and, having satisfied himself that the French were not
to westward, sailed again on the 24th for Alexandria.   July 24.

A week later, on the first of August, he surprised Aug. 1.
the French fleet at anchor in Aboukir Bay. There is
no need to retell the story of the battle of the Nile,
one of the greatest naval victories of all time. It is
necessary for our purpose only to record that the
French fleet was practically annihilated, eleven out of

---

[1] St. Vincent to Dundas, 3rd and 5th July 1798. Dundas's
letter, to which these are written in reply, I have been unable
to discover, but the sense of it may be gathered from St. Vincent's
answer.

1798. thirteen ships of the line and two out of four frigates being taken or destroyed. The blow was crushing; and Bonaparte, though he met it with a firmness and constancy which restored the drooping spirits of his army, realised its severity to the full. He and his force were prisoners in Egypt; and there was no great confidence in the words which he wrote to

Aug. 21. Kléber a few days after receipt of the fatal news: "If the English relieve this squadron by another, and continue to flood the Mediterranean, they may oblige us to do greater things than we wished." From such a man there could hardly be franker avowal of blunder and miscalculation.[1]

Here therefore was a great and famous success achieved by the British fleet. The next question was how it should be followed up; though it must be remembered that the news of the victory did not reach Naples before the 4th of September nor London until the 2nd of October. Nelson himself, though severely wounded in the head, lost no time in repairing his own and the French ships after the action; and on the 14th of August six prizes and seven British ships

Aug. 15. of the line sailed for Gibraltar. On the following day urgent orders reached him from St. Vincent to return to the westward with his fleet for an attack upon Minorca. Accordingly, leaving Captain Hood with three ships of the line and as many frigates to blockade Alexandria and to interrupt the communications of the French on the coast of Egypt and Syria, he sailed on

Aug. 19. the 19th with his three remaining vessels for Naples. The attack on Minorca was, however, in spite of St. Vincent's orders, not to take place for some months; for, though Dundas wisely appointed Stuart to command the expedition, the latter did not receive his instructions until the 29th of August nor leave England until some days later. But in any case Nelson's three ships were so much crippled that they were bound to remain in Naples for some time to refit, and in the meanwhile

[1] *Correspondence de Napoléon*, iv. 369.

he could do no more than take measures for the
blockade of Malta by Portuguese and British ships.
On the 22nd of September he finally arrived at Naples,
where his influence, subjected to other influences, was
destined to produce such fateful results.

At this point it will be convenient to summarise
the events that had passed in Europe since Bonaparte
had initiated his schemes of aggression on the Continent
at the beginning of the year 1798. Switzerland, in spite
of a gallant resistance on the part of the old Cantons,
had been forced by French bayonets to reconstitute
herself as the Helvetian Republic; but France still
refused to withdraw her troops or to recognise the
ancient Swiss neutrality. Indeed Talleyrand said
openly that only an offensive alliance would satisfy
the Directory or deliver the country from new
pecuniary exactions. The confiscation of ecclesiastical
property roused the religious feeling alike of the clergy
and of the people; and a trifling cause brought about
a savage fanatical rising in Schwytz, Unterwalden, and
Niederwalden, which was only suppressed by the French
with difficulty and heavy loss of men.

In Italy the Cisalpine, Roman, and Ligurian Republics were one and all ripe for revolt, owing to the
system of pillage and robbery carried on by the Agents
of the Directory. In Piedmont again the French had
intervened to prevent the Sardinian Government from
repressing an insurrection, and Brune had since the
28th of May taken military possession of Turin. The
next victim was Naples, from which the Directory
extorted by threats a large contribution and an annual
tribute, besides insisting on the dismissal of the chief
minister, the Englishman Acton. By yielding to these
wrongs the miserable King Ferdinand hoped that he
had purchased peace; but his Queen, Caroline, a sister
of Marie Antoinette, was of a less submissive nature,
and her spirit of resistance was quickened by the
appointment of a regicide as French ambassador at
Naples. Resenting this insult, she caused troops to

1798. be raised, and persuaded Austria to conclude on the 19th of May a defensive alliance with the kindom of the Two Sicilies. These measures, however, brought no relief from the heavy hand of France. Revolutionary agents from the Roman Republic continued to make mischief in the Neapolitàn dominions, and the Directory took the Court of Naples to task for allowing Nelson to use the port of Syracuse while on his search for the French fleet. At last, in August, King Ferdinand wrote to the Emperor Francis that the situation had become intolerable, and that the only chance of successful resistance was to anticipate the enemy in attack ; to which end he requested the services of General Mack to command the Neapolitan troops. In answer, Thugut at once consented to send Mack, being glad to be rid of him ; and he added that though the defensive alliance lately concluded was not binding on Austria if Naples should take the offensive, still in the circumstances the Emperor would support King Ferdinand without looking too closely to the letter of the treaty.

This was a great concession from Thugut, who, though long since seriously alarmed at the Directory's proceedings in Italy, had felt constrained to walk warily. Without an ally and without money he dared not break with France ; and England would not hear of any further dealing with him unless he consented to sign a treaty, already rejected by him, for repayment of a former loan. Pitt and Grenville had not forgotten the occurrences of 1794, and were in no mood to supply Austria with millions to spend upon her own aggrandisement without thought of the common cause. The only alternative ally was Russia ; and the Tsar Paul was not too friendly to Austria, because he had failed in an attempt to reconcile her with Prussia. The poor half-crazy creature had, during Catherine's life, been kept under so strict restraint that the sudden change from impotence to omnipotence had turned his head ; and, when Austria and Prussia had refused to

become friends at his bidding, his indignation against 1798.
both parties was boundless.   Bonaparte's capture of
Malta, however, was an insult which swallowed up all
others, for Paul had set his heart upon obtaining that
island for Russia as a base for future operations against
Turkey.   So intense was his animosity towards France
after this occurrence that, on the 16th of July, he July 16.
decided definitely to employ an army of sixty thousand
men against her, to be paid either by Austria or by
England.   Moreover, a few days later, he ordered his July 25.
fleet in the Black Sea to proceed to Constantinople and
to offer its services to the Sultan in any operations that
the attack upon Egypt might move him to undertake
against France.   The Porte was nothing loth, for
Bonaparte's designs to avert its hostility by diplomatic
means, whatever they may have been, had miscarried;
and his unprovoked attack upon the Sultan's dominions
was deeply resented.   Accordingly, on the 1st of
September, the Sultan proclaimed a holy war, in concert with Russia, against France.   Thus Russia was
at last definitely drawn into the great contest against
the Revolution.

Next, let us look for a moment at France itself,
where the consequences of six long years of folly,
rascality, and misrule were making themselves felt with
increasing intensity.   Since the dissolution of the
Constituent Assembly, practically nothing had been
done towards the re-establishment of internal order
and the restoration of good government.   All over
the country roads, bridges, and canals were going or
gone to ruin from want of ordinary repairs, while an
alarming prevalence of highway robbery and brigandage
bore witness to the absence of all internal police.   The
people at large were sunk into a dull and apathetic
despair, waiting against hope for the peace that never
came.   The plunder of her neighbours had enabled
France, by extraordinary exertions, to struggle on so
far, but even that resource was, by bad husbandry,
nearly exhausted.   Moreover, the process of pillage

1798. had been fertile in demoralisation to all concerned, from the Directors down to the private soldiers, though, of course, those that were highest in authority and lowest in merit had gained most profit, while many of those that had borne the burden and heat of the day had gone away empty.   The finances of the country were in such appalling disorder that honest men found themselves powerless to check the frauds of contractors ; while the rapacity even of able generals, such as Masséna, and the low greed of such ruffians as Brune, set the worst possible example to all ranks of the army. Discipline was very seriously relaxed, and the officers of every grade dangerously insubordinate.   The men, unclothed, unfed, and unpaid, were sick of war. Desertion had attained to formidable proportions. Voluntary recruits were not to be obtained.   The twelve hundred thousand men called out under the decree of 1793 had been exhausted ; and the Directory was afraid to raise new levies by compulsion.   France had barely one hundred and fifty thousand soldiers at her disposal, of whom ten thousand were in Holland, twenty-five thousand in Switzerland, forty thousand on the Rhine, and seventy thousand in the Cisalpine and Roman Republics, all of them scattered among strange nations, whom oppression and plunder had goaded into formidable discontent.

Such was the situation when Nelson returned to Naples, and brought to a chafing and oppressed Continent the news of the battle of the Nile.   His reception in the city itself was enthusiastic beyond description, for the fleet at Toulon had long been the dread of the Neapolitans ; and the fame of Bonaparte was swallowed up in that of the sailor who had wrecked his enterprise in the East.   But this would have been a small matter had not there been added to the acclamations of the populace the adulation of two women, Queen Caroline and the wife of the British Ambassador, the celebrated Lady Hamilton.   It is hardly surprising that Nelson's head should have been turned by the flattery of this

pair.   He was but a poor parson's son who had 1798.
lived a life of laborious hardship at sea, and was a
stranger to the ways of Courts.   He was a man of
strong passions and emotional temperament, with a
very large share of vanity ; and lastly, he was suffering
from the effects of a severe wound in the head, and
from the reaction following upon feverish anxiety during
his long quest of the French fleet.   Returning exhausted
in body and mind, he found himself the idol of a
comely, clever, and unprincipled woman, whose early
profession had trained her to the seduction of men,
and whose lust of notoriety could not but stimulate
her to appropriate to herself the hero of the hour.   She
had the advantage also of acting as Nelson's nurse,
the position which sets woman at her strongest in
ascendency over man at his weakest ; and to natural
attention and tenderness in this congenial task she
could add an enthusiastic adoration which was unfortunately only too acceptable to the overwrought sailor.
Through her, too, Nelson gained closer access to a
woman of a type unknown to him, to the daughter of
Maria Theresa, with all her pride of race and station,
high and imperious courage, quick insight and head-
strong impetuosity.   She had long since taken the
direction of affairs from the hands of the feeble and
incapable Ferdinand into her own ; and this was in
itself sufficient to attract a man of Nelson's energy and
activity, and to blind him to her shallowness and
unwisdom.   Nor can the Queen be blamed if she
welcomed this British Admiral, with the scarred face
and mutilated arm, as the man of action long awaited
and arrived at last, who loathed Jacobins upon principle
as fanatically as she hated them for the murder of her
sister, and whose eternal cry was " Down with the
French."

Nelson, though full of ardour to reap the fruits of
his great victory in good time, was painfully aware that
he possessed no resources for the task.   An energetic
General with a thoroughly efficient army was needed,

1798. and the British Government had no troops ready. There was, indeed, the Neapolitan army, whatever it might be worth, and Mack was on his way to Naples to take command of it; but there was still a question whether it was advisable to launch a force, of which so little was known, against the French veterans, few though they were, in the Roman Republic. The Queen was ardently in favour of the movement; but the King, who shrank from trouble of any kind, hung back in timidity and hesitation. All turned really upon the assistance to be given by Austria, and Thugut's last assurances seemed to promise that this would not be

Oct. wanting. On the 9th of October Mack appeared and gave Nelson to understand that, if Naples took the

Oct. 15. offensive, Austria would support her; and a week later Nelson, apparently satisfied that Mack would open the campaign within a fortnight, sailed away to supervise the blockade of Malta.

Nov. 5. Returning to Naples on the 5th of November, however, he found that the General had not yet

Nov. 13. marched; and on the 13th a courier arrived from Vienna with the intimation that Austria would give no help to Naples unless France were the aggressor. The truth was that Thugut was jealous of the lead that England had taken in Europe, irritated that Naples should presume to act on her own initiative, and, above all, annoyed that the Neapolitan Court should have agreed, as lately she had, to make no peace with France without England's consent. Such a covenant, he declared, would make Austria dependent on England in any future negotiations; and, though Sir Morton Eden and the Neapolitan ambassador protested furiously against this renunciation of his former promise, he declined altogether to give way. This discouragement threw back the Court of Naples into agonising doubt; and only the rude intervention of Nelson brought it to a decision. Mack, after inspecting the Neapolitan troops, declared them to be the finest in Europe, in which estimate

Nelson, so far as his knowledge went, was disposed to 1798.
agree ; and the Admiral bluntly told King Ferdinand
that the only alternative to a bold advance was to
"stay quiet and be kicked out of his kingdom." Still
Mack hesitated, until on the 23rd came false news that Nov. 23.
the Austrians had come to blows with the French in
the Grisons ; whereupon, on the 24th, he marched upon Nov. 24.
Rome, while Nelson embarked four thousand men and
sent them with three men-of-war to capture Leghorn.
Despite all his eagerness for Mack to advance, the
Admiral recollected what had happened at Toulon, and
mistrusted the issue ; and he proved to be right.[1] Within
a month the thirty thousand finest troops in the world
had been scattered to the winds by fifteen thousand
French under General Championnet, almost without
the firing of a shot.   On the 22nd of December the Dec. 22.
Court of Naples fled to Palermo on board Nelson's
squadron ; on the 23rd of January 1799 the city
surrendered, after a brave but futile resistance by the
lazzaroni ; and the dominion of King Ferdinand incon-
tinently became the Parthenopœan Republic.

Nelson has been much blamed, and not unreasonably, for the precipitation with which he hurried Naples
into war ; yet it may be questioned whether, looking
to Mack's eulogy of the Neapolitan army, he was not
justified in taking the risk.   It was all important to
follow up the victory of the Nile while its moral effect
was at its highest ; and there was always the chance
that some initial success might encourage Austria to
immediate action.   Switzerland was only waiting to be
rallied in a solid phalanx under the Emperor's banners
against the French ; and though Austria might not yet
be fully equipped for war, it was certain that France
was still more unready and in yet sorer need of time
for preparation.   The person chiefly to blame was
Thugut, for the jealousy and hesitation which led him
to neglect so favourable an opportunity..

Meanwhile, however, Stuart had arrived at Lisbon Sept. 18.

[1] Nelson's *Despatches*, iii. 170, 184-185.

1798. and completed his preparations with all secrecy for the attack on Minorca. The first instructions as to the despatch of the troops to India had been altered, and a single regiment only, the Fifty-first, had been sent upon that service. He was therefore able to withdraw the Twenty-eighth, Forty-second, Fifty-eighth and Ninetieth regiments from Gibraltar, and finally embarked

Oct. with them at the end of October. A sloop was sent forward to cruise off Point Mahon for intelligence, but returned without having made any discovery of importance ; and Stuart then decided at all risks to hazard

Nov. 7. a disembarkation. Accordingly on the 7th of November the fleet made for the north coast of the island ; the line-of-battleships standing in towards the port of Fornells to make a diversion, while the transports sailed a little further to the east and dropped anchor in Adaya Bay. As the armament approached the shore, signals were seen flying in all directions ; and it was evident that, though Stuart had most carefully kept his destination secret, his coming was no surprise to the Spaniards. Indeed the General subsequently ascertained that the authorities at Minorca had been warned of his project quite five weeks before his arrival, doubtless owing to the usual leakage from Dundas's office.

However, the boats were at once hoisted out, whereupon the enemy blew up a small battery at the entrance to the bay and retired. Eight hundred British soldiers were soon landed, but were almost immediately threatened by some two thousand Spanish troops from different directions. Aided, however, by the fire of a British frigate, they held their own until the rest of the force had been disembarked, when the enemy at nightfall retired. Nearly one hundred deserters had already come in from a Swiss regiment which formed part of the Spanish garrison, but they could give no intelligence as to the enemy's movements, though they stated his strength to be four thousand men. Stuart was at a loss to know how to proceed. The country was rugged, mountainous, and

easily defensible, and the roads so bad that any move- 1798.
ment was extremely difficult.   But there were at least
two certain facts, namely, that the principal strongholds
of the enemy, Mahon and Ciudadella, were at opposite
extremities of the island, and that by the occupation of
Mercadal, an elevated pass in its centre, the communication between them could be cut off.   The General Nov. 8.
therefore sent Colonel Thomas Graham with six
hundred men to seize this important point, who by
great exertions reached it very shortly after the main
body of the enemy had traversed it on the way to
Ciudadella.   Several Spanish officers and soldiers were
taken prisoners and some small magazines captured;
and on the following day Stuart brought up his main Nov. 9
body to the same spot, two hundred and fifty blue-
jackets helping, with the usual zeal of their service, to
drag the battalion-guns.

Ascertaining that Mahon had been nearly evacuated
by the enemy, Stuart detached Colonel Paget with three
hundred men to the town, where the garrison of one hundred and sixty men at once surrendered.   Thereby the
harbour was opened to the British fleet, several Spanish
stragglers were captured, and a good number of animals
obtained for the transport of the army.   Intelligence
was then brought in that the enemy's troops were
entrenching themselves at Ciudadella, whereupon Stuart
recalled Paget and two hundred of his men from Mahon
and resolved to carry the entrenched position on the
night of the 13th.   The roads leading to Ciudadella
were two, the northern or old Spanish road, and the
southern, known by the name of a former English
Governor as Kane's road.   A detachment under Colonel
Moncrieff was at once sent forward to Ferrerias to
secure this latter line; and the main body, reinforced
by ninety marines and six light guns from the fleet,
was about to march along the northern road when
news came that four Spanish ships of war were in sight
to westward, evidently steering from Majorca to
Minorca.   With noble unselfishness Commodore Duck-

1798. worth agreed to sail in chase of them without re-embarking the bluejackets and marines which were serving
ashore; and Stuart, having advanced on the 12th, came
Nov. 13. on the following day before the enemy's entrenchments,
his own and Moncrieff's troops presenting the appearance of two powerful columns. Overawed by their
aspect, the Spaniards evacuated their entrenchments
and retired within the walls of the town. Waiting till
darkness could conceal his movements, Stuart now
pushed out a second detachment to his right or northern
Nov. 14. flank, and on the next morning drew a little nearer,
apparently strengthened by a third powerful column.
Having not a single heavy gun nor the slightest
material for a siege, he now summoned the Spaniards to
surrender.   This, however, they hesitated to do, having
very reasonably some doubt whether they were not
superior in number to the British.   Accordingly,
during the night Stuart solemnly threw up two batteries
within eight hundred yards of the town and as solemnly
armed them with three light twelve-pounders and as
many light howitzers ; these weapons, which were really
Horse Artillery-guns, being all that he had been able
Nov. 15. to bring with him.   Then, when the day broke, he
formed the main body of his troops with great parade
before the enemy's batteries, connecting them cunningly
by picquets with the two detachments upon each flank
so as to present an imposing line, partly, as he said,
real and partly imaginary, four miles in length.   The
Spanish commander fired a couple of shots from two
of his heavy guns ; but Stuart, without taking the
slightest notice, invited him to another parley, which a
few hours later resulted in a capitulation of the whole
island upon condition that the garrison should be at
once shipped to the nearest Spanish port.

The total number thus embarked was over thirty-
six hundred of all ranks, not counting those captured
at Mahon and nearly a thousand Swiss, who, having
been taken prisoners from the Austrian Army by the
French in Italy and by them sold to the Spaniards at

two dollars a head, deserted joyfully to the British.[1] 1798.
The numbers of Stuart's troops I have been unable
exactly to ascertain, but they were certainly far inferior
to the enemy's, and probably did not amount to more
than three thousand. The General, in fact, simply
cowed his enemy into surrender by rapidity of movement and confidence of bearing ; and though the feat,
being bloodless, has been absolutely forgotten, it forms
one of the most striking examples in our history of
the powers of impudence in war. Had the Spaniards
really met the British with serious opposition, Stuart's
difficulties might have been considerable, for the
carriages of the six battalion-guns which accompanied
the expedition were so rotten that one and all of them
broke down before they reached Mahon. Stuart was
naturally furious at this neglect of the Office of
Ordnance, as well as at the carelessness or treachery
which had betrayed the secret of the expedition ; but
it is needless to say that he gained no satisfaction for
his complaints. Such shortcomings in the sixth year
of the war were not calculated to inspire Generals with
confidence.[2]

However, the solid fact remained that Minorca had
been taken ; and though for the present its garrison was
too weak to dispense with special protection from the
fleet, the immediate question was to what use it could
most profitably be turned. Stuart wished to increase
the force there at once by bringing over de Roll's
Swiss regiment from Lisbon ; for he was already preparing to enlist the thousand deserters from the Swiss

---

[1] Delavoye's *Life of Lord Lynedoch*, pp. 158-159.

[2] Stuart to Dundas, 26th September, 20th October, 18th
November 1798, and 13th April 1799. The Board of Ordnance,
as usual, evaded the true issue, but Stuart asked for a special enquiry
and sent home a damning report of the condition of the guns, with
the characteristic remark that it was forwarded "not in opposition
to the fact of their being apparently good, nor denying that they
were examined, repaired, and painted in England, but in formal
proof of their being unfit for any sort of service when landed in
Minorca."

1798. regiments of the Spanish garrison into a new battalion, and hoped that the presence of an actual corps of their compatriots might attract even more to the British service. But to this the Court of Lisbon raised strong objections. The attitude of Spain was still threatening; and, though the Portuguese were slowly bracing themselves to resistance, the feebleness of their rulers was such that they shrank from any action without the support of a few hundred British bayonets. Dundas's original idea, as has been told, was that Stuart, as soon as he could collect a sufficient force, should attack Carthagena; but the General had already ascertained that the place was well garrisoned and fortified, and had added a very necessary and significant warning. "Let no persuasion of the Navy," he wrote, "lead you to conceive that its reduction could be accomplished by a handful of men"—words which should have been painted in large letters on the walls of Dundas's office.[1]

1799. Dundas, however, remained wedded to the project, conceiving meanwhile that, with a very small reinforcement, Stuart might keep the Spanish coast in such constant alarm as to prevent any attack upon Portugal. But at the same time he deplored the weakness of England through the want of an efficient offensive army, without, apparently, the slightest consciousness that he was mainly responsible for it. The Portuguese had lately asked for a British officer to take command of their forces; and Dundas was so anxious that Stuart should accept the appointment that he actually promised him two whole regiments of British cavalry, if the negotiations with the Court of Lisbon should come to a satisfactory conclusion. "Eighteen hundred British cavalry would doubtless add much to the strength of any army," he wrote with ludicrous solemnity, though he was perfectly aware that the Portuguese host was no army at all. Nor does he seem to have realised for a moment that France and not Spain was the enemy to be attacked, that she had already a line of communi-

[1] Stuart to Dundas, 13th December 1798.

cation three hundred miles long down the peninsula 1799.
of Italy, that this would be increased to five hundred
miles if she invaded Naples, and that the whole length
of it was assailable on either flank through the British
command of the sea.   Such an opportunity revived in
him no confidence, stimulated him to no exertion.   In
vain had Calvert urged again and again in 1794 that
England must depend upon herself; in vain had Stuart
in October dilated upon the need for spirited military
action to turn Nelson's splendid work to account; in
vain had he added emphatically, "We must fight to
negotiate with effect."   Dundas's only answer was that
"it would be extremely desirable if some well-disciplined European force could be got somewhere on
the Continent to add to the general strength."   Never
was there a more miserable confession of helplessness.
These things should have been thought of before
Nelson was sent to the Mediterranean, and the well-
disciplined force should have been under preparation in
England.[1]

Happily Stuart was equal to his situation, even
if Dundas were not.   Hearing, in the first days of
January 1799, of the dispersion of Mack's forces Jan.
and of the flight of the Court of Naples to Sicily,
he realised that the value of Minorca was thereby
greatly enhanced, and that Spain would spare no
effort to recover it.   He lost, therefore, not a
moment in taking his measures for its defence.   In
framing the capitulation, he had been careful to do
away with certain political and religious difficulties
which had embarrassed the British Government during
its former possession of the island, so that he was
on good terms with the inhabitants; and he had
sent an emissary to make friendly overtures to the
Dey of Algiers, from which country the Minorquins
drew their supplies.   Throughout the month of
January the Spaniards pushed forward preparations
at Majorca with unusual energy; but gradually they

[1] Dundas to Stuart, 5th and 24th January 1799.

1799. realised that the recapture of Minorca would be a long and therefore most hazardous operation. British troops in those days did not love work with the spade, but for Stuart they would do anything ; and he wrote with just pride that the industry of the Twenty-eighth and Ninetieth had rivalled that of Caesar's legionaries in separating Helvetia from the

Feb. Jura. By the middle of February he was able to report that the Spaniards had abandoned all idea of an immediate attack ; and shortly afterwards there reached him, after undue delay, a reinforcement of two battalions, long ago promised by Dundas, from Ireland. These, the Thirtieth and Eighty-ninth, were in no very satisfactory condition, two hundred of them being sick, and two hundred and fifty of the remainder freshly released from the Irish gaols after conviction of rebellion and still more serious crimes. But their arrival was timely, for it enabled Stuart to act on the side where action was really important, that of Italy.[1]

From the moment when he took the Royal family of Naples on board his flag-ship, Nelson may be said to have transferred himself and his force to the service of King Ferdinand. Affairs to eastward he had left to the Russian and Turkish Navies, which, however, instead of joining Captain Hood for the blockade of the Egyptian coast, had employed themselves in the recapture of the Ionian Islands. Moreover, to the great and natural indignation of both Nelson and St. Vincent, Sir Sidney Smith had arrived in the Mediterranean at the end of 1798, with instructions from the Admiralty which appeared to place him in independent command of the ships upon the Egyptian seaboard. The mistake was speedily set right, but it added one more to the many worries which the situation in general, and his own infatuation in particular, combined to heap upon Nelson. By the

[1] Stuart to Dundas, 12th December 1798 ; 4th January, 10th and 24th February, 1st March 1799.

middle of February the apparent spread of republican 1799.
principles through Calabria alarmed him seriously for
the safety of Sicily; and on the 16th of February Feb. 16.
he wrote a despairing letter to Stuart, lamenting that
a thousand British troops could not be spared to hold
Messina and so to secure the whole island. This
was a very broad hint; but Nelson knew Stuart
well, held his ability in the very highest estimation,
and was perfectly sure that, if he could spare a couple
of battalions, he would not be deterred from sending
them by the fear of a Spanish attack.

The Admiral did not reckon in vain. Stuart at once
embarked the Thirtieth and Eighty-ninth, and arrived
with them in person at Palermo on the 10th of March.
Nelson was quite overcome by his promptitude; and the
King and Queen of Naples being accustomed, as Stuart
said, to the greatest sloth in the transaction of business,
were amazed at his inflexible determination to proceed
to Messina at once. They begged for time; but
Nelson and Sir William Hamilton seconded the
General; and within five hours Stuart had started
for Messina, with full powers in his pocket to command and take his own measures in the east of
Sicily. The troops proceeded thither by sea, but the
General rode on horseback by land to acquaint himself with the people and with the country. He found
the inhabitants to be all that he could wish, a hardy,
laborious race of peasants, well affected to their King,
attached to the English, and detesting the French.
At Messina he formed the like favourable judgment of the townsfolk, every soul of whom assembled
to welcome the British transports and to salute the
General as he rode in at the gates. He seized the
moment of enthusiasm to raise his two battalions to
a strength of two thousand men by the enlistment
of Sicilian recruits, and resolved that this should be
the beginning of a firm connection between Sicily
and Great Britain.

The summons of Nelson and Sir William Hamilton

1799. had not been the only inducement that had drawn Stuart to Messina. With deeper insight than the Admiral, he had marked not only the value of the harbours of Sicily to the British Navy, but also its internal resources, its bountiful supplies of food, and its admirable situation as the headquarters of a military force to act either in Egypt or in Italy. Free to strike against either coast of Italy, such a force could by a diversion either aid the advance of Austrian troops from Tyrol, on the side of the Adriatic, or menace the French flank and rear on the side of Genoa. And in order that it might be free, he sketched for Sir William Hamilton a masterly plan for the defence of Sicily by its own people. It was useless, he urged, to try to teach an undisciplined peasantry stiff military movements; the people should be armed and organised in small groups under their own leaders for the defence of their own little properties. An extended line from Palermo to Catania and Messina should be chosen by the most skilful officer that could be obtained; and magazines should be established at different points to feed smaller depots nearer the coast. Districts should then be formed upon this line under experienced partisan-leaders, who would take charge of the various groups within their sphere of command, and show the people how to make the best use of their superior knowledge of the country. Nor must the authorities believe that the capture of Palermo or Messina might signify the loss of the island, for, by the proper use of guerilla-bands, such a capture might be made the seat of famine rather than a prelude of further success. If the enemy should advance inland, the mountains, torrents and ravines made natural defences, and the peasantry should never cease to harass him in front, flanks, and rear. But, above all, the officers selected to command these people must not be the slaves of frippery or etiquette, but must content themselves with showing them the simplest and shortest way

of destroying the enemy and saving themselves. 1798.
"Essential military operations," he wrote, "are too
often avoided, neglected, and misarranged from the
false idea that they can only be effected by disciplined
troops, whereas in many cases, in many countries,
and particularly in Sicily, the joint efforts and exertions of armed peasants are more likely to prove
effectual."   After a hurried visit to Malta, where,
while heartily commending the dispositions of Captain
Ball of the Royal Navy, he warned him not to
be too sanguine in expecting an early surrender,
he left Colonel Thomas Graham in command at
Messina, and returned to Minorca.   From thence,
with health utterly broken down, he set out for
England, and in June arrived in London.   He had
done more in six weeks to shape a good military
policy for England than the whole of Pitt's Cabinet in
six years.[1]

Meanwhile, great events had gone forward among Dec. 29.
the monarchies of Europe.   The Tsar, stirred up by an
adroit appeal of Lord Whitworth to place himself at
their head, signed at the end of December 1798 a
treaty with England, whereby, in return for £225,000
paid down and a subsidy of £75,000 a month, he
agreed to furnish forty-five thousand men.   Paul also
signed formal alliances with Naples and with Turkey, Jan. 3.
promising to help the latter with twelve ships of the
line and eighty thousand soldiers ; and on the 5th of Jan. 5.
January England joined the Russo-Turkish Alliance,
engaging herself to support Turkey by sea while the
Sultan undertook to set on foot one hundred thousand
men against France.   A fortnight later Turkey made Jan. 21.
a league also with the Two Sicilies, pledging herself
to supply ten thousand Albanians to assist in the
expulsion of the French from Naples.   In a word,
another coalition was fairly set on foot, though, as

[1] Stuart to Dundas, 1st and 27th March ; 13th April ; to Sir
William Hamilton, 28th March 1799.   Nelson's *Despatches*, iii.
267, 289.

1799. yet, neither of the two great German powers had joined it. Pitt and Grenville were, as usual, rightly anxious that Prussia should be included. King Frederick William the Second had died in November 1797, and there was some reason to hope that under her new king, Frederick William the Third, she might be more ready than under his feeble predecessor to take part in the great struggle against the Revolution. Accordingly, Thomas Grenville was despatched in December 1798 to Berlin to negotiate a treaty ; the idea being that the allies should devote part of their energy to the liberation of Holland ; after which England, with the consent of the other powers, would be prepared to grant to Prussia a preponderant influence in that country, or even to make it over to her altogether.

The Prussian Minister, Haugwitz, was inclined to join the coalition upon these terms, but he had no great ascendency over the stupid and cautious Frederick William ; and there were many influences and accidents adverse to the success of Grenville's mission. In the first place, all communication between London and Berlin was severed for many weeks by a very severe frost which closed the German Ocean to navigation ; and from this cause Grenville did not reach the Prussian capital, after shipwreck and infinite hardship and danger, until late in February. In the second place, Thugut, still insanely jealous of Prussia, was working with might and main to make mischief between her and Russia, and to exclude her from the coalition. Thus the party which upheld Prussia's old policy of selfish neutrality had not only time but encouragement to work upon the feelings of a king who, as Grenville said, was more weak than wicked ; and the British negotiation had failed even before it was opened. By the end of March the Russian Government was definitely informed that Prussia declined an offensive alliance ; and, though Grenville lingered on at Berlin until June in the vain hope that some accident might yet induce

the King to change his mind, the miserable monarch 1799.
still persisted in his most fatal decision.[1]

The Tsar was so furious at Prussia's refusal to join
him that, as was usual when his wishes were crossed,
he nearly declared war against her on the spot, and
sent a force of sixty thousand men under General
Nummsen to watch the frontier of Prussian Poland.
Nothing could better have pleased the suspicious
mind of Thugut ; but he too, meanwhile, had felt
the hand of the imperious Paul.   Through the whole
of December he had abstained so scrupulously from
any act of hostility, in the hope of wheedling France
into the cession of additional Italian territory to
Austria, that he was actually suspected of a secret
agreement with the Directory.   He denied the fact
vigorously ; but no one, not even his former friend,
Sir Morton Eden, would believe so notorious a liar.
At last Paul threatened to recall the auxiliary force
which he had promised to Austria, unless she would put
an end to the empty negotiations, which were still proceeding at the Congress of Rastadt, and declare
definitely for war.   Thus pressed, Thugut at last,
on the 24th of January 1799, gave the declaration
required of him.   More than this, he very cleverly
turned his concession to good account by offering to
place the Austrian troops in Italy under Russian command, if Paul would appoint the veteran Suvorof to be
general-in-chief and would add another corps of Russians
to that which he had already engaged himself to provide.   Paul, greatly flattered, joyfully gave his consent, although Suvorof was at the time in disgrace ;
and thus, though England was still firm in refusing
to advance another penny to Austria until the treaty for
repayment of her former loan should be signed, the new
Coalition became formally complete.   On the one side
stood Austria, Russia, Turkey and England ; on the
other, France, Italy, Spain, Holland and Switzerland.
The Coalition, by the mouth of Paul, proclaimed the

[1] Sybel, v. 396.   *Courts and Cabinets of George III.* 431-441.

1799. war to be one of principle, and the motive of the powers to be wholly disinterested; but this was true rather in word than deed. Austria still hoped for acquisitions in Italy; the Tsar, having been elected Grand Master of the Knights of Malta, was extremely covetous of the island; while England expected not only to keep some of the colonies captured from France and Holland, but was decidedly jealous of any extension of Russian influence in the Mediterranean. Thus, as always, the Coalition carried within itself the seeds of its own dissolution.

1798.   As to France, her financial condition was nearly desperate, but her military resources had been improved since 1798 by the passing of a new law of conscription. This measure, which had been brought forward first by General Jourdan in the spring but was not finally Sept. adopted until September, made military service compulsory for all men between the ages of twenty and twenty-five, dividing them into five classes, of which the youngest were called up first. The importance of this enactment to France in the following years was incalculable. An autocrat, newly risen to power and unwilling to risk great unpopularity, might have hesitated to forge such a weapon; but Bonaparte was to find it ready to his hand. When the new law was first put into execution in the autumn and winter of 1798, the numbers called up were two hundred thousand men, besides eighteen thousand volunteers, so called, from Switzerland. But the resistance to the levy was most violent. In Belgium it was impossible to enforce it without military coercion; and the authorities resorted not only to the shooting of all fugitives, but to the confiscation of the property of themselves and their families. In France itself there was like difficulty both with refractory conscripts and deserters; and in La Vendée and Brittany the peasants were only awed into obedience by a considerable military force. This was an additional reason why Austria should boldly have drawn the sword in the autumn of 1798, but, as

has been seen, she did not ; and, while she stood idly 1799.
by, the troops were levied which very soon were to
humble her to the dust.

Nevertheless, the forces of France at the beginning of 1799, though formidable on paper, were in
actual fact small. On the Upper Rhine, Jourdan and
Bernadotte had fewer than fifty thousand men to
meet ninety thousand under the Archduke Charles ;
Masséna in Switzerland had but thirty thousand
French and ten thousand Swiss to face over seventy
thousand Austrians in Vorarlberg and Tyrol ; while in
Italy Schérer could collect only fifty thousand men
on the Adige to make head against over one hundred
thousand Austrians and Russians under Suvorof. It
was not until the first week of March that the French
and Austrians came to open hostilities, but from that
moment events marched rapidly. Masséna gained at
first brilliant successes in the Grisons ; but on the 25th
of March Jourdan was defeated by the Archduke at March 25.
Stockach, whereupon the beaten army retired to the
west of the Rhine, and its two commanders, Jourdan
and Bernadotte, hurried to Paris to visit their wrath on
the Directory. This retreat uncovered Masséna's left
flank, and forced him also to retire ; and the Archduke
was preparing to crush him, when Thugut intervened.
The British Government had succeeded in persuading
Paul to consent, if a good understanding with Prussia
were attained, to remove Nummsen's corps of observation from the Prussian frontier and to send
it to Switzerland. This sufficed to revive once again
Thugut's suspicions of Prussia ; and he kept the Archduke inactive at Stockach, so that his force could watch
Prussia and Bavaria. The Archduke, in bitter vexation, asked for leave of absence, but Thugut was
obdurate ; and, since the English insisted that
Nummsen's corps should move to Switzerland, the
stubborn Minister resolved that not an Austrian
should enter that country. Meanwhile, Masséna,
having received the command of the army of the

1799. Rhine from the Directory, had withdrawn the greater part of it to Switzerland, and was now in a position to make a very formidable resistance. The Archduke, having resumed command, invaded that country in defiance of Thugut's orders, and, though unsuccessful June 2. in an attack upon Masséna at Zürich, forced him, none the less, to retreat. Thereby the Archduke secured his communications with the Imperial Army of Italy; whereupon the Swiss flew to arms, and the work in that side needed only one vigorous push to complete it.

In Italy, matters had gone even better. Schérer, having been severely defeated by General Kray at April 5. Magnano on the 5th of April, resigned his command April 29. to Moreau; and, on the 29th, Suvorof, having forced the passage of the Adda with heavy loss to the enemy, entered Milan in triumph. He now laid his plans for beating the French armies in Italy in detail, and for a joint movement with the Archduke Charles to annihilate Masséna; and, following up his success, July 26. drove Moreau back upon Genoa, and captured Turin. On entering Piedmont, however, he had issued a proclamation calling upon the Piedmontese to rise and restore their King, who had been driven by the French from his old capital to Sardinia. This proceeding was highly offensive to Thugut, who by no means wanted the King of Sardinia to receive the whole of his dominions intact, but to yield Novara to Austria. Upon the fall of Turin, therefore, orders came to Suvorof from Vienna to halt and devote himself to the siege of Mantua, since Switzerland was not to be invaded until Nummsen's corps should have arrived there. From that moment all cordial relations between the Russian General and the Imperial Court were at an end.

While affairs were thus prospering in the north of Italy, their aspect was no less favourable in the south, where Nelson was working with fanatical energy to stir up a counter-revolution in Naples. At the end of January Cardinal Ruffo was sent to Calabria to rouse

the people against the French, and met with complete 1799.
success.   Apulia followed Calabria in revolt, and the
French troops were everywhere attacked.   Championnet
found himself unwillingly obliged to disperse his force,
with the usual demoralising result to its discipline.   He
was recalled by the Directory ; and Macdonald, who succeeded him on the 4th of March, tried, though in vain, March 4.
to restore order by excessive severity.   But the news of
the disasters on the Adige and Adda called him away
to northward ; and on the 27th of May, after leaving May 27.
garrisons in Capua and Gaeta, he hurried with all
speed, through a population everywhere hostile, to
join Moreau.   A month later, having been reinforced June 5.
by a few men from the Russian and Turkish fleets,
Ruffo marched upon Naples, entered the city on the
13th, and on the 15th drove the enemy to take refuge
in the forts.   On the 19th the French and their June 19.
followers surrendered, upon a capitulation which
Nelson declined to recognise ; and, by his order,
the leading democrats were arrested, and Admiral
Caracciolo, a principal man among them, was tried by
court-martial and hanged.   Thus, within seven weeks
of Macdonald's departure, the republican edifice erected
by the French in Naples had fallen to the ground.

In the north the success of the Allies continued.
Macdonald was beaten by Suvorof on the Trebbia with
the loss of half his force ; and, on the 20th of June, June 17-20.
the citadel of Turin surrendered.   In all Italy there
was now left to the French no more than Civita
Vecchia, Rome, Ancona, Mantua, Coni, Alessandria,
Tortona, and the Riviera of Genoa.   It remained only
for Suvorof to drive the French from the Riviera, and
the work of the Allies would practically be done.   But
on the 21st of June arrived a tactless message from
Vienna, which irritated Suvorof into asking for his
recall ; while simultaneously his Imperial Master, also
hurt by a slight which he deemed to have been put on
him by Austria, countermanded for a time the march
of Nummsen's corps upon Switzerland.   And now

1799. once more Thugut stepped in with his old jealousy of Prussia. He was anxious above all things to keep the Archduke's army free to put pressure upon that State, but he wished at the same time to withdraw the Russians from Italy, where they might interfere with his plans of territorial aggrandisement. He therefore proposed to call the whole of the Russians to Switzerland, and to place Suvorof in sole command there, while the Archduke should move down the Rhine upon Mainz, and, supported by British operations in Holland, should call Belgium to revolt. Paul was delighted with the idea, and Grenville, on England's behalf, approved it, for he had a sentimental desire for the liberation of Switzerland, and judged Suvorof to be the General best fitted to achieve it. By the end of July all was arranged upon this footing, and Thugut hastened to communicate the new plan to the Archduke; but, unfortunately, he failed to make him understand that the Austrians were not to be withdrawn from Switzerland until the Russians had replaced them. It was bad enough for this jealous, purblind minister to have delayed the invasion of France till another campaign; but it was criminal to add to this the appalling blunder with regard to Switzerland.

June 18. In France, meanwhile, the news of defeat after defeat had brought about the expulsion of the old Directory and the appointment of a new one; whereupon measures were taken for stricter enforcement of the conscription. Under the energetic impulse of Bernadotte, the new Minister of War, thirty thousand men were hastily collected to form an army of the Alps, and fifty thousand more to create a new army of the Rhine; but, strangely enough, Italy was allowed to take care of itself, and Masséna in Switzerland was ignored. In Italy, however, the fall of Alessandria and Mantua on the 25th and 29th of July again released Suvorof for active operations; and on the 15th of

Aug. 15. August he utterly defeated the army of Italy, now under General Joubert, at Novi. He was about to

follow up his victory, which would probably have given
him peaceable possession of Genoa, when he was again
distracted by the political quarrels of the Allied powers.
Thugut still thirsted for Italian territory ; and, on the
16th of August, orders came to Suvorof from Vienna
for eight thousand Austrian troops to be detached to
Tuscany, for another Austrian corps under General
Klenau to join them there from the Riviera, and for
Suvorof himself to take Tortona.   Maddened by this
interference, the Russian General not only suspended
all operations, but allowed Klenau to advance unsupported against the French in the Riviera, and to
be defeated by their superior numbers.   However, the
new plan of campaign gave him full excuse for leaving
Genoa untouched, and taking his whole force to
Switzerland ; though he did not fail to complain bitterly
to his master of the Austrians, and to nurse a bitter
grudge against them himself.

Nor was this the only quarter in which discord
showed itself among the Allies.   All Italy had risen
against the French in rear of Suvorof as he advanced ;
but the people were by no means inclined to welcome
the Austrians as their new masters.   The Neapolitan
dominions were in such a state of anarchy, owing to
the armed but undisciplined bands that had accomplished the counter-revolution, that the restoration of
order and of the old monarchy by some external force
had become urgently necessary.   But it was Suvorof
and not an Austrian general who was entreated to
furnish and to lead that force.   At the beginning of
August, therefore, the ruling powers at Naples bethought them to turn the superfluous energy of their
armed men against Rome and Civita Vecchia, where
the French garrisons were still present and formidable,
in the hope that the occupation of these two places
would exclude the detested Austrians.

For help in this project they turned, of course, to
Nelson, whose infatuation for Lady Hamilton and the
Queen of Naples had by this time sadly blunted his

1799. sense of duty and discipline.   The Admiral grasped
eagerly at the project, for he had never forgiven the
Austrians for not acting in support of Mack's advance
in 1798, and was therefore the more zealous to benefit
Naples at their expense.   But this line of action
brought him also into direct conflict with the wishes
of Russia.   The Tsar was anxious for the force under
Nelson's control to act with greater energy against
Malta ; but the Admiral absolutely forbade the Russian
fleet to take any part in the blockade.   He desired
Malta to be surrendered to himself, not from any sense
of its value to England, but because he wished to
deliver it to the King of Naples.   He was ready to
employ the Russian fleet to aid in the recapture of
Rome and Civita Vecchia ; but here again he had
no idea of taking those places for any one but King
Ferdinand.   In his impatience to anticipate both
Austrians and Russians, he wrote to General Sir James
Erskine at Minorca, adjuring him to spare him a large
part of his garrison for two months.   " The Roman
State," he wrote, " with insurrections and daily murders
is still under the French flag, with not more than
fifteen hundred regulars in the whole state, except
Ancona.   In Civita Vecchia are about a thousand
regulars, with the whole country against them ; but
such mobs are going about plundering that they (that
alone being their object) are sometimes good Republicans
and sometimes their bitter enemies. . . . If you can
spare from the garrison of Minorca twelve hundred
good men for two months for the taking possession of
Civita Vecchia and Rome, with my life I will answer
for the success of the expedition."

To this incoherent effusion Erskine answered with
quiet good sense.   After first stating the danger of his
own position at Minorca owing to the absence of a
squadron, he passed to the difficulties of transport and
supply attending such an expedition, and the notorious
unhealthiness of Civita Vecchia at that season of the
year.   He then urged the general objection that twelve

hundred men would be too few for an enterprise which 1799.
was to begin with the reduction of a regular fortress
and end with a march through a country full of armed
mobs.   What proportion (he asked) of the twelve
hundred would be left for this last dangerous duty,
when weakened by casualties and by detachments left
in captured places ?   Again, assuming the success of the
expedition against Civita Vecchia and Rome, how were
those places to be garrisoned, if the British troops
were wanted for two months only ?   To put down the
anarchy in the Roman States was a task beyond the
power of any but a regular armed force ; and a single
brigade would never suffice for the defence of an extensive district where detachments must be distributed
far and wide.   In fact, though Erskine did not put
the matter so crudely, twelve hundred men employed
as the Admiral desired might easily have entered the
Roman States, but would never have returned from them.
To this Nelson made no reply, for indeed there was no
reply to be made.   The latest of his biographers makes
it a merit in him that he uttered no word of dissatisfaction with Erskine on account of his refusal to comply
with his request.   The truth is that Erskine's firmness
saved him from adding one more to the many follies
which he had already committed.   It was already too
much that he had hazarded the safety of Minorca, and
had sacrificed alike obedience to his commanding officer,
the general service of England and her good relations
with her allies, for the sake of a couple of worthless
women.[1]

Altogether the relations of the coalesced powers
were becoming everywhere strained, and by the end
of the autumn the tension had reached the breaking
point.   The causes that parted Russia from England

[1] Erskine to Dundas (enclosing Nelson's and Sir W. Hamilton's
letters of 29th August and his reply of 5th September), 5th
September 1799.   Mahan, *Life of Nelson*, 409.   See also for
Nelson's jealousy of Russia, *ibid.* p. 357, and of Austria also,
p. 408.   *Nelson's Despatches*, iii. 452.

1799. shall appear in the chapters next following. Those that severed her from Austria must now be very

Aug. briefly summarised.   At the end of August news reached the Archduke Charles that the French had again crossed the Rhine ; whereupon, pursuant to his orders, he drew all his troops from Switzerland to meet them. Thugut meanwhile was jubilant. He opened his mind to Lord Minto, the new ambassador at Vienna, revealing that Austria designed to take Piedmont and part of Savoy, and to give Belgium to the King of Sardinia in exchange ; a project which Grenville declined to entertain for a moment. Thugut then assumed a haughty tone to the Tsar, who was already irritated to the last degree against Austria, and informed him that, if he would not support her in her claims to territory in Italy, the Emperor would reopen the whole question of the partition of Poland. As usual, he was dividing the spoil before beating the enemy, or even taking the simplest precautions to beat him ; and meanwhile he was overtaken by the Nemesis of his previous blunder. In Switzerland a large proportion of the Austrian force was withdrawn before the Russians had arrived to replace them ; and in September, Masséna, finding an inferior force before him, took the offensive with a vigour that wrecked Suvorof's plans. The Russian General himself, on crossing the pass of St. Gothard, found himself isolated, and only by superhuman efforts and very heavy loss contrived to extricate his army. He then refused to act further in co-operation with the Austrians ; and thus the campaign ended with the triumph of the French, and with discord twenty-fold intensified between Austria and Russia.

Oct. 9.   On the 9th of October, the very day upon which Suvorof ended his campaign, Napoleon Bonaparte landed in France, having successfully eluded the British cruisers on the coast of Egypt. Since the battle of the Nile he had passed through many troubles. First there had been a serious insurrection at Cairo on the

21st of October, 1798, which he had repressed with his usual ruthless severity; and in December there had come the news that a large Turkish force was advancing through Syria under Djezzar Pasha to attack him by land, while another expedition was assembling at Rhodes to descend upon Egypt by sea. He at once decided to invade Syria, with the double object of crushing Djezzar and of depriving the British cruisers of their supplies by occupation of the ports. It seems also that he contemplated the possibility of still wider operations, for he wrote at this time to Tippoo Sahib, reporting his arrival on the shores of the Red Sea with an innumerable and invincible army, and requesting him to send a trustworthy messenger to Suez to concert measures for the overthrow of the British in India.[1] His march through Syria was triumphantly victorious until he reached Acre, the best port and fortress on the coast, where he met with his old enemy, the British men-of-war, under the command of Sidney Smith. On the 18th of March Smith captured the French siege-train, which was travelling by sea; and the guns thus obtained enabled him, by the very skilful help of Phélippeaux, a French royalist officer of Engineers, to plan and maintain the defence of Acre. The siege lasted nine weeks, in the course of which period Napoleon utterly defeated a Turkish army of relief at Mount Tabor; but his assaults were one and all beaten off by the garrison of Turks and British blue-jackets. Finally, on the 20th he was fain to retreat, having lost some five thousand men killed, wounded, and plague-stricken before Acre.

His failure banished not only his visionary dreams of Oriental conquest, but even the still dearer hope, which he had long cherished, of an early return to France. It is true that a week before his retreat the British naval commanders had been thrown into consternation by the escape of Admiral Bruix's fleet from Brest, and by its appearance in the Mediterranean at a

1799.

Jan. 25.

March 18.

April 15.

April 20.

[1] *Correspondence de Napoléon*, v. 278.

1799. moment when the British squadrons were scattered in all directions. But Bruix made no use of his opportunity ; and indeed it is doubtful whether his cruise was designed for the relief of the French force in Egypt at all. Moreover, it did not better suit Bonaparte to return to France as one rescued from peril by others than as a defeated General. Fortune, however,

July 10. was kind to him, for on the 10th of July a large body of Turks from Rhodes landed at Aboukir Bay under the guns of the British and Turkish fleets, occupied

July 25. the fort and entrenched themselves. On the 25th he attacked this force and, after a sharp struggle, killed or captured every man. Such a victory was sufficient to bring him back to France with honour ; and the latest news from Europe, which he obtained by adroitly playing on the vanity and indiscretion of Sidney Smith, showed him that for his own sake he could not return too

Aug. 22. soon. He embarked, therefore, by stealth on the 22nd of August, without a word to his army, leaving written orders to General Kléber to command in his stead.

Nelson had always vowed that not a ship nor a man of Bonaparte's expedition should ever return to France, and the probability is that, if his orders had been obeyed by Sidney Smith, his vow would have been fulfilled. Whether or not Bonaparte was justified in quitting his army, after the destruction of one-half of it in useless enterprises, is a question which does not concern us here. The fact remains that he did desert it like a thief in the night, after his victory over the Turks at Aboukir. But if a British force had been brought to Sicily, as Charles Stuart had urged, and had acted in concert with those Turks, there was every reasonable probability that Bonaparte would have been defeated, his army and himself made prisoners, and his reputation so far damaged that France would never have accepted him for a master. There was a British force at disposal for the task, had the British Ministry chosen to employ it ; but, as must now be told, it was diverted to unprofitable operations in a different quarter.

CHAPTER XXIII

IT has already been related that, by the end of the year 1799. 1797, the ordinary sources for the supply of recruits had failed. This was owing not a little to mismanagement, but partly also to the rapid development of the manufacturing industry in England through the removal of all competition in France and the countries which had been overrun by the armies of the Revolution. Since the voluntary system had broken down, it followed necessarily that a compulsory system must be substituted for it. The ballot for the Militia provided a form of compulsion for service at home, and the only resource was to convert the Militia if possible into a fountain of recruits for service abroad. The first step was taken in this direction in January 1798, when an Act was passed to enable any person duly appointed by the Commander-in-chief to enlist a certain proportion of militiamen for an appointed number of regiments of the Line; the proportion not to exceed one-fifth of the Supplementary Militia in any county, and the total number enlisted to be limited to ten thousand men. This, however, in the circumstances of the time, was a measure adopted rather for the reinforcement of garrisons in Ireland and elsewhere than for any other service. No particular inducements were offered to attract recruits from the Militia; no exemption from the dreaded and detested service in the West Indies was promised; and men were shy of condemning themselves to death by yellow fever. Only in Norfolk did the Supplementary Militia come

1799. forward in numbers to fill the ranks of its county regiment, the Ninth Foot ; and it was rewarded for its patriotism by a gratuity which raised the bounty granted to the men to ten guineas apiece. Elsewhere the Lords-Lieutenant set their faces against the scheme ; and it was a total failure.[1]

After the suppression of the Irish rebellion and the victory of the Nile, however, all danger of invasion disappeared ; and the Ministers, rightly deciding to reassume the offensive, found themselves crippled by the want of a striking force.   They had no hope of raising one by the time-honoured methods which had served, though only indifferently well, for the past century ; and yet without such a force it was practically hopeless to attempt to bring the war to a satisfactory close. There was, however, one encouraging sign.   From the 9th of January 1799 onwards there came from Ireland a succession of offers from British Fencible Regiments and Irish Militia to serve abroad ; and it was not the least satisfactory feature in these offers that the great majority emanated originally not from the officers but from the men.   In the first six months of 1799 eleven battalions of Fencible Infantry, two regiments of Fencible Cavalry and seven battalions of Irish Militia volunteered for service in any part of Europe ; seven other battalions of Irish Militia volunteered to serve in Great Britain ; and one battalion of Militia, one of Fencibles and two regiments of Fencible Cavalry nobly offered to go wherever the King might choose to send them.   The condition, made by so many corps, that their wanderings should be confined to Europe, showed plainly that they would have nothing to do with the West Indies, and gave Ministers a valuable hint for future guidance.   Meanwhile, however, time was passing, and the Government's preparations for the united movement of Europe to crush France had been confined so far entirely to

[1] *C.C.L.B.*, A.G. to Sir Charles Grey, 8th June 1798 ; *ibid.* 22nd and 25th June.

the sphere of diplomacy. As has already been told, 1799.
Thomas Grenville's mission to Berlin had proved
abortive, King Frederick William having signified in
May his definite refusal to join the Coalition. But
early in June the Government received intelligence
that Prussia might at any moment call upon France
to evacuate Holland upon pain of an immediate invasion ; in which case she would certainly summon
the English to co-operate with their fleet and to seize
the island of Walcheren. Sir Ralph Abercromby was
thereupon summoned, by a letter of the 8th of June,
from Edinburgh, to take command of the troops
which were to be held ready for this purpose. Moreover, Lord Grenville's weapons of persuasion were not
yet exhausted ; for in that same month he flattered the
Tsar's vanity by proposing a joint expedition of Russia
and England to recover Holland, hoping that Prussia,
whose prize that country was designed to be, might
thereby be still further tempted to move. Paul
readily accepted the proposal ; and on the 22nd of June 22.
June a treaty was signed whereby England engaged
herself to provide thirty thousand men, and to pay
for eighteen thousand Russians more for the recapture
of Holland.

It is extraordinary that Pitt should so boldly have
promised thirty thousand men for this expedition, when
he knew that he had not more than ten thousand ready
to his hand. The means for supplying them had, however, been already considered ; and on the 12th of July July 12.
an Act was passed to reduce the numbers of the Militia
in all counties, as could now safely be done, and to
increase the Army by allowing militiamen to enlist in
certain regular regiments.[1] It was stipulated that these
regiments should not serve out of Europe during the
continuance of the war and for six months after, nor in
any case until the lapse of five years ; that the men

---

[1] The regiments named were the 4th, 5th, 9th, 17th, 20th, 31st,
35th, 40th, 42nd, 46th, 52nd, 62nd, 63rd, 82nd. *Circular of
Commander-in-chief*, 17th July 1799. *Grey Papers.*

1799. could choose their own corps and not be drafted from them against their will ; and that they should receive a bounty of ten pounds. Any man volunteering for service on these terms was entitled to discharge from the Militia, provided that the number of such volunteers did not exceed one-fourth of the full quota of each county. The King was further empowered to disembody the Supplementary Militia or any part of it, in which case the men so discharged might enlist in the regulars. If any man did so voluntarily, no ballot was to be held to fill his place, though if he failed to do so he might be recalled to the Militia. Such was the first enactment in the direction of compulsory service in England, passed, as has been said, on the 12th of July in order to make up a force which was to take the field in September. The Ministers, after all the bitter experience of the past six years, had not yet learned the difference between an army and an assembly of men in red coats.

July.   Meanwhile, such few regiments as were in some degree fit for service were collected together on the Kentish coast ; and their numbers were made up to some ten thousand men by volunteers, attracted from other battalions by a bounty of a guinea and a half.[1] Sir Ralph Abercromby assumed command of this force ; and upon him devolved the duty of planning the campaign in concert with the strategists of the Cabinet, Pitt and Dundas, both of whom took up their residence for the time at Walmer Castle. The avowed object of the expedition was clear enough, namely, the reconquest of Holland north of the Waal and the restoration of its independence under the House of Orange ; but how those objects were to be attained was another question, for the best of the campaigning season was already far spent. Abercromby reviewed the situation and quickly came to a conclusion. The most advantageous point of attack, in the abstract, was undoubtedly the mouth

[1] *C.C.L.B. Circular of Commander-in-chief,* 11th July 1799.

of the Meuse, for from thence the British could take 1799. in rear the lines of the Yssel and of the Vecht, which July. defended Holland against attack from the south and east; and the conquest of that province, thus made easy, would probably lead to the submission of the Dutch Netherlands. But the two mouths of the Maas were barred, the northern channel by the fortress of Brielle, the southern by the fortress of Helvoetsluys, both of them situated on the island of Voorne, which lies between the two channels. If a sufficient force were provided to attack Voorne and effect a landing on the mainland simultaneously, then all might be well; but, if no disembarkation could be accomplished without previously gaining possession of Voorne, then the operation would be hazardous; for the enemy could collect his force while the British were engaged with the sieges of Brielle and Helvoetsluys, and throw grave difficulties in their way. Finally, Abercromby expressed a decided opinion that no attempt should be made upon Holland until the first division of the Russian contingent was on the spot and ready to co-operate in the field.[1]

This blunt and practical opinion was by no means to the taste of Pitt, who was eager for action; and it was all the less so since the Russians were not expected until the end of August. A variety of schemes was now put forward, the first of them being a return to the original idea of seizing Walcheren. Abercromby freely conceded that this island would be most valuable, if the Prussians crossed the Rhine and Meuse and penetrated into Brabant; but without Prussia's co-operation it was useless to Great Britain, would require a large garrison and a squadron to protect it, and was, moreover, extremely unhealthy. It was then proposed that the force should land at Scheveningen, a few miles to north of the Hague, on an open beach where ships would be unsafe in a strong west wind, and where the troops, after disembarkation, would find the whole

[1] *Memo. of Abercromby*, 6th July 1799.

1799.
July.
army of Holland upon their left flank and rear. This plan was summarily dismissed by Abercromby. Another idea was to occupy Walcheren, Goree, an island immediately south of Voorne, and Ameland, a spit of sand off the north coast of Friesland, to support an insurrection. Abercromby, suppressing his contempt, declared quietly that such support would be worthless. The next suggestion was to land fifteen thousand men from the Ems on the shore of Groningen. This being the district where the feeling for the house of Orange and against the French was strongest, the plan had no doubt something to commend it. It was very probable that the force might succeed in recovering Groningen, Overyssel and part of Friesland and Drenthe ; but, before it could proceed to attack the Western Provinces, it must necessarily capture the fortress of Koevorden, on the Vecht, which could hardly be accomplished before the winter set in. In that case there would be a danger not only lest the troops should perish of cold, but also lest communication with England should be interrupted by ice, which would be absolutely fatal to the expedition.

Abercromby therefore pronounced decidedly in favour of the attack on the Maas as the only really serviceable plan, whether the Prussians should co-operate or not. For the success of the invasion in that quarter, however, the possession of Voorne was a preliminary that could not be dispensed with ; and the capture of the island promised to be an extremely difficult and hazardous operation, for the water on the western shore was too shallow to admit ships large enough either to cover a disembarkation or to carry materials for a siege. Abercromby did not conceal these difficulties, which he evidently judged to be insuperable by the force that was to be employed ; and he did not dissemble his opinion that the object of the whole expedition was not worth the risk. Pitt, who had evidently not forgotten the part played by Abercromby in Ireland, became more and more

impatient. " There are some people who have pleasure 1799.
in opposing whatever is proposed," he remarked upon July.
one occasion ; but Abercromby with quiet dignity
suffered this petulant rudeness to pass unnoticed, and
continued to insist upon his opinion.

The root of the whole matter was that Pitt was
about to commit again the old, old blunder of invading
a country with an inadequate force, relying upon an
insurrection of the inhabitants to do the work which
could really be accomplished only by an army. Herein
strangely enough he was abetted by Grenville, usually
the least sanguine of men, who for some reason had
formed extravagant hopes of Prussian assistance and
of an immediate desertion of the Dutch troops from
the French service to the British. " The operation
will be rather a counter-revolution than a conquest,"
he wrote to Dundas. " Make your preparations to
*pre*occupy the Netherlands." Dundas, however, for
once took a wise and sober view of the situation.
" Unless the Dutch co-operate with us cordially and
actively," he answered, " I do not think it possible to
do as much by mere force of arms in this campaign as
we flatter ourselves. I cannot forget the American war
and the disappointment of our hopes." But, in spite
of this belated recollection of past experience, he yielded
to Grenville, whose ideas he knew to be shared by
Pitt, and consented to write to Abercromby that he
was going out, not to conquer a country, but to aid a
counter-revolution ready to burst out in it. More
than this, though he himself had no faith in these
words, he added that they were meant to serve for
Abercromby's justification in case " he should be
led to dash more than military rules and tactics
would warrant." Thus weakly and against his better
judgment did Dundas suffer his colleagues to embark
upon a dangerous enterprise upon the strength
of a mere phrase. Moreover, not content with
choosing one loose corner-stone upon which to build
the conduct of a campaign, Pitt must needs add a

1799.
July.

second in the shape of a visionary Prussian Army; not realising, in his intense ignorance of war and of the world at large, that an edifice balanced between two such tottering foundations must inevitably collapse. Abercromby had not fought through the campaigns of 1793 and 1794 without learning something both of the Dutch and of the Prussians; and in this instance, as formerly in Ireland, his political as well as his military judgment was far sounder than that of Ministers.[1]

Nor were these Abercromby's only difficulties, for he was anything but satisfied with the preparations for his force. His troops, even on the 1st of August, were far short of their estimated strength. The volunteers which were arrived or arriving to fill his battalions needed some days for their equipment, and three of his regiments were judged unfit for immediate service. The naval preparations were behindhand; the tonnage required for the embarkation had not yet been obtained; and the naval force itself—eight ships of sixty-four or fewer guns, and five frigates—was insufficient to carry the number of flat-boats required for disembarkation. Above all, he was uneasy upon the question of transport, no sufficient provision of horses having been made even for the large train of artillery which he had rightly judged to be essential for such operations as were enjoined upon him. "The British troops want the means of conveyance for artillery, sick, baggage and provisions," he wrote at the end of July, "and you know we have not a foot on the Continent till we acquire it. I hope it is not a crime to state such facts." A return of the Russian troops, with an enormous train of waggons, gave him the text for a second discourse upon the same subject two days later. "The Emperor of Russia may make a general into a private man by his fiat, but he cannot

---

[1] Grenville to Dundas, 30th July; Dundas to Grenville, 29th and 31st July 1799. *Dropmore MSS.* Abercromby's Memo., 20th July 1799. Dunfermline's *Life of Abercromby*, 140-149.

make his army march without their baggage. It is 1799.
only in a free country like ours that a Minister has Aug.
absolute power over an army. We are too inconsider-
able to resist. . . . It is self-evident that an army is
not a machine that can move of itself; it must have
the means of moving. . . . As our numbers increase
so must our arrangements; and rest assured that an
army cannot move without horses and waggons." In
his anxiety Abercromby represented the matter to the
Duke of York, who brought it before Pitt and received
from him full powers, that is to say, full powers to
make his requisition to the Treasury and to hope that
it might be timely fulfilled. But Abercromby still
retained his doubts whether the importance of the
question was really understood by the Government;
and he was right.[1]

Dundas was so far impressed by Abercromby's
representations as to the insufficiency of his numbers
that he inclined for a moment to delay the expedition
unless a larger force could be despatched with him.
But political considerations, both domestic and foreign,
prompted him, according to his own account, to urge
the departure of the first division of the army as soon
as possible; and on the 3rd of August he issued to Aug. 3.
Abercromby his instructions. Herein, ignoring the
General's strong recommendation that nothing should
be done in Holland until the arrival of the Russians,
he declared it to be expedient and necessary for divers
unspecified reasons, that the expeditionary force should
sail in several divisions, of which Abercromby's ten
thousand men had been appointed to be the first. The
duty assigned to it was to secure on the mainland of
the United Provinces a safe rendezvous and a favourable
position for future operations, which of course should
permit of free communication with England. With this
object the instructions suggested the capture of Goree
and Overflakkee to south of Voorne, of Rosenburg to

[1] Abercromby to Huskisson, 29th July and 1st, 3rd, 4th August
1798.

1799.
Aug.

north of it, and of Voorne itself, as a means towards obtaining some place on the mainland where reinforcements could land without opposition, and where Abercromby could maintain himself until their arrival. Maassluis, Schiedam, Rotterdam and Dordrecht were named as places suitable for the purpose; and a reinforcement of four thousand British troops was promised to him immediately upon the capture of any one of them. If, on the other hand, he should secure the islands above named but fail to establish himself on the mainland, the reinforcements would be delayed until the arrival of the Russians should enable them to proceed in great strength. Dundas further hinted that the operations might be furthered by naval diversions both northward towards the Texel and southward about Zealand; and to this end he enclosed a proclamation and an address from the Prince of Orange, which were to be published as earnest of England's honourable intentions. But he was careful to add that Abercromby was at liberty to abandon these projects altogether if, on arrival in the Meuse, he should think them impracticable or unduly hazardous or costly.[1]

All this was in the highest degree unsatisfactory, for there seemed every probability that the expedition would reduce itself to a voyage to the Meuse and back again. Goree and Overflakkee had been suggested as landing-places, apparently, by some Dutch refugees of the Orange party; but not one of them could give the slightest intelligence respecting these islands. In fact, the only information which Abercromby could obtain to guide him was that of a Dutch prisoner of war. On the 6th of August Dundas, Abercromby, and the Naval Commandant, Vice-Admiral Mitchell, met in council to talk over the matter, with the help of Captain Flyn of the Royal Navy and a foreign officer, both of whom were supposed to be well acquainted with the navigation of the Meuse. Aber-

[1] Dundas to Abercomby, 3rd August 1799.

cromby was very ill pleased with the result. The 1799.
Admiral talked blindly of the fleet forcing its way Aug.
through every obstacle ; while Flyn was cautious, and
afraid of committing himself.   Ultimately, it was
agreed that to gain possession of Voorne the island of
Rosenburg must first be taken, though it was plain
that, from the difficulties of navigation and other
causes, the success of the operation must be most
precarious.

At this stage matters remained until the 10th of Aug. 10.
August, when Abercromby again complained of his
want of intelligence, and warned the Government
against building too much on the exertions of the
Orange party.   His letter was crossed by a fresh set
of instructions.   Dundas, though somewhat infected
by the sanguine hopes of Pitt and Grenville, still mistrusted the success of the operations already contemplated, and was unwilling to let the General sail without
offering him a further choice of alternative enterprises.
He, therefore, directed him still to make the capture
of Goree his first business, and, after effecting it, to
proceed to the attack of Voorne ; but, if this should
prove to be impracticable, he urged upon him, as
the object next in importance, to obtain possession
of Texel Island and the Helder at the extreme north
of Holland.   Should this operation likewise prove
impracticable, he was to enter the Ems, disembark in
the neighbourhood of Delfzyl, and take possession of
Groningen, Friesland and Drenthe.   But the capture
of the Helder was set down as far more desirable, if it
could be attained, as securing alike a footing in
Holland, the navigation of the Zuider Zee, and
probably the control of the Dutch fleet at the Texel.
None the less, it was urged as essential that troops
should, if possible, be left at Goree, since it was upon
the presence of such a force that the loyal inhabitants
had "probably" built their plans of co-operation.
Finally, after recounting all these alternatives, the
instructions left it to the discretion of the General

1799.
Aug.
and Admiral to do practically whatever they might think best for the King's service.[1]

It has been judged necessary to set forth all these orders at some length, so as to show the extreme vagueness and indecision of the Ministers' intentions in despatching this expedition. They professed to count upon a rising of the Dutch, yet could give the General no certain intelligence of the designs of the insurgents. They had, when seeking Abercromby's advice, made the co-operation of a Prussian army a principal factor for the guidance of his calculation ; yet that factor vanished altogether before the expedition put to sea. Finally, they hurried the General and his ten thousand men out of England with no definite plan of action, but merely with a hazy purpose that he should go to Holland and do something.

Aug. 13.
Abercromby sailed accordingly on the 13th of August, having evidently already made up his mind to go to

Aug. 14.
the Helder. On the following day he announced his intention to Dundas, saying that an attack on the Maas was absolutely out of the question, and that he abandoned it the more readily since the persistence of Prussia in her neutrality had removed the principal reason for advocating it. Dundas at once approved cordially of his decision, though he made no effort to explain why the Government had saddled the General with a responsibility which it ought to have taken upon itself. In his usual breezy fashion he assumed that Abercromby's sphere of attack embraced not only the Helder itself, but Texel Island and the mainland south of the Helder as far as Haarlem, or, in other words, a coast-line of from fifty to sixty miles ; and already he had visions of an early fall of Amsterdam.[2]

[1] Dundas to Abercromby, Abercromby to Huskisson, 10th August 1799 ; Dundas to Grenville, 3rd and 11th August. *Dropmore MSS.*

[2] Abercromby to Dundas, 14th August, three letters ; Dundas to Abercromby, 16th August 1799.

Bad luck, however, dogged the expedition from the very beginning. The fleet was overtaken by a westerly gale of unusual violence, which was ominously noted by Abercromby as certain to delay the arrival of the Russians. Happily, the transports were able to keep company, thanks to bright moonlight, and on the 21st the whole armament approached the coast of the Texel. Preparations were made for disembarkation, but on the next day a second gale forced every sail again to sea ; nor was it till the 26th that the transports could be anchored in the stations appointed for them opposite the shore a little to the south of the Helder, between Kycksduin and Kallantzoog. Water and provisions were already so short in the fleet that, had not the gale moderated on the 26th, Abercromby and Mitchell had determined to abandon the attempt on the Helder and to sail for the Ems. However, at two o'clock on the next morning, the signal was made to prepare for disembarkation, though the surf was still high, and the enemy, having had sight of the fleet for six days past, could not have failed to make preparations for defence. Moreover, owing to his ignorance of the precise duty required of him by the Government, Abercromby had been unable to arrange every detail of his attack before sailing, as he had wished ; and, since the Ministers had failed to provide the flat-bottomed boats for which he had asked, he was obliged to rely upon the boats of the men-of-war only, which could not convey more than three thousand troops at a time. Lastly, the operation of disembarking a force in presence of an enemy was strange to the Navy, whose officers hardly understood the importance of keeping companies and battalions together, and of landing them in the order which they were to preserve on shore.

In such discouraging circumstances did Abercromby approach his adventure. Behind him were the orders of an ignorant and negligent Cabinet ; before him a long row of sand-hills concealing he knew not what

1799.
Aug.
enemy behind them. North Holland is indeed no ordinary country. Lying below the level of the sea, it is preserved, about its northern extremity, only by a gigantic dyke some five miles in length from inundation and destruction by the German Ocean. Along the western coast the part of this dyke is played by a chain of sand-dunes, varying from half a mile to four miles in width, which runs, with but a single break, all the way along the shore from the Helder to the mouth of the Maas. The break in question occurs about fifteen miles south of the Helder at Petten, and extends for some three miles southward to Kamp, between which points the waves are shut out by another huge dyke. From Petten for some five miles northward the dunes are high, and gradually widen out from a breadth of half a mile to a mile and a half at Kallantzoog. North of that point they suddenly contract once more to a breadth of eight hundred to a thousand yards, and, rapidly decreasing in height, present, opposite to the village of Groete Keten, an absolute gap in the barrier of sand. At this point the beach is wide, and the outer bank of the dunes little more than ten feet high, so that from the main-top of a frigate a man could obtain a narrow glimpse of the reclaimed fen called the plain of North Holland.

The nature of that plain is well known to travellers. To the eye a perfectly open expanse of meadow land, it is in reality as strongly enclosed country as there is in the world. At every hundred yards, or less, it is intersected by broad ditches or canals, some of them created to carry off the water, others to mark boundaries and do the duty of fences ; for the northern corner of this strange territory is almost entirely grazing land. Military movements are practically impossible, except on the roads, which without exception are carried along the dykes. With such a description of country Abercromby had become familiar during the campaign of 1794 ; but the sand-dunes, which were all that he could see, were an unknown quantity, and he had

not the slightest idea what force the enemy might 1799,
keep hidden behind them.   Marking, however, the Aug.
gap before Groete Keten and the low dunes to north
of it, he determined, in default of better guidance, to
make that part of the shore his place of landing.

Meanwhile General Brune, who held supreme command in Holland, had, of course, been apprised of
the approach of the British fleet, and, thanks to the
weather, had found. ample time to reinforce the troops
in the north.   On the 27th of August there were at
the disposal of General Daendels, the actual commander about the threatened point, ten thousand
men ; but his was no easy task.   Though the gap
at Groete Keten was the obvious place for a disembarkation, and the shore to the north of Petten
far more favourable for the purpose than that to the
south, there was still no natural obstacle to prevent
an enemy from landing at any point between the
Helder and Alkmaar.   He therefore decided to
disperse his force along the whole of that line.   Apart
from the garrisons in the forts of the Helder, one
brigade lay between Kallantzoog and Petten ; two
battalions, with a third in reserve, were stationed in
the middle of the dunes opposite to the hamlet of
Kleene Keten ; two more were between the village
of Groete Keten and the sea, facing to north, and
three more, with two squadrons of cavalry and four
guns, stood before Huisduinen, a little to the south
of the Helder itself, facing to south-west.   Recognis-
ing that the cannon of the fleet could scour the whole
beach with shot, Daendels had decided to refuse his
centre, and to attack the British upon both flanks
when entangled in the dunes.   The position of
Kleene Keten was probably chosen for the reserve,
because at that point the plain east of the sand-hills is
dry for a few hundred yards, and gives a little space for
the massing of troops on the open ground.

At five o'clock in the morning the men-of-war, Aug. 27.
at a signal from the flagship, opened a tremendous fire

1799.
Aug. 27.

upon the beach ; and the whole line of boats, carrying Coote's brigade and apparently a part of Macdonald's, under the command of Sir James Pulteney,[1] pushed off together for the shore about the gap and to north of it.   The landing was effected in much confusion. Several boats were upset by the surf, and not a few of the seamen and soldiers were drowned.   The men had to scramble through the waves as best they could ; companies and battalions were intermixed, and there was much trouble in dissentangling them.   Nevertheless, Daendels, doubtless dreading the effect of the cannonade, kept his men under cover, and made no attempt, except by distant and dropping fire, to molest the disordered British soldiers as they hurried to and fro to find their places in the ranks.

Abercromby had been careful to select for his disembarkation a slight curve in the strand, where the sand-hills, drawing closer to the sea both to north and south, gave some protection to his flanks.   But it should seem that, in the general confusion, the right of the landing force did not extend itself far enough

---

[1] The force was brigaded thus :—

> *1st Brigade.*—Massed grenadiers of the Guards, 3/1st Guards —Major-general D'Oyley.
>
> *2nd Brigade.*—1/ Coldstream Guards, 1/3rd Guards—Major-general Burrard.
>
> *3rd Brigade.*—2nd, 27th, 29th, 69th, 85th—Major-general Coote.
>
> *4th Brigade.*—2/1st, 25th, 49th, 79th, 92nd—Major-general John Moore.
>
> *Reserve.*—23rd, 55th—Colonel Macdonald.

This differs slightly from the brigading as shown by Bunbury (*Great War with France*), but is taken from the return enclosed by Abercromby to Dundas in his report of the action.   The full strength of the infantry on 4th August was 497 officers and 11,820 non-commissioned officers and men, of whom 753 were sick.   There were also on board :—

> 18th Light Dragoons.—13 officers, 208 N.C.O.s and men.
>
> Royal Artillery.—26 officers, 417 N.C.O.s and men, and 157 drivers.

The guns requested by Abercromby (20th July) were 36 6-prs. (battalion guns), 20 12-prs., 30 24-prs., 18 $5\frac{1}{2}$-inch mortars, 8 8-inch mortars, 19 10-inch mortars.

to southward, being possibly blown from its right course by the south-west wind ; and for this reason a number of troops were cramped within an unduly confined portion of the beach.   This increased the confusion ; and the formation of the British was still, apparently, incomplete when Pulteney, possibly in order to gain more room for the rear battalions, gave the order to advance.   The forward movement must have begun a little to north of the gap, for it instantly brought down a very heavy fire of musketry and light artillery from the enemy, showing that Daendels had brought down his detachment from Kleene Keten to meet them.   Thereupon it seems that the British, after climbing the outer ridge of sand-hills,[1] charged straight upon the two leading battalions, forced them gradually back upon the third, which formed their reserve, and finally drove all three to southward in confusion upon Groete Keten.

Hotly pursuing them, the British came upon the gap in the dunes, where there is a curious pan[2] of flat sunken ground, measuring about five hundred yards north and south by one hundred east and west, from which they scrambled up a steep bank some ten feet high, in no very good order, to debouch upon the plain beyond.   No sooner, however, did they emerge from the sand upon the grass than they were met by a withering fire of grape from the guns, hitherto concealed, of a French detachment on the two roads which lead inland from this outlet.   Thereupon they fell back hastily into the sand-hills ; and Daendels at once launched the two battalions, which he held concealed from view at Groete Keten, upon Pulteney's right flank, called up more troops from Kallantzoog to support them, and sent orders to his regiments

[1] For some distance north of Groete Keten the dunes consist of an outer ridge towards the sea, and an inner ridge at the edge of the plain, with practically open ground between them.

[2] This hollow is so sudden and abrupt that a superficial observer would declare it to be the worked-out clay-bed of an old brickfield.

at Huisduinen to fall forthwith upon the British left flank. This counter-attack from Groete Keten was most dangerous and formidable. Pulteney's troops seem to have been huddled together in the pan above described, where he tried to change the front of his right-hand battalion to meet the flanking attack, but, owing to the narrowness of the space, could only do so with difficulty, and could form no second battalion for its support. The British right was therefore borne back in great disorder; and the consequences might have been most serious had not the enemy forsaken their shelter to pursue them, when, being enfiladed by the guns of the men-of-war, they were forced to retire with very heavy loss.[1]

Abercromby, however, now landed with D'Oyley's brigade of Guards to support Pulteney; while on the left Moore, who had at first been set ashore with only three hundred mixed men from every regiment under his command, was gradually reinforced by the disembarkation of the greater part of his brigade. Taking up his position opposite the Helder, his skirmishers engaged the enemy's riflemen, and seem to have checked the attack ordered by Daendels upon the British left flank. Elsewhere the two armies were engaged in a long and confused struggle among the sand-hills, which lasted until five o'clock in the evening; the French and Dutch making effort after effort to force the British back, and the British, though without artillery, refusing obstinately to give way. At last the enemy on the centre and right, being fairly worn down, gave up the contest, and retired in good order to a position some four miles to the southward.

Thus the landing was won, but there still remained some two thousand Dutch in the batteries of the Helder, which needed to be mastered without delay. Aber-

---

[1] The position of the regiments can be fixed only by conjecture, for the action was extremely confused. From the casualties I guess that the 23rd and 55th were on the right, and Coote's brigade immediately to left of them.

cromby accordingly ordered that they should be attacked
at daybreak on the following morning by the brigades
of Moore and Burrard.   Moore, however, noticed some
movement about the Helder in the evening, and keeping
careful watch, saw the enemy's troops march off at
nightfall by the eastern coast, as if making for the road
to Alkmaar.   Pushing forward his patrols, he learned
that the batteries were evacuated and the guns spiked;
and in the course of the night he took possession both
of the forts and of the town.   At daylight the Dutch
men-of-war, which were lying close under the guns of
the Helder, weighed anchor and retired eastward, with
the exception of seven lying in the Nieuwediep, which
surrendered at once.   Admiral Mitchell employed the
two following days in buoying a channel by which to
approach the main body of the Dutch fleet, and, sailing
in on the 30th, summoned the Dutch Admiral, Story,
to hoist the Orange flag and transfer his ships to the
service of the Allies of the British Crown.   Story
thereupon yielded up his fleet, alleging that his men
refused to fight; and twenty-five more men-of-war,
seven of them ships of the line, together with the naval
arsenal of Nieuwediep, with all its stores and ninety-
five guns, passed into possession of the British without
the firing of a shot.

So great and speedy a success exceeded the wildest
expectations alike of those who projected and commanded the expedition.   Abercromby, in announcing
his intention to hazard a disembarkation, had warned
the Government that to anchor two hundred sail upon
an unsheltered beach, exposed to the prevalent winds,
and then to throw a large force upon a hostile shore,
was an operation beyond the rules of prudence and
common-sense.   Six days' warning had given the
enemy ample time to prepare for resistance; the
means for landing troops were, through no fault of
Abercromby, inadequate; the disembarkation had consequently been disorderly; the first advance, whether
through the eagerness of the troops or the fault of

1799. Pulteney, had been too precipitate ; and the action, after
Aug. long wearing an ugly aspect, had terminated finally
in no very decided success.   Moore, who, it is true,
was always something of a pessimist, looked for a
re-embarkation as almost inevitable if his attack
upon the Helder on the morning of the 28th should
have failed.   Yet, by miraculous good luck, all had
gone well, and the first great object of the expedition
had been secured with, in the circumstances, comparatively small loss.   Three officers and about sixty men
were killed, and twenty men drowned ; twenty-four
officers and three hundred and eighty men were
wounded or missing.   The regiments that suffered
most heavily were the Twenty-third and Fifty-fifth,
upon whom fell nearly one half of the total casualties.
Among the wounded officers were Pulteney,[1] Abercromby's second in command, and John Hope and
George Murray, his two principal staff-officers.   The
losses of the enemy appear to have been far greater,
though it is not clear why they should have been so ;
but they are set down by French historians at not fewer
than fourteen hundred men—an enormous proportion
to the total number engaged.

Meanwhile throughout the month of August the
recruits from the militia had been pouring into the
appointed camp at Barham Downs in the uproarious
condition which, in those days, was inevitably produced
by a large bounty.   Such a sight has rarely been seen
in England, even after the paying off of a fleet.   The
possession of ten pounds filled the majority of the
men with a pride which forbade them to walk to the
rendezvous.   They rolled up to the camp, riotously
drunk, in post-coaches, post-chaises and six, caravans,
and every description of vehicle, leaving the officers to
plod on foot with such few luckless men as had already
lost or spent their money.   Even when arrived at their

[1] Pulteney was hit in the arm, which afforded him the satisfaction of having been wounded in both arms and both legs.
Bunbury's *Great War with France*, p. 47.

destination they were utterly intractable, for, as gentle- 1799.
men who rode in post-chaises, they thought it beneath
them to attend drill or parade.   They knew that they
were to embark almost immediately for active service,
and they were determined to be happy while their
riches lasted.   It was only with difficulty that their
names and the regiments from which they came were
ascertained, while all the efforts of the tailors failed to
alter such a multitude of facings in time for embarkation.   Upon the news of Abercromby's success, Pitt
and Dundas very injudiciously announced that they
would visit the troops on the following evening, to
witness a march past and the firing of a *feu de joie*.
The officers spent the next twenty-four hours in a raid
upon Canterbury and the surrounding villages, and by
three o'clock on the appointed afternoon had swept
into camp every man who could stand or walk.   Not
more than one man in twenty was sober, and the *feu de
joie* was, in consequence, so outrageously jubilant that
it was judged prudent to dismiss the troops without
venturing upon a march past.   Yet these men, knowing
nothing of their comrades, nothing of their serjeants
and officers, nothing of their regiments, were in a few
days to stand in face of an enemy in the field.   A
month before they had been well-drilled, orderly
militiamen ; with three months' training in their new
corps they would probably have been good, and with
six months' training, excellent troops.   Every soldier
knew this, and there were undoubtedly soldiers who
mentioned it to Ministers ; but it was vain to urge
such matters upon Pitt and Dundas.

The first reinforcement of these new levies reached
Abercromby on the 28th of August.   It consisted of Aug. 28.
seven battalions organised in two brigades, and counting altogether rather over five thousand of all ranks,
but with only fifty-seven lieutenants and fourteen
ensigns among the whole of them.[1]   With them, or

[1] Major-gen. Don's Brigade : 17th and 40th (each 2 batts.).
Major-gen. Lord Cavan's Brigade : 20th (2 batts.), 63rd.   147

1799. very soon after, came the Eleventh Light Dragoons. The arrival of these troops was welcome, for it offered Abercromby the hope of improving his success. He was extremely anxious to advance, but an army, as he had said, cannot move without horses and waggons; and he had neither the one nor the other. For four days the troops bivouacked in their chosen position in the sand-hills, exposed to constant wind and rain, without any camp-equipment, and, in Abercromby's words, labouring under a precarious subsistence from want of horses to draw their provisions from the Helder. At length a few horses and waggons were found, and, on Sept. 1. the 1st of September, Abercromby moved southward and took up a strong defensive position, with his right at Petten on the German Ocean, and his left at Oude Sluis on the Zuider Zee.

Following the bank of the Zype Canal, the line of defence ran from Oude Sluis obliquely south-westward for about twelve miles to the hamlet of Krabbendam, from which point it turned back sharply north-westward along the bank of a branch canal which ended at Petten. Thus the front was covered for its whole length by a canal; but a great dyke beyond it was presently made the first line of defence, additional bridges being constructed over the Zype to facilitate the access to it. The principal approach to the position was at the salient angle of Zype Sluis, with its adjacent post of Krabbendam; for it was at these points that the great northern canal from Amsterdam and Alkmaar, and the high road upon the great dyke, entered the lines. Accordingly, the two hamlets were placed in a state of defence, strengthened by redoubts, and committed to the charge of the Twentieth Regiment. To westward of it, along the branch-canal to Petten, there were transverse dykes which gave access to the main dyke; and this space being the right of the line, was occupied by the two

officers, 4967 N.C.O.s and men, of whom 204 sick. The 2/17th and the 40th had not a single ensign. *Return*, in Dundas to Abercromby, 22nd August 1799.

brigades of Guards.   North-eastward from Krabben- 1799.
dam, the next passage of the Zype was by the village Sept.
of St. Maarten, which also was fortified and held by
the Fortieth Regiment under Colonel Spencer ; and
the remainder of Moore's and Don's brigades, less two
battalions left to guard the Helder itself, were stationed
either between Krabbendam and Oude Sluis or as a
reserve in rear of the centre.   Every important point
was covered by field-works ; the troops were quartered
under good shelter in Schagen, Harenskarspel, and other
villages in advance of the Zype ; and, thus secured,
Abercromby resolved, until reinforcements should reach
him, to stand on the defensive.[1]

For this inaction he has incurred severe censure
from the French historian, General Jomini, yet it is
difficult to see what else he could have done.   He
had, it is true, from sixteen to eighteen thousand men
with him, but, with the exception of the Guards and
Ninety-second Highlanders, the regiments that he had
brought with him were imperfect in coherence and discipline.   One and all had been hastily completed by
drafts, and Don's and Cavan's brigades were simply
unformed militia.   The force was very ill-equipped in
every respect, and the only transport that had been
shipped to him so far consisted of thirty-five bread
waggons, with four horses apiece, and a single forge-
cart.   In the country itself the waggons and teams
were few, and the inhabitants unwilling to part with
them.   The Government had counted on water-carriage
to supplement these defects ; but a series of south-
westerly gales made it so difficult for boats to pass from
the Helder through the narrow channel which led to
Oude Sluis and so into the Zype Canal, that it was impossible to form magazines even along the length of the
chosen position.   Moreover, even if such magazines had
been formed, the boats of the Zype Canal were too large
to enter the great northern canal, and the enemy had

---

[1] *Diary of Sir John Moore*, i. 345.   Bunbury's *Great War with France*, pp. 6-7.

1799. been careful to destroy or remove all the smaller craft as they retreated. Lastly, the country itself presented every possible difficulty to an advancing force. No corn was grown on the land, which, being given up wholly to grazing, produced no supplies beyond a limited quantity of meat. Again, the maze of dykes and canals, interspersed at every hundred yards with wet ditches, rendered the movement of troops impossible except by a few roads, which could easily be obstructed either by breaking down the bridges or, in some cases, by inundation. Thus every advantage lay with the defending force, which could with comparatively few troops cover a very wide front, extending practically from sea to sea, and therefore affording no chance for a turning movement. An invasion of North Holland from the Helder signified, in fact, a campaign of frontal attacks along parallel lines of causeways.[1]

General Brune naturally used the respite granted to him by Abercromby's halt to summon every man from the eastern provinces, to call up the National Guard, and to provide for the defence of Amsterdam by collecting a flotilla of gun-boats in the Zuider Zee, and by covering with batteries the peninsula of Buiksloot, Sept. 2. over against the town. On the 2nd of September he joined Daendels, who had taken up a position from Alkmaar eastward nearly to Hoorn, with the outposts on his left pushed forward to within a mile or two of Sept. 8. those on the British right. On the 8th he was strengthened by a reinforcement which raised his total numbers to twenty-one thousand men, two-thirds Dutch and one-third French; whereupon he resolved to attack Abercromby at once before more troops could reach him from England. His plan was to turn the British right, for which purpose seven thousand French under General Vandamme were to debouch from Schoorl, a village about five miles north of Alkmaar, and advance through the dunes by Groet and Kamp upon Petten.

[1] Abercromby to Dundas, 4th September 1799.

On Vandamme's right a second column of six thousand   1799.
Dutch under General Dumonceau were to march by
Schoorldam, a little to eastward of Schoorl, up the
great canal upon Krabbendam, master the bridge and
carry the salient angle of the lines.   On Dumonceau's
right a third column of almost the same force under
Daendels was to assemble at St. Pankras, about three
miles north-east of Alkmaar, and thence advance northward upon Eenigenburg.

The attack was fixed for daybreak on the 10th, but Sept. 10.
Abercromby had been warned of Brune's intention to
take the offensive.   The French movements on the
night of the 9th also were not conducted so silently as
to escape the attention of the British picquets, and
Moore's patrols were ready to move forward as soon
as it was light.   Vandamme's column came first into
action while it was still dark, covering its attack, as
usual, with a cloud of skirmishers, while the Grenadiers
rushed forward with the bayonet.   Nothing could
exceed the impetuous gallantry of this assault—four
companies of the Grenadiers actually gaining the edge
of the small canal at the foot of the dyke which was
lined by the British.   But the fire of Burrard's brigade
was cool and steady, the French column was completely
shattered, and the four intrepid companies were killed
or taken to a man.   After an hour and a half Vandamme's column retired, beaten, with very heavy loss.

Further to eastward the attack was delayed by some
mismanagement which brought part of Dumonceau's
column on to the same road with that of Daendels,
and caused much confusion.   Fearful of losing precious time, Dumonceau launched one of his brigades
at Eenigenburg, and, leaving Daendels to turn his
force further northward against St. Maarten, hurried
forward with the rest of his men to the storm of
Krabbendam.   Here again the vehemence of the
assault and the gallantry of the assailants were conspicuous.   The brigade was parted into two columns,
of which the smaller dashed forward along the road,

despite the enfilading fire of two British guns, gained the first houses of the village and filled them with skirmishers, while the main body made a rush to seize the entrenchments on the dyke.   Misled by the attack on Eenigenburg, Abercromby had detached the Second battalion of the Twentieth to that quarter; and consequently the whole brunt of Dumonceau's onslaught fell upon five companies of the First battalion. For a short space these were borne back, and the situation wore so serious an aspect that Abercromby dismounted and placed himself at their head.   But, though hastily composed of militiamen from half-a-dozen counties besides Devon, to which the regiment was by title affiliated, the Twentieth had an excellent Colonel, George Smyth, who had already made it worthy of its old reputation.   The five companies behaved with the steadiness of veterans, repelling attack after attack until the Second battalion returned to their assistance, when Dumonceau's men broke and fled, and Colonel Macdonald pursuing them with the Reserve captured a gun, pontoons, and several prisoners.

At St. Maarten, Daendels was met with equal firmness by the militiamen of the Fortieth under Brent Spencer, and soon retired.   At Eenigenburg the enemy carried the village but dashed themselves in vain against the entrenchments.   In brief, Brune was repulsed all along the line, and retreated with a loss of over two thousand killed, wounded, and prisoners.   The casualties among the British barely exceeded two hundred killed, wounded, and missing of all ranks; and of eleven officers wounded six belonged to the First battalion of the Twentieth.   Brune's chances of success, unless by singular favour of fortune, were in fact remote; though the extraordinary advantages promised by a victory may be held to have justified him in hazarding the attempt.[1]

[1] Lieut.-col. Anstruther to Colonel Calvert, 11th September 1799.   Notes on the expedition in *W.O. Orig. Corres.*, 65.

The prosperous issue of this day greatly strengthened 1799.
the confidence of the British troops in themselves and
in their officers ; and it was with high hopes that they
welcomed the arrival, within the five following days, of Sept. 12-15.
three more brigades of British infantry, a few more
squadrons of British cavalry, and two divisions of
Russians.   In all, the reinforcements numbered thirty-
three thousand men, with the Duke of York for Commander-in-chief, David Dundas as a General of Division, and Lord Paget, who is better known by his later
titles of Earl of Uxbridge and Marquis of Anglesey,
in command of the Seventh Light Dragoons.[1]   As to
the quality of these troops it can only be said that the
British infantry were, like most of the regiments already
on the spot, militiamen of excellent but unshaped
material.   The Russians, who numbered twelve
thousand men, were also imperfectly trained and
disciplined ; for, though the Tsar Paul had busied
himself immensely with military improvements, the
results had not been commensurate with his spasmodic
energy, and the Muscovite soldier was not yet such a
man as he proved himself later to be at Eylau.   Of
General Hermann, who commanded the two divisions
in Holland, it can only be said that, with a great deal of
boasting and pretension, he was no better than his men.
As regards the Duke of York, his deficiencies in the
field had been sufficiently shown in 1793 and 1794 ;
and his appointment was beyond doubt chiefly due to
the imperative need of a commander-in-chief whose
rank and authority the Russians could not venture to
question.   But, though it may well have been essentially necessary (as in Abercromby's opinion it was), the
choice of the Duke was unfortunate ; and the methods
selected by Ministers for making good his defects were
more unfortunate still.   For he was required by his

[1] These troops were : Lord Chatham's brigade, 4th (3 batts.),
31st; Maj.-gen. Manners's brigade, 9th (2 batts.), 56th ; Prince
William of Gloucester's, 5th, 35th (each 2 batts.) ; also the 7th Light
Dragoons, a detachment of the 18th Light Dragoons, and Artillery.

1799.
Sept.
instructions to guide himself upon all important occasions by the advice of a Council of War, consisting
of Abercromby, David Dundas, Pulteney, the Russian
commander, and Major-general Lord Chatham.[1]   The
three first of these were thoroughly competent soldiers,
the fourth might or might not be so ; but the addition
of Lord Chatham, a man of notorious indolence and
incapacity, was nothing short of an insult.   Still even
if one and all had been Heaven-born generals, the
arrangement could not but have been utterly vicious ;
and it would have been far better to give the Duke
absolute control, with Abercromby or Moore for the
chief of his staff.   As regards the operations to be
undertaken, the Government wisely left to the Duke
a wide discretion, merely prescribing the recovery
of Holland and of Utrecht southward to the Waal, as
the principal object, and hoping that his force would
enable him to send detachments also to the eastern
provinces.[2]

The Duke had now some forty-eight thousand men
under his command, of whom three-fourths were British ;
but the first sight of many of them filled him with
dismay.   In the haste to despatch the troops from
Deal and the scarcity of tonnage, many necessary
articles had been left behind.   Some of the men were
almost naked ; two whole brigades did not possess a
great-coat among them ; and the result, in a season
of incessant wind and rain, was that seventeen hundred
of Abercromby's force were already in hospital.   The
arrangements for transport and supply gave him even
more anxiety.   In respect of land-transport the full

[1] Bunbury, *Great War with France*, p. 43. I have found no
trace of these instructions as to a Council of War in the papers
(otherwise very perfect) in the Record Office ; but there is con-
firmation of the statement in a letter of Lord Grenville to Lord
Buckingham (*Court and Cabinets of George III.*, ii. 449) : " The
Duke of York has, I really believe, had no other fault than that of
following, perhaps too implicitly, the advice of those whose advice
he was ordered to follow."   There is no sign, however, of any
share taken by Lord Chatham.

[2] Dundas to York, 5th September 1799.

allowance ordered by the Government for a force of 1799.
practically fifty thousand men was one hundred bread- Sept.
waggons, as many forage-carts, twenty hospital-waggons
and ten forge-carts—an allowance which, on the scale
of the present day, would be wholly insufficient for
a division of infantry and a brigade of cavalry, counting together less than thirteen thousand men. Moreover, these waggons were not yet on the spot, fully
half of them being in England and quite possibly still
in course of construction. In the matter of ammuni-
tion-waggons, again, the Office of Ordnance, from
motives of economy, had sent out a number of the old
pattern which had been so strongly condemned by the
Duke of York himself in 1793. So cumbrous, unstable, and unmanageable were they, that the success of
the action of the 10th of September was imperilled by
the difficulty of bringing forward ammunition ; and
men and officers rejoiced to see half-a-dozen of these
" vile and ridiculous " vehicles knocked to pieces.

To add to these difficulties, not a single sutler had
joined the army, and there was consequently not a drop
of spirits to be obtained for the men. Fuel was wanting and was only supplied, pending the despatch of
coal from England, by breaking up some of the captured
Dutch ships. There were no store-houses for the
housing of the supplies accumulated at the Helder,
and it was necessary to substitute store-ships for them.
Again, the Treasury had contrived to reduce itself to
hopeless confusion over the provision of bread for the
army. On the 9th of September there was but six
days' supply in store, and the Chief Commissary could
think of no better remedy than to write a long and
solemn letter to Abercromby explaining why his forces
must starve. Lastly, the medical arrangements were
absolutely chaotic. The authorities had not taken the
trouble even to form a hospital in England for the
reception of invalids from Holland ; and, when requested to appoint a place for it, they named Deal,
where all the unfortunate wounded must have been

1799. landed from small boats on the beach with infinite torture and risk to broken limbs. Fortunately, a leading medical authority, Sir Jerome Fitzpatrick, interposed, and insisted upon the choice of a port where hospital-ships of large draught could come alongside a jetty. But it is abundantly evident that the Ministers and the Public Departments, with the single exception of the Commander-in-chief's office, were as hopelessly incompetent for the conduct of war as in 1793. The Ministers were so busy planning campaigns, of which they understood nothing, that they could spare no time for the humble details whereby an army is kept efficient in the field.

There was yet one more burden laid upon the Commander-in-chief—that, namely, of arming and organising the Dutch who were to bring about the counter-revolution in favour of the House of Orange. High hopes had been built by Pitt and Grenville upon such a national movement, owing to the representations of the British Agent in the United Provinces, Mr. Bentinck, whose name sufficiently explains the reasons for his appointment. The Greffier Fagel, to whom Lord Grenville at the end of 1798 had submitted some of Bentinck's letters, declared that he had never heard the names of the persons whom the Agent put forward as men of influence and leading, and said plainly that little was to be expected unless the Orange party were favoured by the principal men in the actual province of Holland.[1] The British, when they landed, found the people if not actually hostile, certainly not friendly; but, none the less, the Hereditary Prince of Orange, with the encouragement of the British Government, attached himself to Abercromby and plagued him with projects of every description. " I listen," reported the sagacious old man, " but follow what to me appears to be our interest. . . . I believe the Prince has been deceived in thinking that he has more friends than enemies in this country. If we can advance, every one

---

[1] *Dropmore Papers*, iv. 313.

will be on our side, but there are few who will risk 1799. anything." There was the root of the whole matter. A successful campaign would undoubtedly regain the people of the United Provinces for the House of Orange, not because it was the House of Orange, but because it was the winning side ; and, until the British arms had reconquered Holland, all negotiations with the Dutch were premature.

Such, however, in spite of a dozen lessons within half as many years, was not the belief of the British Ministers. Emboldened by their promise of pay for any levies that he could raise, the Prince of Orange produced a list of nearly three thousand Dutch sailors and deserters, demanded wages and levy-money for them, and proposed to attach them to Abercromby's army with himself at their head. The old General positively refused to encumber himself with such a rabble ; but, none the less, the British Government expressly directed the Duke of York to co-operate with the Prince in raising such levies, so that the British troops should be free to go where they were most wanted. Moreover, Thomas Grenville was sent Ambassador to the Hague to act as the Prince's political adviser ; so that the Duke had every prospect of being hampered not only by the Russian Commanders and his own Council of War, but also by the Prince of Orange, and possibly by the brother of the Secretary of State for Foreign Affairs. Not yet had British Ministers learned, and not yet for ten years were they to learn, that in war all secondary considerations must be postponed to the first and greatest object of military success.[1]

[1] Abercromby to Dundas, 11th September (two letters with enclosures from the Prince of Orange). York to Dundas, 14th (three letters), 16th, 18th September; Dundas to York, 5th and 15th September 1799, enclosing letter from Sir Jerome Fitzpatrick.

CHAPTER XXIV

1799. OWING to the time consumed in disembarking the troops, the Duke of York was unable to advance immediately; and meanwhile Brune had employed the respite thus gained since his defeat on the 10th of September in strengthening his position. He now occupied an oblique line running from the little town of Bergen, which lies about three miles north-west of Alkmaar, north-eastward for six miles to Oukarspel. Bergen itself, nestling close under the highest and steepest range of the dunes and surrounded by little woods and copses, was strongly entrenched; in advance of it the villages of Schoorl, Groet and Kamp were fortified; and commanding positions were taken up on the sand-dunes, so that every inch of the ground on his left should be defensible. To eastward of this, his centre barred the road southward along the Great Northern Canal by the occupation of the hamlet of Schoorldam and of the village of Warmenhuizen, a little to north-east of it; and his right, posted at Oudkarspel, lay astride the great causeway which leads to Alkmaar from the north. At each and all of these points he had multiplied the many natural obstacles of the country by breaking up the roads, making abatis and palisades, and constructing redoubts at the heads of the dykes; but, though outnumbered by nearly two to one, he omitted as yet to inundate the country to east of Oudkarspel for the protection of his right flank.

In a country which was accessible only by a few

causeways, the Austrian system of attack by isolated   1799.
columns was the only possible one ; and the Council Sept. 19.
of War laid its plans accordingly. It was agreed that
the Russians should take the place of honour on the
right, and that General Hermann, with twelve Russian
battalions, Manners's British brigade and the Seventh
Light Dragoons, should drive the enemy from the
sand-hills at Bergen.[1] This was the First Column. On
its left the Second Column, consisting of the two brigades
of Guards, Prince William's brigade, and two squadrons
of the Eleventh Light Dragoons, under David Dundas,
were to force the positions of Warmenhuizen and
Schoorldam and to co-operate with Hermann. On
Dundas's left the Third Column, composed of Don's
and Coote's brigades, with the two remaining squadrons
of the Eleventh, were to carry Oudkarspel. Finally,
a strong detached column, consisting of Moore's,
Cavan's and Chatham's brigades, the Reserve, two
composite battalions of Grenadiers and Light Infantry,
and two squadrons of the Eighteenth Light Dragoons,
under Abercromby's command, were to move wide to
the left upon Hoorn, some twelve miles south-east of
Oudkarspel, and, proceeding thence southward by forced

[1] For the reader's convenience I repeat the list of Brigades :—
Cavalry.—7th Light Dragoons, 11th Light Dragoons, detachment
    of 18th Light Dragoons, 1 troop R.H.A.
First Brigade.—Guards grenadier battalion, 3/1st Guards—Major-
    general D'Oyley.
Second Brigade.— 1/ Coldstream, 1/3rd Guards—Major-general
    Burrard.
Third Brigade.—2nd, 27th, 29th, 85th—Major-general Coote.
Fourth Brigade.—2/1st, 25th, 49th, 79th, 92nd—Major-general
    Moore.
Fifth Brigade.—1/17th, 2/17th, 1/40th, 2/40th—Major-general
    Don.
Sixth Brigade.—1/20th, 2/20th, 63rd—Major-general Lord Cavan.
Seventh Brigade.— 3 battalions 4th, 31st—Major-general Lord
    Chatham.
Eighth Brigade.—1/5th, 2/5th, 2/35th—Prince William.
Ninth Brigade.—1/9th, 2/9th, 56th—Major-general Manners.
Reserve.—23rd, 55th—Colonel Macdonald.
In garrison at the Helder, 1/35th, 69th.

1799.   marches upon Purmerend, to fall on the enemy's right flank and rear.

It is plain that the nicety of combination required for the success of this movement was excessive ; and indeed the whole plan bears the mark of a compromise or, in other words, of a Council of War. The object of the Allies was to penetrate as speedily as possible to Amsterdam, and for that end the first thing requisite was to clear the passage between Alkmaar and the North Sea, so as to reach Haarlem and the Y. It may be affirmed with certainty that Brune could not be ousted from his position except by forcing one or the other of his flanks ; and it therefore followed that in any attack the function of the Allied centre must be chiefly to contain the enemy, while the bulk of their strength was concentrated against a flank. Undoubtedly, the eastern flank, in the direction of Hoorn, was vulnerable ; but a turning movement from that side was so wide as to require a corps of sufficient strength to act independently. Moreover, such a corps would need to be concentrated at Hoorn beforehand, so as to move up on Alkmaar simultaneously with the army on the Zype ; and to this there was the objection that its appearance at Hoorn would betray the design, and cause Brune to check it by inundating the country. All considerations, therefore, dictated the massing of an overwhelming force at Petten so as to force Brune's left or western flank, which would have led the army straight upon Haarlem and Leiden. Instead of this the Council of War, apparently halting between two opinions, concentrated considerable bodies of troops on both flanks and overwhelming force on neither.

The attack was appointed to begin at dawn of the
Sept. 19. 19th ; and accordingly, on the evening of the 18th, Abercomby marched with his division, about ten thousand men, for Hoorn. The distance to be traversed did not exceed thirteen miles as the crow flies, but was increased to more than twenty by the deviations of the road, which, moreover, was in an

extremely bad condition.   Hence his column had a 1799.
long and fatiguing march, but on reaching Hoorn at Sept. 19.
two in the morning found the commandant and his
petty garrison asleep in their beds, and the sentinels
asleep at the gates.   The place was therefore occupied
without difficulty, and one hundred and sixty Dutch
soldiers were captured, which was all to the good.
But the troops were so much jaded by their exertions
during the night, and the roads were so execrable, that
Abercromby did not feel justified in making a forced
march upon Purmerend until he heard how the day was
going on his right.   And things on the right, as must
now be told, were going anything but well.

At two o'clock, or still earlier, in the morning of
the 19th some Russian light infantry and a battalion
of grenadiers under General Schutorff crossed the canal
before Petten, for no reason, apparently, except their
own caprice, and advanced along the sea-shore straight
upon the French lines at Kamp.   General Hermann
was apprised of the fact by half-past two, but made no
effort to stop or recall them ; and, on the firing of
one or two shots an hour later, he declared that,
since Schutorff had begun the attack, he must be
supported.   Thereupon, he ordered his first line of
Russians to advance from Petten along the Slaeper
dyke, parallel to Schutorff and about two thousand
yards east of him.   At the same time he directed two
squadrons of the Seventh Light Dragoons to support
Schutorff and two more to act as escort to a troop of
British Horse-Artillery, at the same time moving
Manners's brigade a little to the eastward from Petten
to wait in reserve.   It was still too dark to distinguish
any object when he ordered the gun to be fired as the
signal for attack, being fully aware, as he confessed,
that he was beginning his work too soon, but unable
longer to restrain the impatience of the troops.

The first line of the Russians therefore advanced in
very fair order along the Slaeper dyke till they reached
the first breastwork erected by the French, when they

sent up a savage yell and rushed forward. The enemy gave way without firing more than half-a-dozen shots, but the whole of the Russians, from front to rear of the column, responded with a tremendous and irregular fire, destructive to none but themselves. In this tumultuous state they pressed on in the dark, carrying the second of the breastworks as easily as the first, but suffering heavily from their own fire. Meanwhile, Schutorff's column could be heard advancing as rapidly on the right through the sand-hills, and Hermann's men raised a wild cry for artillery. This was brought forward, and, though the darkness still forbade all distinction of any definite object, the guns likewise opened a furious and aimless cannonade. Pressing on to the end of the dyke the column parted itself into two divisions, one of which joined Schutorff's force, and with it poured from time to time a heavy fire upon the other division, which followed the road to Groet. This village also was carried with little difficulty, but it was evident that the main force of the enemy was on the east side of this road ; for a heavy though irregular fire was directed upon the Russians from that quarter, which was answered both by Hermann's column and, though far out of range, by Schutorff's, the latter firing indiscriminately both upon the enemy and upon their comrades. Hermann's horse was struck by a French bullet from the east, and he now ascended the dunes towards Schutorff's corps, leaving his own column without directions of any kind. However, both divisions still blundered on in the same irregular fashion. The Russian light infantry had exhausted its ammunition and was thenceforth useless ; but their second line of infantry came up, promptly mingled with the first, and by its impetus carried the whole body forward. The Russian colonels could not find their regiments and had lost all control of their men. From time to time they shouted the order to cease fire, but no one took the slightest notice. The men of the French advanced posts had been rallied upon

three battalions before Schoorl ; but the Russians in 1799.
the road, though still under the fire of their comrades Sept. 19.
on the sand-hills, brushed them aside and floundered
on blindly towards Bergen.

The road now passed through a chain of scattered
houses and narrow copses of very thick underwood, with
occasional openings towards the east,[1] from which a
steadily increasing volume of fire poured upon them
from the French infantry and artillery.   For Brune had
already begun to reinforce his left by calling detachments from Dumonceau's troops across the bridge at
Schoorldam.   Captain Taylor, the British staff-officer
who had accompanied the Russian column on the road,
now entreated the commanding officers to deploy their
regiments and extend them to eastward ; but they seemed
utterly helpless and incapable of more than a wild advance along the highway, with indiscriminate firing to
front and flanks.   They were now within a mile of
Bergen, and plunged into an avenue with dense underwood on each hand, which screened them until they
were within two hundred yards of the town.   There the
underwood ceased on the eastern side, and their advance
was checked by a tremendous fire of musketry and
artillery on their front and left flank.   Crowded together
in a confused mass, they again yelled for guns, which
were with great difficulty brought up, the horses being
scarcely able to crawl.   Then, covered by their fire,
the mob of men again surged forward, still under a
terrible rain of bullets and grape, when General Essen,
Hermann's second in command, at last appeared and
gave the order for the troops to halt and form.

A battalion was then extended to the left, with guns,
to keep down the French fire ; the crowd of men on
the road was re-formed ; and more infantry came up in
the rear under Hermann himself, who apparently had

[1] The character of the road, though the houses are far more
numerous than a century ago, is little changed ; and the course of
the action can be well traced by the traveller who traverses it at
this day.

brought them down from the sand-hills. The column
then advanced again, but was immediately thrown into
confusion by the battalion which had been extended
to the left, and which now fell back in disorder upon
the road. However, though Hermann had now lost
all control of his men, they struggled on to Bergen,
and actually occupied it in a helpless and apathetic
fashion for about twenty minutes, without the slightest
idea as to what they should do next. But by this time
Brune's reserve from Alkmaar had arrived upon the
scene ; whereupon Vandamme, sending forward his
chasseurs to drive back such few Russians as remained
in the sand-hills, attacked the village both from east
and west, and, as the main body fell back along the road,
closed in upon it on all sides. The Russian retreat
now became a rout. Hermann was taken prisoner.
Essen, collecting a few troops, forced his way back
through the avenue under the fire of the French, who
had lined the underwood alongside it, and succeeded in
reaching a small body of men on the sand-hills. Upon
these he rallied his troops, at the same time despatching Taylor in hot haste to bring up Manners's brigade
to his support.

Meanwhile, Dundas's column, which was accompanied by the Duke of York, had advanced as soon as
the light permitted upon Warmenhuizen, throwing out
one battalion towards Schoorldam to cover Hermann's
left flank, and two more to eastward to preserve
communication with Pulteney. His progress was
necessarily slow, owing to the need for throwing flying
bridges over the innumerable waterways that barred his
advance ; but at six o'clock the village was smartly
stormed by the simultaneous attack of three Russian battalions from the east, and of the First Guards from the
west. Supported by three gunboats in the great canal,
Dundas moved next upon Schoorldam ; but, the enemy
having destroyed the roads, he could advance to it
only over a network of canals, and did not reach it
until nine o'clock. He carried that village also, how-

ever, taking several hundred prisoners ; soon after 1799.
which an aide-de-camp came galloping up at the top of Sept. 19.
his speed to the Duke of York.   He brought the news
of the utter defeat of the Russians upon the right.

The Duke at once ordered Manners's brigade to
advance upon Schoorl ; but the French had followed up
their counter-attack with astonishing rapidity, and the
Russians were utterly demoralised.   They were scattered
in scores about the villages which they had taken—
drunk, insubordinate, and pillaging upon all sides.
Major-general Knox, who entered their camp at nine
o'clock, found it full of stragglers wounded and un-
wounded ; while on the sand-hills Russian riflemen were
in sight, with the French chasseurs in hot pursuit.
Seeing that there was nothing to check these chasseurs,
Knox sent two squadrons of the Seventh Light Dragoons
to rally the Russian riflemen, if possible, and galloped
back to the Helder to fetch the Thirty-fifth, which
formed part of the garrison.   Returning to Kamp with
this regiment at about eleven, he met the Russian
General, Essen, who entreated him to stay his drunken,
plundering troops ; whereupon he handed the Thirty-
fifth to him to cover their retreat.   A more trying and
difficult duty for a battalion of raw militia, which had
evidently been left in garrison because it was worse
fitted than the rest for the field, it would be difficult to
imagine ; and it is not surprising to find that it suffered
heavily.[1]

Thus it was that when Manners's brigade reached
Schoorl it found the village already abandoned by the
Russians and set on fire by their plunderers, and was

---

[1] A militiaman, whom I presume to have been of this corps,
left a journal in which he recorded his impression of our Allies as
he first saw them.   "The Russians is people as has not the fear of
God before their eyes, for I saw some of them with cheeses and
butter and all badly wounded, and in particklar one man had an
eit days clock on his back and fiting all the time which made me
to conclude and say all his vanity and vexation of spirit."—*Recollec-
tions of the British Army, Colburn's Military Magazine*, February
1836.

1799.
Sept. 19. soon fully occupied, if not overtasked, with the duty of checking the counter-attack of the French. Great efforts were made to rally the Russians, but without success. They streamed away into their own lines, and dispersed, both officers and men, without the slightest effort to re-form ; and the danger that the French might force the western extremity of the Allied line became pressing. Meanwhile, the bridge over the great canal at Schoorldam had been broken down, and Dundas was unable to send a man to Schoorl until it had been repaired, which took a full hour. Battalion after battalion was then withdrawn from his force to reinforce Manners, while Dundas himself maintained his position at Schoorldam under a very heavy fire with indomitable tenacity. But it was too late. The British were forced back from Schoorl ; and Dundas then retired in good order, covered by the gunboats in the great canal. This seems to have taken place between four and five o'clock in the afternoon, by which time the British had been on foot for thirteen or fourteen hours ; and the retreat, as was natural with weary, half-trained, and incoherent bodies of men, was anything but orderly. Many of the brigadiers, as well as the regimental officers, were without experience, and several battalions filed through the all - important post of Krabbendam without an order to any one of them to take up positions for its defence. In fact, there were no troops to be trusted except the four battalions of Guards and the artillery ; and the Guards, having been heavily engaged all through the day, had lost many men, had expended nearly all their ammunition, and were quite worn out with fatigue. These old soldiers, however, were still unbeaten, and, thanks to their spirit, the French did not venture on an attack upon the lines.[1]

[1] According to Bunbury the situation was saved by a Grenadier of the Guards, who, when his Colonel hesitated to march the weary battalion back to Krabbendam (through which it had already passed), said, "Give us some more cartridges, and we will see what can be done." Thereupon the Colonel gave the order to march. *Great War with France*, p. 19.

Meanwhile, Pulteney, after struggling with infinite 1799. difficulties before Oudkarspel, had at last contrived to Sept. 19. carry the redoubt which barred his progress along the great causeway. Coote's brigade, which he had detached to turn the French position, had found it absolutely impossible to make its way over the obstacles presented by the marshy meadows. In front, he himself could advance no further than to a cross-dyke, from behind which he engaged in a savage duel of musketry and artillery with the Dutch, hoping that time might yet give him a favourable opening. At length, after the lapse of many hours, the enemy imprudently attempted a counter-attack, which was heavily repulsed ; and the British, pursuing, entered the redoubt upon the backs of the fugitives, and drove them from it, with the loss of sixteen guns and seven hundred prisoners. The Dutch retreated in confusion south-westward to Koedyck, and Pulteney, after advancing for a short distance in that direction with the hope of renewing the attack on the morrow, bivouacked for the night. At eleven o'clock he received an order from the Duke of York to retreat without delay to the lines of the Zype, which he did, after first destroying the captured guns ; and thus the whole of the advantage which he had gained was thrown away.

Abercromby's division never moved nor fired a shot throughout the day. The first message which he received from the Duke of York came at noon and announced Dundas's success at Warmenhuizen, but added that nothing was known of Pulteney. The General thereupon took steps to ascertain whether he could march across country to the westward, but found that such a step was impracticable owing to the breadth of the canals that barred the way. At four o'clock in the afternoon a second messenger arrived with the news that Pulteney had captured Oudkarspel, but that the Russians had been beaten, and that the division was to return to its original station immediately. Leaving the Fifty-fifth to occupy Hoorn, where the inhabitants had been very friendly, he started at dusk along the road by which he had come. The rain began to fall in torrents directly afterwards; the road became one mass of mud, and the march was terribly arduous. The two battalions of flank-companies from the Line, being composed entirely of militiamen, left an enormous number of stragglers on the road, one company returning to quarters with only twenty men out of one hundred and ten.[1] At every point was proved the danger of throwing half-trained men suddenly into active service.

The casualties of the British were six officers and one hundred and twenty-seven men killed; forty-four officers and three hundred and ninety-seven men wounded, and four hundred and ninety men missing, exclusive of three hundred and fifty men of the First battalion of the Thirty-fifth, whose fate was stated to be unknown, but who were certainly taken. This was the unfortunate battalion that had been hurried forward from the Helder, when the retreating Russians first began to stream into Petten. The total of casualties was therefore rather over fourteen hundred of all ranks, of whom five hundred belonged to Manners's brigade; from which it is evident that the covering of the Russian retreat cost far more men than the attacks of Dundas and Pulteney. Against this the Duke of York could show three thousand prisoners captured, the bulk of them by Dundas in his capture of Schoorl-dam, and sixteen French guns destroyed. The loss of the Russians was set down at between two and three thousand men, the latter figure being the more probable; and they left twenty-six guns in the hands of the enemy. The loss of the French and Dutch can have been little if at all smaller than that of the Allies; and, altogether, neither side had very much to boast of.

---

[1] Of these twenty, fourteen were old soldiers, of which there were only fifteen in the company. The remaining six were rebels captured at Vinegar Hill. Colburn's *Military Magazine*, Feb. 1836.

None the less, the moral advantage gained by the 1799. French was immense. The British had lost all confidence in the Russians; and the Russians, though their misfortunes were entirely of their own making, of course attributed them to the backwardness of the British in giving them support. Since the Duke of York had sacrificed nearly a thousand men to save them, their complaints did not render the British feeling towards them more cordial. Beyond all doubt, the Russians were responsible for the day's failure, for, if they had but gone through their antics two hours later, as had been arranged, the Duke's plan, faulty though it was, might have proved successful. Even so, however, their plunder and destruction of the Dutch villages would have done, as it actually did, untold mischief by alienating the inhabitants; for, in this respect, the behaviour of the British had so far been exemplary. Lastly, the British had lost confidence in their Commander-in-chief, and the Commander-in-chief had lost confidence in his troops—in neither case without good reason. The Duke's hasty recall of both Abercromby and Pulteney, instead of holding on to Oudkarspel, and using a part of Abercromby's force to support it, showed that he had lost his head for the moment; and this was not calculated to encourage the troops. On the other hand, the disorder of the retreat on the right and the helplessness of the brigadiers in that difficult duty were enough to discourage any General.

Two days later Admiral Mitchell took a flotilla of Sept. 21. gunboats into the Zuider Zee, and paid visits to Medemblick and Enckhuisen, where the inhabitants hoisted the Orange standard; while another detachment of the like craft sailed across and made a raid upon Lemmer, on the west coast of Friesland. There was, however, little profit in these operations, and, indeed, the Admiral seems to have been no very enterprising officer, or he would long before have prepared his gunboats, as Abercromby had urged,

and have threatened Amsterdam.[1]   However, on the
24th of September a new corps of from three to four
thousand Russians from Kronstadt was disembarked,
and at about the same time there arrived also three
troops of the Fifteenth Light Dragoons, and a company or two of riflemen from the Sixth battalion of
the Sixtieth—a battalion not yet two months old,
and, of course, composed of foreigners.   The Duke
of York, therefore, lost no time in making preparations for a second attack.   The plans which he submitted
to Abercromby and Dundas were three.   The
first was to detach a strong corps to eastward to
threaten the French right, and in co-operation with
the fleet to alarm Amsterdam.   This Abercromby
rejected on the ground that this detachment, if raised
to a proper strength, would leave too few men to
hold the lines of the Zype.   A second proposal, to
hold the present position, and send seven thousand
men to hearten the Orange party in Friesland and
Groningen was rejected both by David Dundas and
Abercromby, as promising no certain result and
giving the enemy time to gather reinforcements.
It was, therefore, decided to adopt the third plan,
namely, to make a second general attack upon the
enemy's position, directing an overwhelming force
upon his left, and entrusting the hardest of the work,
namely, the advance along the sea-shore from Petten,
to the best of the British troops with Abercromby in
command.

The attack was fixed for the 29th of September,
and the columns were actually formed up at daybreak ; but a heavy south-westerly gale made the
march of troops along the beach impossible, and drove
the sand so furiously before it in the dunes that
no troops could have fought against it with success.
Further operations were therefore unavoidably delayed
for three days, which Brune did not fail to turn to
account by perfecting his defences.   Warmenhuizen

[1] Abercromby to Dundas, 4th September 1799.

was indeed abandoned, but Oudkarspel was further 1799.
strengthened by inundations. Koedyck, a village on
the great canal about three miles to south - east of
Schoorl, and Schoorl itself were fortified by additional
entrenchments; and the reclaimed fens called the
Schermer, Beemster and Purmer, to east and south-
east of Alkmaar, were flooded, thus effectually covering his right flank and rear. Finally, a reinforcement
of four French squadrons, four French and several
Dutch battalions made good to him his losses in
the last action, and raised his force to about twenty-
five thousand men.

The Duke of York laid his plans for the attack
in four principal columns.

The First or Right Column consisted of D'Oyley's,
Moore's, and Cavan's brigades, and Macdonald's
Reserve, in all about eight thousand bayonets;
together with one troop of Horse Artillery and
nine squadrons of the Seventh, Eleventh, and
Fifteenth Light Dragoons, making seven hundred
and fifty sabres, under Lord Paget. It was ordered
to march along the beach against Egmont-aan-Zee[1]
and to turn the enemy's left flank.

The Second Column was composed wholly of
Russian troops, eight thousand of them infantry,
and two hundred Cossacks, under their own General
Essen. It was directed to follow the road under the
eastern face of the sand-dunes, which Hermann had
traversed on the 19th of September, through Groet
and Schoorl upon Bergen, keeping a detachment
under General Sedmoratzky on its eastern side so
as to cover its left flank and maintain communication with the next column.

This, the Third Column, under command of David
Dundas, was formed of Chatham's, Coote's and
Burrard's brigades, with one squadron of the Eleventh
Light Dragoons; in all about forty - five hundred

---

[1] The form most familiar to Englishmen is Egmont-op-Zee, bu
I adhere to the name as given on modern Dutch maps.

1799. bayonets and one hundred sabres. Of these, Coote's
Sept. brigade was to follow the advanced guard of Abercromby's column to Kamp, and there turning eastward to take in reverse the defences which barred
the advance of the Russians, and to cover Essen's
right flank.   Chatham's brigade was to follow in
support of Essen's corps for the attack on Bergen,
and in conjunction with Coote's to endeavour to
maintain communication with Abercromby. Burrard's
brigade was to move on the eastern side of the Great
Northern Canal and combine with Sedmoratzky's
corps in the attack on Schoorldam, being assisted by
seven gunboats, specially prepared and protected for
the purpose, upon the canal itself.

The Fourth Column, under Pulteney, consisted
of Prince William's, Don's, and Manners's brigades,
two battalions of Russians, and two squadrons of
the Eighteenth Light Dragoons. It was posted so as
to cover the left of the British position to the
Zuider Zee, threaten the enemy's right, and take
advantage of any favourable opportunity that might
offer itself. It numbered forty-eight hundred bayonets
and one hundred and fifty sabres, and was stationed
chiefly at Schagen.[1]

The attacking army, excluding the Fourth Column,
was reckoned at twenty-two thousand bayonets and
sabres, or, making allowance for officers and sergeants,
about twenty-five thousand of all ranks.

It will be observed that the greater part of this force
was to act in the sand-dunes, the one space unbroken
by dykes, ditches, and canals in Brune's line of defence ;
and it is therefore necessary to describe them somewhat minutely. From Kamp southward to Bergen,
a distance of about four miles, the dunes rise to a
larger scale than at any other point on the coast.
Beginning with a breadth of two or three hundred

[1] I have taken the numbers from the plan enclosed in the Duke
of York's letter to Dundas of 25th September, corrected by the
slight alterations that are shown in his despatch of 6th October.

yards at Kamp itself, they widen rapidly to more
than a mile opposite Groet, to about three miles
opposite Schoorl, and to close upon four miles midway between Schoorl and Bergen.   In this last space
they attain to the dignity of true hills, with a height
of fully one hundred and fifty feet, and with unbroken ridges, four or five hundred yards in length,
covered with heather and stunted coppice.   On
the seaward side they rise abruptly, like cliffs, for
some eighty feet sheer above a broad beach.   To
landward they descend, for the most part, as abruptly
to the level plain of the fen, covered with long strips
of dense scrub and coppice, chiefly birch, which,
where fully sheltered from the westerly wind, grows
to a respectable height.   Between the two outer ridges
to seaward and to landward lies a chaos of lower
sand-hills, for the most part bare or held together
by coarse grasses, but frequently presenting narrow
valleys of nearly level ground, dotted with heather
and low creeping shrubs, and broken by occasional
patches of dense stunted birch from a quarter to
a half of an acre in extent.   These little valleys are
in places fully half a mile long, and from fifty to
one hundred yards broad ; and it is important to
note that they are to be found, for the most part,
immediately within the two outermost ridges.   Hence,
if a force were advancing in line through the dunes,
the two flanks, unless constantly checked, would
inevitably soon outstrip the centre.

It must be remarked also that, once within this confusion of sand-hills, a man is practically shut off from
the world without.   A company advancing just within
the seaward ridge, and another company advancing
along the beach within three hundred yards of it would
be out of sight, and, from the roar of wind and sea,
out of hearing of each other.   The only means for
preserving communication between them would be
for one man, or a few men, to follow the comb of
the outermost ridge itself, ascending and descending

1799.
Sept.

knee-deep in loose sand, along a surface where hardly three consecutive steps would be upon the same level. Troops summoned from the beach to the dunes would equally have to climb up a sheer ascent of eighty or a hundred feet knee-deep in sand, no very easy matter to men burdened with a heavy musket and a pack. Finally, within the dunes themselves, an officer could rarely see to any distance either to front or flank without a laborious scramble to the summit of some ridge or hummock, where his figure would stand clear against the sky-line, an easy mark for sharp-shooters, who even within a few yards of him could find ample means of concealment. It will, therefore, be gathered that it was difficult to move infantry, and quite impossible to move artillery through the dunes. Hence, Abercromby could take no guns with him except a single troop of horse-artillery and two six-pounders, which were practically tied to the beach; and freedom of movement even on the beach, owing to quicksands and other obvious causes, was dependent on the state of the tide.

So much for the difficulties of the advance and the maintenance of communication between the beach and the dunes. Scarcely less formidable were those that beset the communication between the dunes and the reclaimed fen to landward. The road from Kamp to Bergen runs at first about five hundred yards distant from the foot of the sand-hills, draws closer to them at the village of Groet for a few hundred yards, recedes again for a short distance, and finally returning to them at the village of Schoorl hugs them closely all the way to Bergen. At Groet there begins on the eastern slope of the sand-hills a chain of rough coppice, which continues almost unbroken to Bergen; while that slope itself from Schoorl southward is often for many hundred yards so steep that a man could hardly ride, and could only with difficulty lead, a horse from the road to the summit. A blinder

country, and one more difficult for scouts, it would 1799.
be difficult to find. But this is not all. Immediately
to south of Bergen the width of the dunes suddenly
contracts from four miles to two, and continues to
shrink steadily to southward, until at Egmont-aan-
Zee it hardly exceeds a mile. The hills themselves
also become easier and lower, while the plain immediately to east of Egmont itself, though perfectly level,
is for nearly a mile in width sound, firm ground,
enclosed by banks and free from the ditches that
make the plain of North Holland impassable. It
is, in fact, ground where troops can deploy, where
artillery can move, and where cavalry can act.
There is also a gap in the dunes at Egmont-aan-
Zee, and a road running eastward from it to Egmont-
aan-den-Hoef whereby guns could be easily moved to
or from either flank of the sand-hills. To south of
Egmont-aan-Zee the dunes, though low and scattered,
broaden out once more, while a great number of
little copses on each side of the road afford additional facilities for a force retiring southward to cover
its retreat. A reserve of French troops about Egmont-
aan-Zee and Egmont-aan-den-Hoef could either
prevent an exhausted enemy from debouching from
the dunes on to the plain, and cut them off from
water, or, if forced back, could effectually harass, if
not actually prevent, their further advance.[1]

The morning of the 2nd of October broke fine Oct. 2.
and warm, though the wind still blew too strongly
from the south-west to permit the flotilla on the
Zuider Zee to make a demonstration, as had been
intended, on the right flank of the French. About
six o'clock the tide was at ebb, and Abercromby's
column moved out of Petten, the advanced guard
being formed by a squadron of the Seventh Light
Dragoons with two guns of the Horse Artillery.

[1] I feel constrained to apologise for so lengthy a description of
this little strip of country ; but without it any conception of the
difficulty of the Duke of York's task is impossible.

1799.
Oct. 2.
The French picquet at Kamperduin retired without resistance, merely firing a signal-gun as it went; and Abercromby's column, with the other brigades that followed it, passed on to the sand-hills and deployed. Coote's brigade, pursuant to its orders, turned sharply to eastward, making for the road to Schoorldam. Macdonald's Reserve, strengthened by two composite battalions of the Grenadiers and Light Infantry of the Line, and by three hundred Russian Light Infantry, also turned to the east, its duty being to cover the left flank of Abercromby's main column. Moore's brigade, which formed the advanced guard, likewise entered the sand-dunes, keeping its right flank on the hills that rise immediately from the beach, while the rest of the column followed the beach itself,[1] the right flank of the cavalry being constantly in the water. The enemy was visible in small bodies both on the shore and among the dunes; and a few skirmishers presently engaged and annoyed the Reserve. Thereupon Macdonald, who has been described by one of his contemporaries as a " very wild warrior," strayed away to eastward in pursuit of them, leaving the flank of Abercromby's column uncovered. Unable to discover what had become of the Reserve, and finding his flank galled by the French light troops, Abercromby was obliged to delay and weaken his advance by throwing out a flank-guard. Moore accordingly detached the Twenty-fifth and Seventy-ninth for this duty, taking command of them in person.

He had scarcely formed them before the French attacked them in earnest, but were driven back by a charge with the bayonet, though not before Moore had been struck in the thigh by a bullet. He continued

[1] The *British Military Library*, ii. 111, says that Cavan's brigade (which was commanded by General Hutchinson) followed Coote's brigade and advanced along the heights overlooking the road to Schoorl. All other authorities point to its having been on the beach, but I can find no trace of the part that it took in the action, and its casualties were slight.

however, to command his brigade, and the advance was 1799.
resumed, the French light troops retreating before him, Oct. 2.
but skilfully using all the innumerable advantages of
the ground to harass and oppose him. Gradually more
battalions were thrown out to bear back the pressure on
Moore's left flank and rear,—first the Royals and Forty-
ninth, and later the Grenadier battalion of Guards
from the beach ; and thus it came about that, the
difficulties both of the ground and of the enemy's
attacks being greatest upon his left, Moore's whole
brigade was drawn out into a long irregular echelon, the
Twenty-fifth leading it on the right at a considerable
distance in advance of the other battalions. However,
after five hours' march in these trying circumstances,
Abercromby's column arrived within about a mile of
Egmont, where the enemy stood in force in a strong
position.[1]

Their officers quickly noticed Moore's disordered
battalions, and forthwith launched upon them their
own fresh and unwearied troops. The Twenty-fifth
was struck heavily in front and flank, and three companies of the Ninety-second, coming to their assistance, were clumsily led straight through the hottest of
the fire. The whole began to give way, and at this
critical moment Moore was struck down by a bullet
behind the ear, and fell to the ground stunned and
helpless. The rest of the Ninety-second, however,
backed by the First Guards, came up on the right of
the Twenty-fifth ; the Royals, Forty-ninth, and Grenadiers of the Guards hastened to close up to their left ;
and the fight was renewed. A confused struggle
followed, which lasted the best part of an hour ; small
bodies of men on both sides closing with each other,
and, unable to use their weapons in the unstable sand,

[1] After close examination of the ground I and my companion
came to the conclusion that this position was exactly opposite the
village of Wimmenum, where a transverse ridge of very steep sand-
hills, with a multitude of little copses, cuts across the dunes from
east to west. But, in truth, the whole of the dunes form one continuous defensive position.

1799.
Oct. 2. betaking themselves to their fists.   At length, wearied
out, the French retired to their first position,
the British halted over against them, and, as if by
tacit agreement, the contest ceased in this part of the
field.[1]

In this situation Abercromby found himself as the
sun began to decline.   Moore's brigade, the only one
except the Guards which was composed of trained
soldiers, was utterly exhausted by fighting, and
weakened by the loss of nearly seven hundred men
and of forty-four officers, among whom was Moore
himself, the best officer of all.   To renew his attack
he had no trained soldiers except the two battalions
of Guards, of which the first had lost nearly seventy
officers and men in the struggle to rescue the Twenty-
fifth, while the Grenadiers, though they had suffered
far less, had shared in the distressing march through
the sand-hills.   To support them he had only three
battalions of Militia, numbering fewer than eighteen
hundred men.   The enemy in his front was in great
force ; reinforcements were visible marching to join
them ; and their artillery, far surpassing his own in
weight and number of guns, had already made itself
felt among the troops on the beach.   Of the rest of
the British army he could see nothing and hear
nothing.   From Macdonald he had received not a
word except one note written some hours before, to
say that he was at Groet, which was at least three
miles from where he ought to have been.   Weary in
body, for two horses had been killed under him,
perplexed and harassed in spirit, Abercromby was fain
to halt, and, while making a show of a bold front, to
look for a position against the coming of night.

Nor had the other columns fared much better.
Coote's brigade duly scoured the sand-hills on the
right of Essen's column, while Sedmoratzky and
Burrard cleared the plain on their left ; but though
the French retired without much resistance from

[1] *Narrative of a Private Soldier in the 92nd Foot*, pp. 46-48.

Groet and Schoorl, they stood for some time at 1799.
Schoorldam, until driven out at about eleven o'clock Oct. 2.
by Sedmoratzky and Burrard.   At this point, however,
Essen halted the whole of the Russians and declined to
budge further, thus preventing Burrard from moving
forward against Koedyck, and leaving only Coote's
and Chatham's brigades to Dundas for the capture of
Bergen.   Coote's battalions were at the time above
Schoorl, extended at wide intervals into the sand-hills
and making little progress.   Dundas therefore passed
Chatham's brigade to the right of Coote's, and moved
it forward so as to threaten the left flank of the French,
who retired to the heights above Bergen itself, from
whence they opened a heavy cannonade upon Dundas's
line.   The British, easily finding shelter among the
dunes, suffered little ; and an attempt at a counter-
attack from the French along the avenue that led into
Bergen was repulsed with heavy loss by the Eighty-
fifth.   Dundas now passed three battalions of Coote's
brigade to the right of Chatham's ; and these unexpectedly found their right in contact with Macdonald's
Reserve, which had been floundering aimlessly among
the sand-hills all day.   The whole were therefore
formed in line, Coote's and Chatham's brigades to east
of the road from Bergen to Egmont, and Macdonald's
battalions to west of it.   A general advance swept the
enemy from the sand-hills on the right front ; and the
eleven battalions established themselves astride of the
road, thus cutting the direct communication between the
French on the beach and their comrades in Bergen.

Meanwhile Abercromby, though remaining halted,
had pushed his troop of Horse Artillery well in advance,
its escort of dragoons standing dismounted a little in
rear of it and hidden from the enemy's view by a
sand-hill. General Vandamme, who had just brought
up two battalions and a squadron of hussars from
Alkmaar, perceiving the guns to be unprotected, sent
forward the hussars to make a swoop upon them ; and
so swiftly and cunningly did these French horsemen

advance that they were actually in the midst of the
battery before they were discovered. But a dozen
English sergeants and officers, among whom were
Paget, Robert Wilson, and Colonel Erskine of the
Fifteenth, had remained in the saddle; and this handful of horsemen galloping straight at the hussars
engaged them so vigorously as to gain time for the
escort to mount. The British Light Dragoons speedily
came up to their assistance and every man of the
French squadron was cut down or captured.

This closed the action on the western flank. Far
away to eastward Pulteney had played his part in
threatening Oudkarspel and the French right with
sufficient skill and prudence; and at nightfall the
divisions of Dundas and Abercromby bivouacked on
the ground that they had won, Macdonald bringing
his weary and jaded men into Abercromby's lines at
dusk. The action had lasted for over twelve hours,
and the men were terribly fatigued. They had by
the Duke's order left their packs behind, and carried
only a blanket or a great-coat and three days' provisions;
but, parched by the wind and by the salt and sand with
which it was loaded, the men had emptied their water-
bottles by noon, and there was no water in the bivouac.
Suffering agonies from thirst, they were unable to touch
their salted rations, and lay down in misery until, as
had already happened in every twenty-four hours of
this campaign, the rain presently came down in torrents
and gave them relief. Wringing their dripping clothes
into their hats they drank the water greedily; and
when the morning came, it was found that Brune
had withdrawn his army from its position between
Oudkarspel and Egmont and retreated. He retired,
however, at his leisure and in perfect order, only to
take up a shorter and more formidable line from Wyk-
aan-Zee on the west through Beverwyk to Purmerend.
The action had not accomplished much towards the
conquest of Holland.

However, the Duke of York could justly claim a

victory, and the name of Egmont-op-Zee is still borne 1799.
on the colours of the regiments engaged.   But it was Oct. 2
the kind of victory which ruins an army.   The loss of
the British amounted to over fifteen hundred officers
and men,[1] and of the Russians to over six hundred
officers and men killed, wounded, and missing, making
over two thousand casualties altogether.   Considerably
more than half of this loss fell, as has been said, upon
Abercromby's Division, and chiefly upon Moore's
brigade, wherein the Ninety-second Highlanders alone
counted fourteen officers and two hundred men fallen,
besides forty more missing.   Macdonald also had contrived in the course of his foolish wanderings to throw
away nearly three hundred men of the Reserve ; his
raw troops having suffered heavily from the French
riflemen.[2]   The loss of the French was at least as
great ; and they left seven guns, besides a few hundred
prisoners, as trophies to the Duke.   But there can be
no doubt that the British in the sand-hills were out-
fought throughout the day by the enemy, for the simple
reason that the French had an active and well-trained
light infantry, whereas the British had none.   Moore
himself was obliged to drive off the French skirmishers
with the bayonet, having no skirmishers of his own
with which to meet them ; and the huge militiamen
of the massed grenadier-companies exhausted themselves in rushing up sand-hills after the nimble little
Frenchmen, who indeed always retired, but were seldom
if ever overtaken.   This was one cause of the general
failure of the attack.   Others, which chiefly contributed
to it, were the sulky refusal of the Russians to advance,
and the powerlessness of Abercromby upon his arrival

[1] 11 officers and 226 men killed ; 74 officers, 1033 men wounded;
5 officers and 218 men missing ; 125 horses killed, wounded, and
missing.

[2] Surtees, *Twenty-five Years in the Rifle Brigade*, pp. 16-20.   The
author at the time was in the light company of the Fifty-sixth.
From his account it is plain that the Reserve became broken up,
and that there were companies of it scattered along the whole line
from Bergen to the sea.

1799. before Egmont owing to the vagaries of Macdonald. But, in truth, even the most highly-trained troops under the best of officers might easily have come to misfortune over a plan of operations which was necessarily complicated owing to the enormous difficulties of the country.

On the days following the action Abercromby moved forward to the south of Egmont-aan-Zee, the Russians to Egmont Binnen on Abercromby's left, Dundas to Alkmaar and to Heiloo on the road to Haarlem, and Pulteney to the space between Alkmaar and Schermerhorn, with Prince William's brigade detached to Hoorn. But these dispositions were made in the most careless and slovenly fashion, and for two days Abercromby remained isolated at Egmont without a man between him and Alkmaar.[1]   Meanwhile Brune, having been reinforced by six French battalions from Belgium, had fortified a triple line of posts, the foremost running from South Bakkum through Limmen to Akersloot and the Lange Meer, the next from Heemskerk to Uitgeest, and the third from Wyk-aan-Zee to Beverwyk; while Daendels held the passes through the inundations to eastward at Knollendam and Purmerend, with a reserve in rear of the latter at Monnikendam.

The Duke of York, somewhat elated by his victory and in difficulties over supplies for his army, was anxious to force the position of Beverwyk before Brune could fortify it effectually; and, ignorant of his true dispositions, ordered the advanced posts on his right to move forward on the morning of the 6th and to occupy the villages in their front.   Accordingly, so far as can be gathered, a part of Abercromby's division advanced through the sand-hills on the coast, Essen's Russians moved upon South Bakkum, and Coote's and Burrard's brigades upon Limmen and Akersloot respectively.   All three of the villages were captured with little difficulty, five companies of the Coldstream

Oct. 6

[1] *Diary of Sir John Moore*, i. 358.   Bunbury, *Great War with France*, p. 31.

and Third Guards making a brilliant charge at Akers- 1799.
loot and capturing two hundred prisoners.   But Essen, Oct. 6.
not content with this, insisted upon wandering still
further south, unaware that Brune had been concentrating upon his second line of defence; and upon
reaching Kastrikum, on the road a little to southward
of South Bakkum, the Russian General found his easy
progress arrested by a sharp resistance from three
French battalions.   Instantly he sent for reinforcements.   Battalion after battalion of his own troops
hurried forward to join him; Abercromby also came
forward on the west; and the French commander,
finding that Abercromby was gaining way and likely
to outflank him, evacuated the village and fell back
to a position in the sand-hills.   From Egmont Binnen
southward to Kastrikum and beyond it, the dunes again
widen out to a breadth of fully three miles, no longer
separated by a hard line from the cultivated plain, but
gradually merged in it, in a tangle of little hills,
enclosures, and copses.   Here, therefore, the French
held their own till Brune came to their support with
the greater part of a division; and then for three
hours a stubborn conflict was maintained with little
advantage to either side, until Brune observed British
troops, presumably Burrard's brigade, moving from
the east to the help of Essen.   Thereupon he detached
three battalions to hold Burrard in check, and, massing
the remainder in close columns, fell upon the Russians
with the bayonet, and drove them headlong back to
Kastrikum.

Here Essen rallied his broken battalions, calling
urgently to Abercromby for help; but hardly had he
succeeded in forming about four thousand men and
posting his guns to command the approaches to the
village, when the French division came upon him in
pursuit.   A sharp struggle followed; but Brune's
men, pressing on with the impetuosity of success,
speedily captured his guns and again drove him back
along the two roads to South Bakkum and Limmen.

The French cavalry followed them up keenly on the western road, until a small party of British horse, apparently of the Seventh Light Dragoons under Lord Paget, crashed in upon their left flank from an ambush in the dunes and sent them galloping back in wild confusion upon the French infantry.[1]   The effect of this unexpected charge of a few score of resolute men was astonishing.   The panic of the French horsemen communicated itself to the French foot, and the whole, some two or three thousand strong, gave way and ran back to Kastrikum.   It was but just in time, for an unbridged stream lay in the rear of the Russians, and their destruction was almost inevitable.   The attack of the dragoons, however, gave them breathing-time and recovered for them their guns.   Abercromby appeared in person with one brigade from the west, and two of Dundas's battalions from the east.   The bridge was repaired ; the stream was passed ; and the fight ended at the villages of Bakkum and Limmen, whence both sides retired in the darkness to their first positions.

It is difficult to know what to make of this strange scramble of an action.   It seems certain that the Duke of York had intended only to drive in the French out-posts on the 6th, and to advance in force on the following day ; and the British blamed Essen for carrying his troops too far forward in contempt of the Duke's orders.   Since Essen, by all accounts, refused to have any dealing with the Duke and made a point of dis-obeying his commands, this may well have been the case ; but the fact remains that the Duke allowed the whole of his force to drift into a general action for no particular object, without the slightest idea how to control it.   He was, in fact, in Alkmaar, with one of

[1] This charge of the Seventh Light Dragoons (for, putting the various accounts together, I think it certain that the credit of the action belongs to them) must have taken place where the road passes actually through a belt of the dunes a little to the north of South Bakkum.   There is a small open space, just large enough for a couple of squadrons, adjoining the road but invisible until actually entered, where they were probably formed.

his staff perched on the top of the church-spire and 1799.
with aides-de-camp flying in all directions to discover Oct. 6.
what had become of his army.   The country, as has
been told, was extremely difficult and intricate ; the
rain was falling in torrents ; the smoke hung thickly
among the trees ; and in all directions were bodies of
troops engaging whatever enemy came first to hand,
and advancing or retiring, sometimes in great disorder,[1]
according as they were the weaker or the stronger
party.   Yet it seems that the Duke had notice of the
first serious encounter of the Russians with the French
from Abercromby, with a warning that the enemy
seemed to intend a general attack.   No notice, however, was taken of this ; and the Duke being at
dinner, only invited the messenger, a certain Major
James Kempt, to join him at table.   Fortunately Brune
did not meditate a general attack ; but the engagement was sufficiently costly.   The Russians returned
a loss of over eleven hundred of all ranks, and the
British casualties amounted to over eight hundred
killed and wounded, and over six hundred prisoners.[2]
The brigade that suffered most severely was Chatham's,
in which the three battalions of the Fourth lost nearly
one hundred and fifty officers and men killed and
wounded, and over five hundred, including thirteen
officers, prisoners ; while the Thirty-first lost over
one hundred killed and wounded and thirty-three
prisoners.   In what part of the field these battalions
were engaged I have been unable to discover, but under
so incompetent a brigadier they were likely to come to
misfortune in any position.   According to one authority
Chatham himself was wounded, but not, apparently,
in time to save him from wrecking his unfortunate
troops.   Far heavier work fell upon Hutchinson with
the Twentieth and Sixty-third, who was left to hold

[1] See the account of the rout of the grenadier-companies before
Egmont Binnen in Surtees, pp. 24-25.
[2] 4 officers, 91 men killed ; 36 officers, 696 men wounded ;
19 officers, 593 men missing.

1799.
Oct. 6.
his own against superior forces in the dunes while Abercromby was extricating Essen's disordered battalions. Hutchinson himself was struck in the thigh by a bullet; the Sixty-third lost nearly two hundred of all ranks, one-fourth of them missing, and the two battalions of the Twentieth over one hundred and eighty more; but the brigade did its difficult duty well. The loss of the French was probably somewhat smaller than that of the Allies, though they too left five hundred prisoners in the hands of the British. But there could be no question that with them lay the advantage of the day.[1]

On that night Abercromby, David Dundas, Pulteney, and Hulse, the four Lieutenant-generals with the army, went to the Duke of York, and told him that he must retreat; and both they and he wrote to Henry Dundas their reasons for the necessity. The army since landing had fought five considerable actions, costing altogether nine to ten thousand men, but had made little or no progress. The country was singularly difficult; the sand-hills afforded neither fuel nor cover; the plain of North Holland, always low and marshy, was so soaked by continuous rain that troops could not be encamped, even if there had been means of transporting tents; and all movements were confined to dykes and roads, of which the latter had been much damaged by the enemy. So far the army's supplies had been carried on the canals; but even so it had been impossible ever to keep more than two days' victuals in hand, and seldom even so much. The canals had now come to an end, and, owing to the want of wheeled carriage, every step in advance increased the difficulties of transport and supply. Moreover, it was well known

[1] Few modern actions are so obscure as this last, not a single English person present, apparently, having left any account of it. The above account is drawn chiefly from Jomini, iv. 67. Moore was not present. Bunbury's narrative is as vague as the Duke of York's despatch of 7th October, wherein he reported the action. Maule, the *Military Library*, and Colburn's *Military Magazine* give few or no particulars.

that, owing to the state of the roads and the lowness 1799.
of the land, military operations generally became im- Oct. 6.
possible in Holland in November.   The Russians were
disheartened, and there was no friendly feeling between
them and the British.   A renewal of the attack would be
hazardous in the extreme, for the French had been reinforced ; and even if they were beaten it would be
impossible to follow them owing to the state of the
roads, the lack of waggons, and the presence of the
Dutch on the eastern flank.   Defeat, on the other
hand, would mean utter disaster.   " Were we to sus-
tain a severe check," wrote Abercromby privately, " I
much doubt if the discipline of the troops would be
sufficient to prevent a total dissolution of the army.
This is melancholy, and is the natural consequence of
young soldiers and inexperienced officers—all-powerful
if attacked, but without resource if beaten." [1]

Accordingly the Duke retreated on the following day, Oct. 7.
leaving his wounded behind him for want of means of
conveyance, and on the morrow re-entered the lines of Oct. 8.
the Zype.   So terrible was the state of the roads after
weeks of rain that his few waggons took two days to
cover nine miles ; but, though the French followed him
closely, the army suffered little loss.   An attack was
indeed made by Daendels upon Prince William's
brigade on its retreat from Hoorn, but this was repulsed with little trouble.   Even within the lines,
however, the difficulties of supplies recurred, there
being but nine days' provisions in store.   The Commissary had sent ships to Hamburg and Bremen for
flour more than a month before, but, owing to foul
winds or other causes, not one had yet returned.
Abercromby thereupon wrote to Henry Dundas that
the sooner the army re-embarked the better, though
even with the best management it could not hope
to evacuate Holland without loss of horses and

[1] The Lieutenant-generals to Dundas, 6th October ; Abercromby to same, 8th October ; York to same, 7th and 8th October
1799.

1799.
Oct.

artillery.   The Helder by itself was untenable, and could not by any means be made secure for the winter. The Zype position, though strong, was so extensive as to throw much labour on the troops, who were already sickening fast ; and it was out of the question for the army to winter there, if only for the reason that the navigation to it was generally closed by the middle of November.   The re-embarkation itself promised to be a most difficult matter, for the Zype was the only position that really covered the port, and as the troops were gradually withdrawn from it, the enemy would have the better chance of attacking it with success. Moreover, the Helder could not be strengthened so as to hold out above three or four days against siege-artillery ; and, if it were captured, every ship in the Mars Diep would be captured with it.   In fact, the situation was as awkward and as dangerous as could well be conceived ; and, to distress the Commanders still further, there came at this time the news of Massena's victory at Zürich on the 11th of September, and of the defeat of the Allies in Switzerland.[1]

Fortunately Brune's officers threw out a hint of an armistice and a convention, which was eagerly caught up by the Duke's staff.   Negotiations were accordingly opened on the 14th, Major-general Knox acting very

Oct. 18.

ably on behalf of the British, and by the 18th a capitulation was agreed upon.   The conditions were that hostilities should cease and that the British should evacuate the country by the 30th of November, yielding up eight thousand French and Dutch prisoners from England, though without prejudice to the cartel already fixed for exchange of prisoners during the past campaign.   The Dutch fleet was to remain in the hands of its captors. Though Brune did not know it, the British had but

Oct. 20.

three days' bread left on the 20th ; and indeed Abercromby looked upon the loss of half of the army as so certain that he could not conceive why the French

[1] Abercromby to Dundas, 12th October; York to Dundas, 12th, 14th, and 18th October 1799.

agreed to such easy terms.   However, fortunately for 1799.
Pitt and Dundas, they did, thanks not a little to the Oct. .
astuteness of Knox.   Further supplies of flour arrived
shortly after the signing of the capitulation ; and with
some difficulty, owing to continual storms, the whole
of the troops were embarked by the appointed day.
By that time sickness had reduced the British to
twenty - four thousand and the Russians to nine
thousand effective men.   Bad luck continued to dog the
expedition to the last, for three ships of war were
wrecked on the Dutch coast, two of them with all
hands, and a transport with over two hundred and
fifty of the Twenty-third on board was also cast away,
and only twenty of the soldiers saved.   However, the
remainder of the troops seem to have reached England
in safety, including the Russians, who, after astounding
the good people of Yarmouth by drinking the oil from
the street-lamps, were finally quartered in the Channel
Islands.   So ended the expedition to the Helder.[1]
   The enterprise is of interest in many respects as
being, in spite of its failure, the first undertaken by
the renovated, or rather of the new, British Army.
The force was of course raw, unformed, hastily assembled, and therefore utterly unfit to be plunged, as
it was, immediately into active service ; but, none the
less, considered as material, it was the best that
England had put into the field since Cromwell's regiments were disbanded.   There was singularly little
crime among the soldiers, in spite of the demoralising
company of the poor underpaid Russians ; and Abercromby declared the Militiamen to be, in his judgment, a superior class of men and a great acquisition
to the Army.   Mingled with them were a certain
number of Irish, hot from the late insurrection ; and
an officer recorded many years later that the best
soldiers during the campaign in his own very strong

[1] York to Dundas, 20th and 21st October ; Abercromby to
Dundas, 19th October 1799. Dunfermline's *Life of Abercromby*,
pp. 197-203 ; Colburn's *Military Magazine*, February 1836.

1799. company were six rebels captured at Vinegar Hill.[1] Unfortunately the officers were not only deficient in numbers, but many were very young and inexperienced men who had been lifted, by the sudden augmentation of the regiments, prematurely to superior rank. In fact, the hurrying of this crude force into the field at a moment's notice was a shameful injustice alike to Generals, regimental officers, sergeants, and men ; and it was creditable to them to have got through the campaign, with all their faults, as well as they did. It was, however, a great point that this new material had been found. " In the spring," wrote Abercromby to Dundas, "you will have a fine army, if the brigades are put under Major-generals who are capable of instructing young officers and training young soldiers. They must remain stationary, and not be allowed to dance all over Great Britain." Here, therefore, was a promise of a future camp at Shorncliffe, though not yet of a Light Division.[2] Nevertheless, as has been seen, there were a few riflemen, actual members of the British Army, who took a share in this campaign ; and this marked a step in advance, which, as shall be seen, was soon to be carried still further.

Another innovation was the appointment for the first time in our history of an officer in supreme command of the Artillery, at whose recommendation Abercromby withdrew the battalion-guns from the infantry and massed them into four brigades or, as we should now call them, batteries, each of four six-pounders.[3] But the campaign was altogether an important one in the history of the Artillery, for it not only brought that arm into the field for the first time with its own drivers, but launched the Horse Artillery likewise into active service, and gave its baptism of fire to the famous Chestnut Battery.[4]

[1] Colburn's *Military Magazine, ut supra.*
[2] Abercromby to Dundas, 11th September 1797. *Military Magazine, ut supra ; Life of Abercromby,* p. 202.
[3] Lieut.-col. Whitworth to Abercromby, 5th July 1799.
[4] Duncan, *History of the Royal Artillery,* ii. 88 *sq.*

Still more interesting was the appearance of a 1799. new corps called the Royal Waggon Train, which, though only formed for the first time on the 12th of August, was at once carried across the North Sea. It consisted of five troops, which on the 21st of September were increased to eight, each of four officers and seventy-one men, of whom sixty were drivers ; and a Waggon-Master-General was placed in command of the whole.   The pay of the Waggon-Train was the same as of the Cavalry, the men being in fact such troopers of the Cavalry as were nearly worn out or " did not match their regiments." [1]   Considering that Abercromby sailed on the day after the order for the formation of this corps was issued, it may readily be conceived that no part of it was ready to accompany him.   But it appears that fragments of it soon reached the Duke of York, and that, by the time when he had decided to re-embark, he had for the first time a sufficient, or nearly sufficient, number of officers and men to deal with the transport of his army.   It seems, in fact, that the Government in this expedition to the Helder despatched the troops first, then the supplies, and lastly the transport ; and, since the difficulties of transport and supply were among the chief reasons urged for the retreat and re-embarkation of the army, it is necessary to enter rather more minutely into this dry and difficult question.[2]

An inquiry was held as to the causes why the main depot of supplies at the Helder had so often been on the verge of exhaustion ; when both the Treasury and

[1] *S.C.L.B.*, 12th August, 21st September ; *C.C.L.B.*, 8th August 1799.

[2] A return of 14th October 1799 shows the strength of the Waggon-Train at that date in Holland to have been 25 officers, 275 officers and men, and 514 horses.   The Duke of York wrote to Dundas on 24th October that " the Waggon-Train has been till now inadequate to the service of the Army."   I may add that at the present time the number of four-horse *vehicles* assigned to an Army Corps of 36,000 men, excluding all pair-horse carriages, six-horse carriages, and pack-animals, is 514, the precise figure of the *horses* at the Duke of York's command.

1799. the Commissary-general were able to produce vouchers showing that between the 13th of August and the 20th of October there had arrived in Holland from England ninety-seven days' supplies for forty thousand men.

Aug. 13. The largest shipment was that which left England with Abercromby, amounting to thirty-five days' subsistence for forty thousand men ; and yet, though Abercromby had no more than at first twelve thousand and, after the 28th of August, seventeen thousand men, his supplies had already run dangerously short by the 9th of September ; that is to say, after twenty-eight days only. This the Commissary-general professed himself unable to explain at the time ; though he was able to account for it triumphantly some months later, when it was discovered that many of the transports on their return to England contained provisions enough to victual the men on board for several weeks. It seems extraordinary that the Commissaries themselves should have been unaware of this fact ; and indeed their ignorance reveals extreme incapacity and want of organisation in this department of the Treasury. But, apart from this, the Commissariat appears never to have calculated for the necessity of retaining at least a month's supplies for the troops upon all the transports, for it was not safe to allow less even for so short a voyage as the passage of the German Ocean. Abercromby's division had been fourteen days on board ship before it could land at the Helder ; and, with the dangerous and intricate navigation of the Mars Diep to be encountered in the face of prevailing westerly winds, it might well have been delayed even longer in its return to England. The only retreat of the British, in case of defeat, lay across the sea, and a General who failed to keep his ships victualled against such an event, to say nothing of possible movements of troops by water in the course of the operations, would have been a madman.

But, even if Abercromby's division were adequately provided for, the same is not true of the Duke of

York's army.   Its strength was reckoned at forty 1799.
thousand men : it numbered actually from forty-eight
to fifty-four thousand ; and the Russians required a
ration of bread half as large again as the British,[1] so
that the number of bread-rations required must be
taken as at least fifty thousand.[2]   At the time when the
Duke of York's army disembarked there had reached Sept. 14.
Holland forty-seven days' bread for forty thousand
men, or say forty days' allowance for fifty thousand.
Of this Abercromby's division had already consumed
the equivalent of at least twelve days' supply, leaving
twenty-eight days' supply only, or about the quantity
that should have been kept on board the ships in case
of re-embarkation.   During the remaining sixteen days
of September there arrived, or were purchased with
great difficulty from the fleet and in the country, small
quantities amounting to a further supply for twenty-
eight days, leaving twelve days' allowance on the 1st
of October.   Between the 1st and 19th of October
arrived twelve days' further supply, in two consign-
ments ; but meanwhile, owing to the accumulation of
three thousand Dutch deserters and other adherents of
the Prince of Orange, the number of mouths had
increased.   Hence on the 13th of October there was,
both on the transports and ashore, bread for only
twenty-three days for the forty thousand men that
remained of the force.   This amount being less than
ought to have been reserved upon the transports against
the event of a disembarkation, it was not untrue that,
when the capitulation was signed, the army was practically at the end of its supplies.

Sheer misfortune was in great measure responsible
for this, for four months' bread-stuffs for forty thousand men had been purchased in the Elbe just before ·

---

[1] 1½ lb. against 1 lb.

[2] I give the figures of Commissary-general Motz, being uncertain
whether he does or does not make allowance for the extra half-
ration required by the Russians.   I am very nearly certain that he
does not ; and if I am right the case against the Treasury is very
much stronger than is here expressed.

1799. Abercromby sailed; but the ships that carried them were wind-bound for five weeks and did not reach the Helder until the 20th of October. But even if they had been delayed for one week only, which should fairly have been taken into calculation, they would not have reached their destination until a week after the army had disembarked; and the season was so far advanced that time was valuable beyond all price. This, therefore, cannot excuse the failure to furnish the Duke with a very large reserve of supplies in the first instance; for want of which he was unable to fill his advanced magazines and to provide adequately for movements upon a large scale. The truth is that the Cabinet came to its decision in a hurry, and left this and many other matters to chance.[1]

When even the comparatively simple business of filling the principal magazine was mismanaged, it is not surprising that the far more difficult task of distributing provisions from that magazine was found insuperable. Abercromby, as has been seen, asked again and again for horses and waggons, but without result. The figures as to the waggons and so forth have already been given and need not be repeated; but it is beyond all question that the Ministers deliberately burked the whole subject of land-carriage, and determined to trust to water-carriage and to luck. They trusted in vain; for the French, as has been told, on learning of Abercromby's approach, removed every boat and waggon that they could; but this was a contingency that should have been reckoned with. Henry Dundas blamed the weather for everything that went amiss in the matter of transport and supply; but, even if his expectations as to water-carriage had been realised, canals no more dispense with the need for wheeled-transport than railways.

In fact it is difficult to decide whether the reckless-ness of the Government was more conspicuous in the

[1] See the voluminous correspondence on this subject in *W.O. Orig. Corres.*, 64, 65.

preparation or in the design of this expedition. The 1799.
dissatisfaction of the public in England over its mis-
carriage was very great ; and the Ministers were therefore driven to find new excuses for it. Their first line
of defence was the weather, which beyond question
was cold, rainy and stormy beyond all human experience, considering the season, and greatly impeded the
progress of the campaign. But rain and tempest
furnished no explanation for putting a raw force into
the field without any transport ; wherefore it was
roundly asserted that all the maritime resources of
England would not then have sufficed to disembark an
army at once complete with the necessary train of
carriages and waggons. This was probably true ; but
the obvious reply was that, in that case, North Holland,
which was known to possess few horses and waggons,
was a very unfortunate field of action to select.

As to the imperfect training and organisation of
the troops, Ministers pleaded that, until the initial
successes of the Allies in Italy and the sailing of the
Brest fleet, they did not feel justified in diminishing the
number of the Militia. But considering that the successes of the Allies were well advanced in April, that
the French fleet left Brest on the 25th of that month,
and that the Act for reducing the Militia was not passed
until July, this plea was merely childish. Moreover,
the Militia could, with a little care, have been made
more effective for home defence when converted into
regular regiments than before. The next step, therefore, was to prove that the expedition was valuable as a
diversion in favour of the Allies, and that it played a
part in weakening the French numbers at Novi and in
Switzerland. Upon this it is sufficient to remark that
the battle of Novi was fought two days after Abercromby sailed, and that Massena's great victory over
Suvorof in Switzerland was won a week after the Duke
of York had begun to move forward in force.

These pretexts being miserably thin, it was necessary
to back them by some military opinion, which was the

1799. more difficult since Abercromby had condemned the whole enterprise from the first. So far, Dundas in his correspondence with the Generals in this campaign had behaved with a candour that did him honour. He had acknowledged to Abercromby after his embarkation that he had required of him an unduly hazardous service ; and he had acquitted the Duke of York in generous terms of responsibility for the misfortunes that compelled him to retreat. But in the House of Commons his courage failed him ; and he or one of his colleagues, prompted by him, quoted a single sentence apart from its context from one of Abercromby's letters, to show that the veteran General had looked forward to a successful campaign. Abercromby strongly remonstrated against such unfair treatment, but in vain. The Ministers wrote him many compliments and offered him a peerage ; but they would not imperil themselves by telling the truth, and allowed the public to believe that they had acted in accordance with the General's advice instead of directly contrary to it. A century has wrought little change in this respect among British Ministers of War.[1]

The Ministers, therefore, escaped payment of the penalty for this as for so many previous military failures ; but meanwhile it is still difficult to discover what was their real design in sending this large force to Holland. It is, I think, absolutely certain that they had no idea of entering upon a regular Continental war and of making Holland the sphere of operations ; otherwise the fleet could have been used to transport the army to the coast of Friesland, thence to strike on Arnheim and to invade the province by line of the Waal. Ministers hoped, no doubt, that at the first appearance of British troops the Dutch would rise,

[1] Dundas to York (private), October 1799. *Life of Abercromby*, pp. 211-215 ; and see four draft memoranda, evidently prepared to defend the action of Government in *W.O. Orig. Corres.*, 64, 65. Whole passages from these occur in the speeches of Ministers in Parliament.

expel the French and restore the Stadtholder ; but this 1799.
was a matter that could very well have waited until
France was brought to her knees by the Allied Armies
and the British fleet, when it would have followed as a
matter of course.   What, then, was the need to hasten
British troops over the North Sea with orders (for such
was the purport of Abercromby's instructions) to land
somewhere and do something ?   The explanation
appears to lie in the intense distrust which the British
Cabinet not unjustly entertained towards the Court of
Vienna ; and in its desire to hold a pledge which should
bind that Court to some approach to honest dealing.[1]
It should seem as though Pitt dreaded lest France should
be crushed and Europe parcelled out by Austria and
Russia without reference to England.   Holland therefore being the country with which British interests
were chiefly concerned, he determined to intervene
there in concert with Russia by military operations, so
as to secure a decisive voice in the ultimate fate of the
United Provinces, and to bring Austria to reason by
threatening to hand them to Prussia.   But, be this
as it may, the fact remains that he did send a powerful
force to the Helder for no sound military object, and
that it was forced to withdraw with disgrace.   That
there were grave military blunders committed by the
Commanders-in-chief both of the British and of the
Russians is unquestionable ; but, in the opinion of the
best judges, the difficulties of the country were so
enormous that a successful invasion of Holland from
the Helder was practically impossible.   The brunt of

[1] " The only right suggestion is that which the King made to
me on Wednesday—that we should make our force sufficient to be
quite certain (at least as much as the thing will admit) of occupying
the whole country ourselves before the winter.   It is only in that
way that we can put ourselves in a situation to talk to Vienna in
the only style which ever succeeds in making them hear reason.
. . . If we decide to return the provinces to Austria, it should, I
think, be only in consideration of her co-operation in the attack on
France.   If we return them to Austria during the war we lose our
only tie on them."   Grenville to Dundas, 27th July 1799.   *Dropmore MSS.*

1799. the blame for the mishap, therefore, must lie with the Ministers who persisted in pursuing their own designs despite the emphatic and repeated protests of their best military adviser.

AUTHORITIES.—The authorities for the Helder Expedition are *W.O. Orig. Corres.*, 61-65, Walsh's *Campaign in Holland, Life of Sir R. Abercromby*, Surtees's *Twenty-five Years in the Rifle Brigade, Narrative of a Private Soldier in the Ninety-second*, Bunbury's *Great War with France, Diary of Sir John Moore*, Major F. Maule's *Memoir of Events in the Campaigns of North Holland and Egypt*, Colburn's *Military Magazine*, February 1836. I know of no French account besides that of Jomini, which is rather unusually full.

CHAPTER XXV

By the failure of the attempt upon North Holland, the 1792. attention of the British Government was perforce brought back once more to the Mediterranean. But before proceeding to follow the narrative of events in that quarter it is necessary first to trace the progress of affairs in the East Indies, the influence of which has already been seen in the hasty despatch of British troops from Portugal to India. The story of the capture of Pondicherry, of Ceylon and of the Dutch East India settlements has already been told, as a part of Pitt's policy in seizing every foreign settlement that could be appropriated beyond the sea. It is now time to enter into the dealings of the British not only with European but with native powers in India.

Our last review of this subject ended with the conclusion of the Treaty between Cornwallis and Tippoo Sahib after the capture of Seringapatam in 1792. The Sultan of Mysore had, it will be remembered, been brought to submission by a triple alliance of the Nizam, the Mahrattas and the British. In other words, the two powers which aimed, consciously or unconsciously, at supremacy over the whole of India had leagued themselves against their most dangerous rival in the south, and had drawn into the quarrel a third power, which, being too weak to stand by itself, was bound to submit itself to one of the three others. Cornwallis, after the fall of Seringapatam, had endeavoured to develop the treaty of alliance into a treaty of guarantee, whereby the Nizam should be assured of protection if

1792. attacked by the Mahrattas or Tippoo, either singly or in combination. Such a treaty was naturally much desired by the sovereign of Hyderabad, but the Mahrattas threw every obstacle into the way of it, and Cornwallis departed from India leaving the matter, which was of vital importance, still unsettled.

The motives of the Mahrattas in obstructing Cornwallis's negotiations are easily explained. The basis of all Mahratta policy was plunder ; and, though the Mahratta Confederacy was at this time dangerously divided, there was within it one great and able chief, Madajee Scindia, who, despite the jealousies of his peers, aspired to unite it and ultimately all other native powers in one great effort to drive the foreigners from India. Up to 1782 he had been thwarted by the British ; but the urgent danger from Hyder Ali had then compelled Warren Hastings to buy him off by the Treaty of Salbye, and he had used his freedom to 1793. good purpose. By 1793 he was not only master of Central India and of North-Western India as far as Aligarh, but also ruler of the Mogul Empire, having military possession of all the strong places from Ujjein to Delhi and Agra. With all this he still professed subjection to the Peishwa, the pageant head of all the Mahrattas, at Poona, and acted ostensibly only as his deputy in directing affairs at Delhi ; but in council his voice was all powerful. Having every intention of plundering the Nizam's dominions, he remonstrated strongly against any further connection with the British ; and he gave a significant clue to his policy when he represented that the weakening of Tippoo Sahib had been a mistake. He soon found a pretext for a quarrel with the Nizam by making a claim upon him for tribute. Sir John Shore, Lord Cornwallis's successor, thinking any evil preferable to war, excused himself by jesuitical arguments from giving assistance to the threatened potentate, even though Tippoo was prepared to assist the Mahrattas in their aggression ; and they were accordingly left free to work their will.

Madajee Scindia died before the actual outbreak of 1794.
hostilities, but his successor, Dowlut Rao Scindia, pur- Feb. 12.
sued his policy, and in March 1795 a single battle 1795.
brought the Nizam to a disgraceful treaty.   Thereby he March.
not only conceded extensive territory to the Mahrattas
but gave up to them his Minister, Azim-ul-Omra, who
had always favoured alliance with the British, and abandoned himself to what seemed to be political extinction.

Much incensed against the Governor-General for
his neutrality, which he interpreted not quite unjustly
as a renunciation of promised friendship, the Nizam
dismissed the two auxiliary battalions furnished to him
by the British Government, and seemed disposed to
break with it for ever.   The rebellion of his son, Ali June 28.
Jah, however, induced him presently to beg that these
troops might be restored to him ; and their prompt
return prepared the way for a reconciliation, which was
presently forwarded by the release of Azim-ul-Omra
by the Mahrattas, and his reinstatement as Minister at
Hyderabad.   For the present, however, the Nizam
decided to strengthen his forces by measures which,
as shall presently be shown, were wholly antagonistic
to British interests.

Tippoo, meanwhile, had watched the proceedings
with the keenest attention, and had engaged himself, in
return for a large extent of territory, to help Ali Jah towards the dethronement of his father.   But the rapid
suppression of the rebellion put an end to these designs,
and he resolved to bide his time until he could obtain
a French armament to assist him.   A few months later, Oct. 25.
the young Peishwa, Madoo Rao Narrain, destroyed
himself, and the Mahrattas were distracted from further
immediate mischief by quarrels over the succession to
his throne.   The British also were intent upon the
conquest of Ceylon and other Dutch possessions ; and
thus all parties were for the time sufficiently occupied
with their own affairs.

But, during the past few years, there had grown up
a new power within the armies of several of the native

1795-96. princes.   Having learned by experience the value of
infantry trained after the European model, they had
sought out officers to form and command regular
regiments for them ; and the greater number of these
officers were French.   Madajee Scindia had taken to
himself M. de Boigne, a Savoyard, who, after serving
both in the French and Russian armies in Europe, had
drifted out to India, where he was successively an
officer in the Madras Native Infantry of the British
Service, in the army of the Mogul Emperor, and
finally, in 1784, in the forces of Scindia, for whom he
raised two native battalions.   These two were gradually
increased to twenty-four battalions, to each of which
was attached a battery of five guns ; and the whole
were organised into three brigades, which, with one
regiment of horse attached to each of them, made up a
force of twenty thousand trained men.   The officers,
so long as De Boigne retained command, were of all
European nations, British not excluded ; and many
of them men of good character and education.   De
Boigne resigned about 1796, giving to Scindia the
parting advice never to excite the jealousy of the
British Government by increasing his battalions, and
rather to discharge them than to risk a war.[1]   His
successor, M. Perron, however, was not of this mind.
He not only advocated increase of the force, but would
accept none but French officers ; and he discouraged
such Englishmen as remained in Scindia's army so
systematically as to convert it practically into a French
force under French commanders.   Moreover, taking
advantage of Scindia's title as Deputy of the Peishwa
in the vicegerency of the Mogul Empire, Perron
called his army the Imperial Army ; from which it is
not difficult to see that any treaty, real or fictitious,
between the French Republic and the puppet Emperor
of Delhi would have given him a sufficient pretext for
invasion of British territory.[2]

[1] Grant Duff, *History of the Mahrattas*, ii. 339 ; iii. 24-5, 175.
[2] Wilks, iii. 352.

Another force, similar in kind though inferior in 1796. efficiency, was that of the Nizam, under the French officer, M. Raymond. Originally it had consisted of two battalions only, which had fought with the British against Tippoo Sahib in 1792 ; but, after Sir John Shore had left the Nizam to fight with the Mahrattas unaided, it was increased to twenty-three battalions which their commander laboured incessantly to bring to perfection. Nor was he unsuccessful, for they were reckoned superior to all native infantry except the Sepoys in the British Service. But this was not all. Raymond was deeply infected with the doctrines of the Revolution. His battalions carried the colours of the French Republic, and wore buttons engraved with the cap of liberty. He had been detected in a correspondence with the French officers who had been taken prisoners at the capture of Pondicherry, with the object of obtaining their services ; and lastly, he had opened communications with Tippoo himself. On every side was evidence that Raymond and his subordinates cherished a determined hostility to the British.

Among all these potential enemies of the British rule in India, Tippoo seems to have steered his course so unskilfully as to have secured none for his allies. Early in 1796, however, he sent an embassy to Cabul to invite the Sovereign of the Afghans, Zeman Shah, to come with his army into the plains, conquer Delhi, and expel the Mahrattas first from Hindostan and then from the Deccan ; after which it would, as he urged, be easy to sweep the rest of the infidels into the sea. Zeman Shah, as a matter of fact, had already moved his forces for an invasion, and, though he was recalled by intestine troubles to Afghanistan, the menace kept the Government of Bengal in constant apprehension. Nor can it be doubted that his march into Hindostan would have served as an important diversion in Tippoo's favour by preventing the resources of Bengal from being employed in the south. But Tippoo's chief

1796. reliance was still on France, as the power that would help him to drive the British out of India. The Frenchmen in his service were careful to point out the superiority of their country's arms over England's, as displayed in the victories of the Revolutionary armies ; and they were able to transmit for him any letters which he wished to send to Paris. He remembered the favourable reception given to his embassy by the French Court in 1788 ; and it appears certain that he invited French help and made formal propositions of alliance to the Republican Government.

Such was Tippoo's state of mind when, early in
1797. 1797, a privateer from Mauritius arrived at Mangalore, dismasted, to beg permission to refit. It so happened that the Sultan's chief officer at the port had been one of his ambassadors to Paris, and had learned enough of the French language to converse with the master of the vessel. This person, François Ripaud by name, wishing apparently to add to his own importance, gave out that he was second in command at Mauritius, that an expedition was waiting there in readiness to expel the British from India, and that he had been specially instructed to touch at Mangalore in order to ascertain Tippoo's wishes regarding French co-operation with him for that object. The Sultan's officers quickly discovered that Ripaud was an impostor, and strongly recommended that no faith should be reposed in him, representing at the same time the danger that would arise from premature revelation of their sovereign's designs against the British. Tippoo, however, had already made up his mind to make use of the man ; wherefore, purchasing his ship for his own service,
April. he despatched it in April to Mauritius with four ambassadors on board, one of whom was to remain on that island, and the remainder to proceed to Paris. Ripaud himself was retained as French envoy in Mysore.

The voyage, however, was delayed by the abscond-

ing of one of the Frenchmen with the money which 1797.
the Sultan had paid for the vessel ; and ultimately the
mission did not start until October, with the envoys Oct.
reduced to two, and Ripaud himself in command of
the ship.   According to Tippoo's instructions, the
ambassadors were to conceal their quality and their
object, and to pose only as merchants ; but upon
their arrival at Mauritius, on the 19th of January
1798, the Governor, M. Malartic, sent officers of high 1798.
rank to wait upon them, and received them himself
upon their landing with a guard of honour and a
salute.   They then presented their despatches, containing the Sultan's proposals for a treaty with the
Government of Mauritius, which were to the following
effect.   The French were to provide for five to ten
thousand European troops, and from twenty-five to
thirty thousand Africans, who were to be met at an
appointed rendezvous by sixty thousand Mysoreans ;
after which the whole would proceed to the conquest
first of Goa, which would be retained by Tippoo, then
of Bombay, which would pass to the French, then of
Madras, then of Nizam Ali and the Mahrattas, and
finally of Bengal.

The ambassadors speedily discovered that Ripaud
had lied, and that no armament for an expedition to
India was either ready or expected at Port Louis ; but
the Sultan's letters were at once forwarded to Paris,
and, in the meanwhile, Malartic bethought himself to
satisfy them by raising a corps of volunteers in
Mauritius and Bourbon.   The Mysorean envoys
protested in vain that their instructions were to bring
a large force and not a small one, and that they had no
money for the raising of a new levy.   Whether from
arrogance or from vanity, Malartic insisted upon foisting
a band of adventurers upon them.   Further, not content
with this, he issued on the 30th of January a public Jan. 30.
proclamation, wherein he set forth at length the arrival
and objects of the Mysorean mission, and the Sultan's
intention, when strengthened by a French force, of

1798. driving the British from India. Finally, after recounting his own inability, owing to want of regular troops, to furnish the succours which the Sultan needed, he invited citizens to enter his service with the assurance of advantageous rates of pay. The reasons which induced Malartic to this most fatuous proceeding, violating as it did Tippoo's injunctions as to secrecy and proclaiming his designs to the whole world, have never yet been fathomed; but the Revolution produced so many men who were alike arrogant and incompetent that the simplest explanation is probably the truest. The unfortunate envoys weakly gave way to the blustering Frenchman; and,

March 7. on the 7th of March, they re-embarked for India with their volunteers, exactly one hundred in number, · including one General of the land forces, twenty-nine officers and sergeants, thirty-six European soldiers, and twenty-two half-castes; one General and six officers of the marine, four shipwrights, and a watch-maker.

April 26. On the 26th of April they arrived at Mangalore, when Tippoo, instead of sending them straight back to Mauritius, welcomed them to Seringapatam. There this precious band organised a Jacobin Club, under the worthy presidency of that approved swindler and pirate, Citizen François Ripaud. They formed a council of discipline to subvert that of their own commanders, brought the national colours to be blessed by Citizen Tippoo on the public parade, planted a tree of liberty, and swore an oath of hatred to all kings except "Tippoo Sultan the victorious"; all of which harmless eccentricities were countenanced with benign amusement by the potentate in question. The officers, or at any rate the two Generals, Chapuis and Dubuc, appear to have taken no part in these antics, having prepared for themselves credentials as

June. envoys to the Sultan's court; and, in June, Dubuc was selected to sail in company with two Mohammedan envoys from Tranquebar on a special mission to the

Directory in Paris.   It is difficult to say which showed 1798.
the greater folly during these months : Tippoo himself June.
or the gang of ruffians who, with matchless impudence,
had intruded themselves into his capital.

Meanwhile the news of Malartic's proclamation,
carried by an American vessel, had reached the Cape of
Good Hope.   From thence it was forwarded east and
west on the 28th of March by the Governor, Lord
Macartney, reaching England on the 14th, and India
on the 18th of June.   Dundas had already received
intelligence which led him to suspect an attack by
Tippoo upon the British dominions ; and he was by this
time satisfied that the destination of Bonaparte's fleet,
which, as will be remembered, had sailed from Toulon
on the 19th of May, was Egypt.   No difficulties, as
he wrote, were likely to deter the " unprincipled
desperate Government of France nor its adventurous
speculative leader " from making an attempt upon
India ; and he had therefore determined to send five
thousand seasoned troops to India as soon as possible.
But since, at the height of the Irish rebellion, not a
regiment could be spared from England, the reinforcement was to be composed of two battalions from
Gibraltar, three more from Portugal, and two from the
Cape.

The three from Portugal were, as has already been
seen, reduced ultimately to the Fifty-first only, which
sailed from Lisbon in the first days of October.   The Oct.
two from the Cape were consequently increased to
three, of which the Eighty-fourth and the Scotch
Brigade were, with the exception of a few companies,
embarked in September, together with two hundred
dragoons.   The whole of these were under the command
of Major-general David Baird, who had stopped at
Cape Town with the skeleton of his own regiment, the
Seventy-first, on his way to England.   The remainder
of these two corps, together with the Eighty-sixth,
sailed from the Cape in the middle of February 1799 ;
and, meanwhile, the Tenth from England and the

1798. Fifty-first from the Mediterranean reached the Cape at the end of December 1798, and proceeded immediately upon their voyage to India.   Considering the delays to which navigation was subject in those days, the difficulty of obtaining tonnage at the Cape, and the numerous embarrassments which crowded upon England in the summer of 1798, the despatch of these reinforcements appears to me to be the best work recorded of Dundas during his direction of the war.   It was not accomplished without reducing the garrison at the Cape to dangerous weakness, and that at a time when the Boers at Graf Reinet were still giving trouble; but the occasion was worth the hazard; and Dundas should receive credit for his courage and his zeal for India.[1]

The situation in India meanwhile was in many respects disquieting for the British; but, fortunately, there had arrived in April, 1798, a new Governor-general, Lord Mornington, who was great enough to cope with it.   He found Perron's troops, as we have seen, tacitly menacing the British frontier on the north, and a further invasion threatened by Zeman Shah; while in the south there were Tippoo, evidently prepared to open hostilities, and Raymond's corps under the Nizam, little less hostile in spirit than Tippoo. The British forces had been weakened by the garrisons required for Ceylon and other less valuable Dutch dependencies, and only by great good fortune had escaped still more dangerous reduction.   In August 1797 a small army of about three thousand British and four thousand native soldiers had been collected at Madras for an expedition to Manilla, under command of Sir James Craig.   One division of it had already sailed to Penang, when, in consequence of

---

[1] Brigadier Fraser (Lisbon) to Henry Dundas, 7th October 1798; Lord Macartney (Cape) to Henry Dundas, 28th March and 18th September 1798; General Francis Dundas (Cape) to Henry Dundas, 23rd January and 6th April 1799; Henry Dundas to Macartney, 18th June, 22nd August, 15th December 1798.

Bonaparte's victories in Italy, and of apprehensions 1798. that Tippoo might seize the opportunity to invade the Carnatic, orders came from England for. it to be recalled.   It will be observed that Pitt and Dundas, not content with exhausting the army of England, wished to exhaust that of India also by their absurd methods of making war.

But though this peril of Manilla had been averted, the army of Madras was dispersed in all directions, not only among the possessions captured from the Dutch, but also, owing to the maladministration of the Nabob of the Carnatic, within the Madras Presidency itself. It was impossible to concentrate it without the delay of several weeks, during which Tippoo might have taken the offensive with every chance of success ; while, even supposing the concentration to have been accomplished, motives of economy, as is usual with the British, had forbidden the maintenance of any efficient organisation for transport and supply.   None the less, two days after the receipt of Malartic's proclamation, Mornington ordered the army to be assembled June 20. on the coast, and instructed General Harris to select a station as a starting-point for a march upon Seringapatam.

His next immediate care was to regain, so far as possible, the former members of the triple Alliance. On the 8th of July instructions were issued to the July 8. Resident at Hyderabad to negotiate a treaty for the increase of the British subsidiary force in the Nizam's Army from two to six battalions, and for the dismissal of Raymond's troops, now under the command of M. Piron.   This was duly accomplished, and the treaty, which stipulated for the mutual defence of the members of the Triple Alliance, and for a mutual guarantee between them, was signed on the 1st of Sept. 1. September.   Immediately upon the conclusion of the negotiations, the four additional subsidiary battalions, which had been stationed near the frontier, marched to Hyderabad to enforce the disarmament of Piron's

1798.   troops. The Nizam, a weak and foolish old man,
hesitated to give the necessary orders ; but the British
Oct. 21. Resident was peremptory, and on the 21st of October
the six British battalions, with their artillery, took up
a position commanding the French lines. The proclamation for the dismissal was then circulated among
the French, and two days later, after some little
trouble, the whole of them were disarmed and disbanded without bloodshed. Thus a body of fourteen
thousand hostile soldiers was removed, and the
Nizam's assistance gained for the coming campaign
against Tippoo.

At Poona no such success was to be expected.
Scindia was quite prepared to throw in his lot with
Tippoo for the prosecution of his own designs of
plunder in the south of India ; and the treaty of
Hyderabad, whereby the British engaged themselves
to mediate in case of any differences between the
Mahrattas and the Nizam, could not be agreeable
to him. He therefore used all his influence, and
with success, to prevent the Peishwa from taking
part in the coming struggle as a member of the
Triple Alliance ; but at the same time he saw that
it would be prudent for him to maintain neutrality.
This was as much as Lord Mornington had expected,
and was for the present sufficient.

Meanwhile the news that the Governor-general
projected a campaign against Tippoo had at first
thrown the Council of Madras into dismay. Not
only was the army unready, but the transport was
reckoned to require twenty thousand bullocks, to
purchase which the Government could show only
an empty treasury and bankrupt credit. From the
earliest days of the British in Madras it had been
the practice in every campaign to buy at any price
the wild and undersized cattle of the Carnatic, and
to attach them to the guns and waggons without
previous training or experienced drivers. Commander
after commander had complained of this, from Eyre

Coote downward, but no effort had been made to 1798.
apply any remedy. It was very soon ascertained
beyond all doubt that an immediate advance upon
Mysore, such as had been at first contemplated by
the Viceroy, was absolutely out of the question, and
that the necessary force could not be equipped and
concentrated before February 1799.[1]

But, apart from this, Mornington was confronted
with a further difficulty. There were many men, including some of excellent judgment, who viewed his
plans with dread and did their utmost to dissuade him
from executing them. Against these Mornington found
the staunchest of allies in General Harris, who was
not only Commander-in-chief, but senior member of
Council in the Presidency. It was he who had insisted on sparing four thousand men to enforce the
Viceroy's policy at Hyderabad, and had overborne
all objections by offering to pledge his private funds
for the necessary expense. The success of this stroke
caused a revulsion of feeling in Mornington's favour,
which was intensified as the campaigning season continued to pass away without any attack from Tippoo.
And meanwhile the British troops were silently but
steadily concentrating at Vellore and Wallajahbad,
from forty to fifty miles west and south-west of
Madras, the latter under the superintendence of
Major-general Floyd, the former under the Viceroy's
younger brother, Colonel Arthur Wellesley of the
Thirty-Third. This latter officer was still only in
his twenty-eighth year, and had arrived in India in
1797, having seen no active service since he fought
under the Duke of York in Holland in 1794.
Harris, who was to command the expedition to
Mysore, we saw first at Bunker's Hill, where he
was severely wounded. He had since taken part in
the brilliant action at St. Lucia in 1778, and ten
years later had accompanied Sir William Medows to
India, where he had learned under Cornwallis in

[1] Lushington, *Life of Lord Harris*, pp. 150, 156, 204.

1798. 1791 and 1792 the difficulties of an advance upon Seringapatam.

On the 31st of October the news of the victory of the Nile reached India ; and, the British preparations being now well advanced, Mornington seized Nov. 8. the opportunity to open negotiations with Tippoo Dec. 10. for a specific settlement. A month later he himself embarked for Madras, so as to be at hand to pursue them in person. A few letters passed, wherein Tippoo seemed to be intent rather on gaining time than on serious entertainment of Morning1799. ton's overtures. But the new Governor-general was not a man to brook any trifling. All intelligence from Egypt pointed to the fact that the French were in possession of a considerable force ; and at last came the news that, after many delays, Dubuc and Tippoo's envoys had sailed on the 7th of February from Tranquebar on their mission to the Directory in Paris.

After incredible difficulties, due chiefly to the cumbrous forms of the military administration in Madras and the encroachments of the civilians upon the powers of the Commander-in-chief, the preparations were completed, and the " ponderous machine," as Arthur Wellesley called the army, was ready to Feb. be set in motion.[1] Early in February, therefore, Harris received his orders to invade Mysore, and therewith the fullest possible authority that could be delegated to him by the Governor - general. Mornington had been strongly pressed by the Council in Madras to accompany the army in person ; but, feeling little inclination thereto, he wisely consulted his brother Arthur, who told him bluntly that if he himself were in Harris's situation and the Governor-general were to join the army, he would quit it. Harris therefore entered upon his task with a free hand and plenary powers.

The army at Vellore numbered close upon twenty-

[1] Wellington, *Suppl. Desp.* i. 191-2, 199.

one thousand non-commissioned officers and men, 1799. of which the European cavalry counted just nine hundred, and the European infantry rather fewer than forty-four hundred; and it was reckoned to be the best equipped force ever seen in India.[1] Marching westward from Vellore on the 11th of Feb. 11. February, it was joined near Amboor on the 20th by the troops from Hyderabad. These included the six subsidiary battalions which had disarmed Raymond's force, with the artillery attached to them, six thousand of the Nizam's Cavalry, and thirty-six hundred of his old French contingent, in all sixteen thousand

[1] *Cavalry.*—Major-general Floyd, 19th Light Dragoons.
    1st Brigade.—19th Light Dragoons, 1st and 4th Madras Native Cavalry—Colonel Steerman, Madras Army.
    2nd Brigade.—25th Light Dragoons, 2nd and 3rd Madras Native Cavalry—Colonel Pater, Madras Army.
884 Europeans, 1751 Natives—Total, 2635 non-commissioned officers and men.
    Artillery :—
    Two companies Bengal, 1st and 2nd battalions Madras Artillery.
Total, 608 non-commissioned officers and men.   Also 1483 Gun Lascars.
    Infantry :—
    Right Wing.—Major-general Bridges, Madras Army.
    1st Brigade.—His Majesty's 12th, 74th, Scotch Brigade—Major-general Baird.
    3rd Brigade.—1/1st, 1/6th, 1/12th Madras Native Infantry—Colonel Gowdie, Madras Army.
    5th Brigade.—1/8th, 2/3rd, 2/12th Madras Native Infantry—Colonel Roberts, Madras Army.
    Left Wing.—Major-general Popham, Bengal Army.
    2nd Brigade.—His Majesty's 73rd, De Meuron's, His Majesty's 33rd—Colonel Sherbrooke.
    4th Brigade.—3 battalions Bengal Native Infantry—Lieutenant-colonel Gardiner, Bengal Army.
    6th Brigade.—2/5th, 2/9th Madras Native Infantry—Lieutenant-colonel Scott, Scotch Brigade.
    1000 Madras Pioneers.
Total, 4381 European, 10,695 Native non-commissioned officers and men.
    The native regiments are designated not by their present but their contemporary numbers.

1799. men.[1]　This last corps, before the territory ot Mysore was actually entered, was placed under the command of Colonel Wellesley, much to the discontent of Baird; and the Thirty-third regiment was added to it.　Thus the forces on the side of Madras amounted in all to thirty-one thousand fighting men, exclusive of the Nizam's cavalry.　Besides these, a force of six thousand men from Bombay had been organised under command of Lieutenant-general James Stuart,[2] and assembled at Cannanore with orders to ascend the ghauts into the province of Coorg.　It marched accordingly from Cannanore on the 21st February, and encamped on the 2nd of March about seven miles west of Peripatam, on the high road to Seringapatam, and not above fifty miles distant from it.

March 2.

Tippoo, meanwhile, after long wavering between resistance and submission, had finally decided to defy the British, principally, it seems, upon the persuasion of the French officers who had come to him from Mauritius.　His forces, including the garrison of Seringapatam, were reckoned at about thirty - three

---

[1] *Hyderabad Contingent* :—

   1 and 2/10th Bengal Native Infantry, 2/2nd, 2/7th,
      1 and 2/11th Madras Native Infantry; 1
      Company of Artillery, 1 Company of Bengal
      Artillery　.　.　.　.　.　6,536
   Nizam's Cavalry 6000, Old French Contingent
      3621　.　.　.　.　.　9,621
                        16,157

[2] *Bombay Army* :—

   Right Brigade.—1/2nd, 1/4th, 1/3rd Bombay Native In-
      fantry—Lieutenant-colonel Montresor.
   Centre Brigade.—His Majesty's 75th, 77th, 103rd (Bombay
      Europeans)—Lieutenant-colonel Dunlop.
   Left Brigade.—2/3rd, 1/5th, 2/2nd Bombay Native Infantry
      —Lieutenant-colonel Wiseman.
   European Infantry and Artillery, 1617 non-commissioned
      officers and men.
   Native Infantry, Artillery, and Pioneers, 4803 non-com-
      missioned officers and men.
   Total, 6420 non-commissioned officers and men.

thousand infantry and fifteen thousand cavalry and 1799.
rocket-men, making a total, with artillery, of fifty
thousand fighting men ; and, on learning that the
British were closing in upon him from both east and
west, he decided, while there was still time, to strike
a decisive blow. Leaving, therefore, a small force to
watch the progress of Harris, and giving out that
he meant to attack him on that side, he led twelve
thousand men of the flower of his troops secretly
and by forced marches upon Peripatam, in the hope
of crushing Stuart while he was still isolated from the
main army. Stuart, for his part, had endeavoured in
compliance with his instructions to find a defensive
position for his force, but this was impossible in a
country almost covered by thick and nearly impenetrable forest ; and he found himself compelled to
distribute his troops into three divisions. Of these
the foremost, Montresor's brigade, was at Sedaseer, on
the frontier of Mysore, near a high hill which commands a view of the country almost to Seringapatam ;
while the six remaining battalions were at two different
points twelve and eight miles distant from it. Stuart
was a good officer, who had marched to Seringapatam
with Cornwallis in 1792 ; wherefore it would be unreasonable to suppose that his dispositions were not,
under the circumstances, the best that he could make,
though in themselves they wear the appearance of
being both unsafe and unsound.

On the morning of the 5th of March a recon- March 5.
noitring party on the hill of Sedaseer remarked the
formation of a large encampment a little to westward
of Peripatam, with a green tent which seemed to
signify the presence of the Sultan himself. Intelligence from Seringapatam reported that Tippoo had
marched with all his forces to meet Harris ; but Stuart
none the less judged it prudent to reinforce Montresor's
brigade by an additional battalion of Sepoys. At dawn
of the following morning Major-general Hartley, who March 6.
held a command in the Bombay Army, discovered that

the enemy's force was in motion, but, owing to the forest and the haziness of the atmosphere, could divine neither their direction nor their object. Indeed, so swiftly and quietly did Tippoo's columns make their way through the jungle that between nine and ten o'clock they fell almost by surprise simultaneously on the front and rear of Montresor's brigade ; interposing five thousand men so as to isolate it completely from its fourth battalion, which was stationed over two miles from the main body. Fortunately, Hartley was able to send intelligence of the attack to Stuart, and meanwhile Montresor's battalions took up the best position that they could. There, though surrounded on all sides by greatly superior numbers, they fought stoutly and held their own.

They were, however, well nigh exhausted by nearly six hours' struggle, when at length Stuart came up at half-past two with the Seventy-seventh and the flank-companies of the Seventy-fifth, and after half an hour's sharp firing routed the division of the enemy that encompassed Montresor's rear. The enemy then lost heart, and before three o'clock retreated in all directions, with a loss of fifteen hundred killed and wounded ; the casualties of Stuart's force little exceeding one hundred and forty killed, wounded and missing. The action was most creditable to the steadiness of the Bombay Sepoys ; but it must be confessed that, alike for his design to crush Stuart and for his dispositions in the attack, Tippoo deserved better success. But for his revelation of his presence by pitching his tent at Peripatam, he would almost certainly have surprised and annihilated Montresor's brigade, and possibly also the greater part of the Bombay army.[1]

By this time Harris likewise had crossed the border of Mysore. From Amboor the main army moved very slowly west and southward to Baramahal, reaching Rayacotta on the 4th of March. From thence detachments were sent out to capture a couple of hill-

[1] *Life of Sir T. Munro*, i. 217.

forts, which being accomplished, the entire force 1799.
moved north-westward to Kelamungalum, and thence
on the 10th by Anicul and Jigginy toward Bangalore,
within sight of which the army encamped on the
14th.   The works of Bangalore and Oossoor had March 14.
been destroyed by Tippoo in order that they might
not serve again as advanced bases or depots to the
British ; but Harris's movement in this direction was
no more than a feint, though a successful one, for the
Sultan's light horse could be seen destroying forage
on all sides to northward.   As in 1791 and 1792,
transport and supply were to be the great difficulties
of the campaign, but in 1799 the situation of the
British was far more favourable, for they possessed the
districts of Baramahal and Coimbatore, in the former
of which a force of over five thousand native troops
was employed in collecting and forwarding provisions.
Had Tippoo taken the initiative by using his cavalry
to devastate Baramahal, he might have delayed the
whole expedition for a year.

Nevertheless, even as matters were, owing to the
necessity for transporting a train of forty-seven heavy
siege-pieces and from thirty to forty days' supplies,
Harris's anxieties were terrible.   The advance was
made always in two parallel columns, the British force
on the left and the Nizam's contingent on the right,
with the cavalry thrown out in front and rear, which
gave the army the formation practically of a parallelo-
gram with two sides of seven miles and two of about
three miles.   Within the space thus enclosed was
crowded an incredible number of beasts of burden.
In Harris's army the baggage and commissariat alone
required sixty thousand bullocks, three-fourths of
them pack-animals, to which the grain-merchants
added twenty thousand more.   In the Nizam's contingent the grain-merchants and military departments
employed thirty-six thousand bullocks, making nearly
one hundred and twenty thousand bullocks in all.
Besides these, there were more bullocks, elephants,

1799.
March.
camels, coolies, and a rabble of followers belonging to private individuals, according to the luxurious fashion of Indian campaigns. The bazaar of Harris's army, according to an officer who accompanied it, equalled that of a populous city in extent and variety of articles exposed for sale; and the followers outnumbered the fighting men by five to one.[1] "I have no scruple in declaring," wrote Wellesley at the time, "that the number of cattle and people in the employment of individuals was double that in the employment of the public." The whole of this gigantic multitude of animals, of course, required forage; and in the first few days after entering Mysore it seemed as if the task of providing for them would break the whole expedition down. The bullocks in the department of the Commissary of Stores began to fail very early, although there was abundance of forage in the country; great quantities of ammunition were lost, and on the 14th of March the outlook was so serious that an investigation was held into the cause. It was then discovered that, as so often happens, these unfortunate bullocks had been starved in accordance with certain absurd regulations of the department concerned. These rules were summarily abolished; a number of superfluous stores were destroyed; and from that moment matters slightly, but only slightly, improved.[2]

Mar. 15-16.
During the 15th the army halted in its position close to Bangalore, and on the 16th turned westward until it struck the road from Bangalore to Cancanhilly at Talgautporam, at which point it wheeled abruptly to the south upon Cancanhilly itself. The Mysorean horse, not expecting this new movement, had omitted to destroy the forage along this road, and

[1] MS. *Journal* of Lieutenant George Rowley of the Madras Engineers. I am indebted to the kindness of the Honourable N. Darnell Davis of British Guiana for the loan of a copy of this journal.

[2] Lushington, *Life of Lord Harris*, p. 267; Wellington, *Suppl. Desp.* i. 203-206.

the army in consequence found abundance of it and of   1799.
water also.   But still the loss of ammunition from the
siege-train continued, and on the 18th the whole force March 18.
was again halted to find further remedy for this evil.
At last, on the 21st, Harris reached Cancanhilly, having March 21.
taken five days to march five and twenty miles ; and
there he learned that Tippoo and his army, having
retreated from Peripatam, were now little more than a
day's march in his front.   Nevertheless, though the
enemy's cavalry were busy in laying waste the country,
forage was still procurable ; and the force, now in
three divisions, turned westward and continued its
slow progress, till, on the 24th, the cavalry and right March 24.
wing, which were in advance, reached the river Mad-
door and encamped on the eastern bank.   Tippoo,
however, made no attempt to dispute the passage,
though the ground offered him every advantage ; and
Harris was further encouraged on this same day by the
receipt of a letter from Stuart reporting his success at
Sedaseer.   After passing the river, the advanced divisions halted on the 25th for the rear to come up, and Mar. 25-26.
on the 26th the whole force encamped five miles east
of Mallavelly.   From the site of the camp the enemy's
advanced parties, with a few elephants among them,
could be seen upon a distant ridge ; and the sight of
fourteen or fifteen guns in motion pointed to the likelihood of a general action on the morrow.

   At daybreak on the 27th the army marched forward March 27.
along the high road towards Mallavelly, Wellesley's
division and the Nizam's contingent moving parallel
to it and somewhat wide on its left flank, so as to
protect the baggage, while Floyd with his two brigades
of cavalry as usual covered the advance.   Within a
mile of Mallavelly the enemy's cavalry was discovered
in force upon the British right, while his infantry
appeared in position on the heights beyond the village,
and his guns were seen to be in motion towards his
southern flank as if with the design of enfilading the
British during their advance.   Wellesley's division,

supported by Floyd's cavalry, was thereupon directed to attack the enemy's right flank, while the right wing under Harris in person advanced upon his centre at the village of Mallavelly, and the left wing was instructed to cover the baggage.

The enemy on perceiving these dispositions at once retired for some distance to a line of heights, whereupon Harris ordered the camp to be marked out beyond the village. The picquets of the army under Colonel Sherbrooke, together with the Twenty-fifth Light Dragoons and a regiment of Native Cavalry under Colonel Stapleton Cotton, thereupon advanced to cover the Quartermaster-general's parties; but the camp had hardly been marked out before two of Tippoo's heavy guns opened fire at extreme range. Cotton cleared some parties of Mysorean horse and rocket-men out of two neighbouring villages, but the main body of the enemy's cavalry on the British right now became so menacing that he was obliged to station himself so as to check them, while Sherbrooke drew the picquets together on Cotton's left, resting their right flank upon a village. The enemy's cannonade increasing, Harris ordered guns to the front to answer it, and bringing forward in succession Roberts's, Baird's, and Gowdie's brigades of infantry formed them upon the left of the picquets; while Wellesley's division, supported by Floyd's First Brigade, came up on the left of Gowdie in echelon of battalions, with the left refused. The whole line then advanced slowly over a low ridge, and descended into low, uneven ground, broken by patches of jungle.

The enemy thereupon with great spirit delivered two nearly simultaneous attacks upon the British left and centre. Ten thousand infantry, supported by cavalry, advanced boldly upon the Thirty-third, at the head of Wellesley's echelon, received its fire at sixty yards' distance, and did not give way until the British bayonets were almost upon them. Then, however, Floyd's First Brigade of Cavalry crashed into them, and cut them down with frightful execution. A body of

Tippoo's infantry also bore down upon the left of Baird's
brigade, whereupon Baird advanced three companies
of the Seventy-fourth with orders to fire and fall back
immediately.   The Mysorean foot swerving from the
volley, the whole of the Seventy-fourth fired and
rushed forward just as a compact body of three
hundred cavalry, breaking out of a patch of jungle,
charged furiously down upon the right of the brigade.
Galloping forward, Baird with great difficulty succeeded in checking the Seventy-fourth ; and meanwhile
the steadiness of the Twelfth and Scotch brigade completely shattered this second attack.   One Mysorean
trooper, however, fell by the bayonets, while another
actually broke through them close to Harris, who for
the moment took personal command of the Scotch
brigade ; but the rest turned and galloped along the
right of the British line, receiving the fire of five
Sepoy battalions without losing a man or a horse.
Had Tippoo supported these attacks, the action might
have been serious ; but he had only sacrificed these
brave men to gain time to withdraw his artillery, for
he fully shared his father's superstition as to the con-
servation of his guns.   His whole force now retired
to a second line of heights where it formed a new
front ; the British infantry following it for about two
miles, while Sherbrooke and Cotton worked round its
left flank to be ready for attack in case he should make
a second stand.   But the Sultan was bent upon nothing
but retreat, and Harris halted his army and returned
to his former encampment, being unable to find water
elsewhere.   The British loss was trifling, being less
than seventy killed, wounded, and missing, of whom
forty-three were Europeans.   The enemy's loss was
later ascertained to have been a thousand killed and
wounded.   The action was typical of the feebleness
which now characterised Tippoo's military operations.[1]

[1] Beatson, *War with Tippoo Sultan*, pp. 78 *sq.* ; *Life of Sir
David Baird*, i. 182-183 ; *Life of Lord Harris*, pp. 277 *sq.* ; Wellington, *Suppl. Desp.* i. 208.

1799.
March 28.

On the following day Harris moved forward about four miles north-west of Mallavelly, where he could find water, as if still intending to follow the main road westward to Seringapatam; but he had already made up his mind to cross the Cavery, if possible, at Sosily, about fifteen miles south-west of Mallavelly, and to attack the city from the westward. One advantage of this plan was that it would facilitate the junction with Stuart's force; a second, that it would assist the forwarding of supplies from Baramahal by the pass of Caveriporam; but the great advantage of all was that an advance by this route would be unsuspected by Tippoo, and the forage in that quarter consequently undestroyed. For, it must be repeated, the whole campaign turned upon the question of forage. If the beasts could not be fed, they could not transport supplies and stores; and, if they could not transport supplies and stores, the army could not be fed, nor could the batteries necessary for the siege of Seringapatam be furnished with ammunition. Keeping his intentions absolutely secret, Harris on the same morning sent a small party to reconnoitre the ford of the Cavery at Sosily, and, having received a satisfactory report, marched

March 29.

thither at daybreak of the following morning. The result exceeded his utmost expectations. The villages on the way were all deserted, but forage in abundance was found in them and in the fields, and the fort of Sosily was discovered to contain a large stock of grain. Moreover its environs were crowded with the fugitive inhabitants and their property, including several thousand head of cattle and a great number of sheep and goats. In the exhausted condition of the gun-bullocks such a supply was valuable beyond estimation.

April 1.

Two days were consumed in the passage of the river, and on the 1st of April Harris marched westward along the Cavery, the enemy's horsemen appearing in his front, but showing themselves less activity than usual in

devastation.   Nevertheless the progress of the army,   1799.
though unopposed, was still miserably slow, and it was
not until the 5th that it at last took up its position about April 5.
two miles from the western face of the fort of Seringapatam, having spent five days in traversing twenty-eight
miles.   However, the force had reached its destination
with its siege-train and abundance of food and ammunition, and the main difficulty of the campaign was
overcome.

The position occupied by the army was extremely
strong.   The right of the camp was on high commanding ground ; its rear was covered by deep ravines, and
its left secured not only by the Cavery, but by an
aqueduct which in its winding course protected much
of the front.   There were, however, beyond it several
ruined villages and rocky eminences which gave shelter
to the enemy's rocket-men and sharpshooters, and
which therefore required to be taken at once.   Accordingly, on the evening of the 5th, two parties were sent
out—one, consisting of the Twelfth and two native
battalions, under Colonel Shawe, to attack the enemy's
post at the aqueduct ; the other, made up of a Bengal
battalion and the Twenty-third under Wellesley, to
clear a grove of trees, known as the Sultanpettah Tope,
on the right front of the British camp.   Both marched
at sunset, and the night fell with an intense darkness
which proved fatal to the enterprise.   Shawe seized a
ruined village which sheltered his men from the fire of
the enemy on the aqueduct, but could do no more.
Wellesley entered the grove at the head of the flank-
companies of the Thirty-third, and was at once
received by the enemy with a hot fire in front and
flank, which killed an officer and struck down several
men.   The two companies gave way, and the remainder
of the battalion, having lost its bearings, was led by its
commander to the shelter of an embankment for the
night ; while Wellesley found his way back alone to
camp at midnight to report, with much agitation, his
misfortunes to Harris.   The young Colonel was deeply

1799.   mortified by his failure,[1] but on renewing the attack on the following morning with the Scotch Brigade, two native battalions, and four guns, he carried the grove with little difficulty. Shawe at the same time made a rush upon the enemy who had foiled him in the night, and drove them out ; and thus the line of the aqueduct was secured for the British advanced posts.

At dawn of the same day Floyd marched with four regiments of cavalry and nearly the whole of the left wing of infantry, to open communication with Stuart
April 14. at Peripatam. On the 14th he returned in company with Stuart's whole army, which had suffered little from the enemy on its march, but was short of supplies and, through some disease among the cattle, had lost four thousand bullocks. Still more alarming was the discovery made on the next day that Harris's store of rice, which had been reckoned on the 5th at thirty-three days' supply for the army on full allowance, had
April 15. through some rascality been reduced by the 15th to eighteen days' supply on half allowance. This decided the General more than ever to hasten the attack ; and, in compliance with the advice of the engineers, the north-western angle of the fort was selected as the
April 16. point to be assailed. On the 16th Stuart's force crossed to the northern side of the Cavery and took up a position with its right to the river, and its left on the ruins of the Eadgah or Mosque redoubt, which had delayed Medows for so long in the assault of the
April 17. 6th of February 1792. On the following day at sunset he sent out the Seventy-fifth and two battalions of Bombay Sepoys under Colonel Hart, supported by the Seventy-fourth and a native battalion from Harris's force, to attack the village of Agrar, over against the north-west angle of the fort, from which the enemy was driven with little difficulty or loss. On the same

---

[1] "Wellesley is mad with this ill success," Lieut. Rowley's *Journal*. The true account of the mishap is in Lushington's *Life of Lord Harris*, pp. 292 *sqq*.

night a battery of six cannon and two howitzers was 1899.
constructed to enfilade the angle above named, and was
christened by the name of Hart's post; while, on the
south bank of the river a first step was taken by
driving the enemy from a watercourse, called the
Little Cavery, running parallel to the western front
of the fortress. A post was here established, which
received the name of Macdonald's post.   A trench
was dug to connect this last with a ruined village on
the aqueduct in rear of it, called Shawe's post, and
therewith, though the town had not been invested, the
siege of Seringapatam was fairly begun.

None the less, Harris's anxiety on account of failing
supplies was extreme. On the 19th, the anniversary April 19.
of the disastrous fight at Lexington in 1775, Stuart
had but two days' provisions in store for his Europeans; and though, by various means, rice had been
collected sufficient to victual the fighting men for a
month, the General on that day sent Floyd eastward
towards the pass of Caveriporam with the whole of the
cavalry and a brigade of infantry to hasten the arrival
of the convoys expected from Baramahal. The work
of the siege, however, progressed. The enemy had
thrown up a line of entrenchments on the western
bank of the river parallel to the western face of the
fort, from which position it was essential to drive them
in order to obtain a site for breaching batteries. A
battery was therefore erected a little to the north of
Sultanpettah to enfilade such portion of it as was not
raked by Stuart's guns, and on the evening of the
20th the enemy were driven from one of their posts
at a powder-mill in advance of this entrenchment, with
a loss of two hundred and fifty killed and wounded.
A first parallel was then dug from the Cavery to the
Little Cavery, and a battery, known as the eight-gun
battery, built a little in front of it; while at the same
time a new battery was marked out on the north bank
of the river. This last measure stimulated the enemy
to a determined attack upon Stuart's position on the

1799.   22nd, which, however, was beaten off with a loss to
April 22. them of six or seven hundred men.   The new battery
was then constructed, and with the assistance of additional batteries on the southern bank the enemy's guns
April 24. on the western face of the fortress were by the 24th
entirely silenced.

On that night a first zigzag was carried forward from
the eight-gun battery, and a new battery was raised,
which in a short time forced the enemy to withdraw
the guns from two towers which flanked the site
of the intended breach.   This zigzag brought the
besiegers within little more than two hundred yards
of the enemy's entrenchments on the west bank of
the Cavery.   These occupied a length of about eight
hundred yards on a narrow slip of ground between the
river and the watercourse, the front being covered by
the bank of the watercourse, and the southern flank
closed by a small circular work.   At sunset of the
April 26. 26th, under direction of Colonel Wellesley, an attack
was made upon this entrenchment by two columns
simultaneously, the first consisting of four companies
of the Scotch Brigade, the second of as many of the
Seventy-third, each of them supported by four companies of Bengal Sepoys.   Both parties entered the
enemy's lines at or near their northern extremity, and
carried them at the first rush ; but, finding themselves
under heavy fire from the circular work at the southern
end, suffered some loss.   A party of the Seventy-
fourth and Scotch Brigade, however, presently joined
them under Lieutenant-colonel Campbell, who without further ado stormed the obnoxious work, and,
following hard upon the flying enemy, actually crossed
the bridge in rear of it into the island of Seringapatam.
There they bayoneted some of Tippoo's troops in their
tents and spiked two guns, after which Campbell, content with having filled the entire garrison with alarm of
a general assault, very wisely retreated.

April 27.   By ten o'clock of the next morning the British had
established themselves firmly on the ground thus

gained, their losses in the action having slightly 1799.
exceeded three hundred of all ranks, killed, wounded,
and missing, the brunt of which fell on the Seventy-
fourth.   The watercourse being found to furnish an
excellent third parallel, ready made, the construction
of breaching batteries against the western face of the
north-west angle was at once begun ; and, on the 2nd May 2.
of May, fire was opened from twenty-nine cannon and
six howitzers.   Early in the course of the cannonade,
a magazine of rockets was exploded within the fort,
and by the evening of the 3rd the breach was reported
practicable.   Harris thereupon decided to assault at
once.   Indeed, he had no choice, for his supplies had
fallen so low that the army was on the verge of
starvation.   So desperate was the situation that the
General had fully resolved, if necessary, to throw his
entire army into the breach, since success was positively
necessary to its existence.[1]

The command of the assaulting column was May 4.
entrusted to Baird, who had volunteered his services
upon this, his third visit to Seringapatam.   The troops
were told off into two parties, which were to enter the
breach together and turn, the one to the left and the
other to the right, upon mounting the rampart.   The
left attack under Lieutenant-colonel Dunlop of the
Seventy-seventh, consisted of the flank-companies of
that regiment, the Seventy-fifth, and the Hundred and
Third, besides the complete battalions of Twelfth and
Thirty-third Foot, ten flank-companies of the Bengal
Native Infantry, and a small body of artillerymen.
The right attack, under Colonel Sherbrooke, was
formed of the flank-companies of the Scotch Brigade
and of de Meuron's Regiment, the Seventy-third and
Seventy-fourth Highlanders, and fourteen flank-companies of Bombay and Coast Sepoys, with also a
handful of gunners.   The whole numbered close upon
five thousand men, of whom nearly three-fifths were

[1] *Life of Sir D. Baird*, i. 200 ; Lushington, *Life of Lord Harris*,
p. 332 ; Lieutenant Rowley's *Journal*.

1799.
May 4.
Europeans.[1] Each column was led by a sergeant and twelve volunteers, followed immediately by twenty-five men under a subaltern, the chosen officers being Lieutenant Hill of the Seventy-fourth in Sherbrooke's party, and Lieutenant Lawrence of the Seventy-seventh in Dunlop's. The troops were all in the trenches by daybreak, having been marched thither in small bodies in order to disarm suspicion ; and Harris had directed that the assault should take place at one o'clock in the afternoon, judging that the enemy would least expect it on the hottest hour of the day. The men were not in high spirits, possibly because they were half starved, but there was every likelihood that they would prove to be savage, for the murder and torture of prisoners by Hyder Ali and Tippoo in former days had not been forgotten. All through the forenoon the batteries played upon the breach incessantly, and at one o'clock, Baird, in the advanced trench, drew his sword, with the words, " Men, are you all ready " ? " Yes," was the answer. " Then forward, my lads " ; and both storming parties instantly rushed forward to the breach.[2]

From the trench to the bank of the river was but one hundred yards. The river itself, rocky and varying in depth from ankle-deep to waist-deep, measured two hundred and eighty yards more ; beyond that again was a low stone wall, then a ditch some sixty yards wide, and finally the breach. A very heavy fire of grape, musketry, and rockets was poured upon the columns as they advanced, causing some of the men to swerve from the ford, which had been marked out for them, into deeper water. But Baird led the way across

[1] 2494 Europeans and 1882 natives are the official figures ; but these do not include sergeants nor havildars, nor, of course, officers. The numbers *of all ranks*, excluding staff officers, were—Europeans, 2862 ; natives, 2003.

[2] These details are from Lieutenant Rowley's *Journal*. He was one of the assaulting party, and records Baird's terse words (which are less theatrical than those ascribed to him by Hook or Beatson) with the comment that they were not in the style of Livy.

the appointed passage, crossing the ditch, which was 1799.
almost filled with the ruins fallen from the breach, May 4.
among the foremost ; and, within six minutes, the
British flag was waving on the ramparts.   The sup-
porting companies quickly came up, and the two
columns separated, Sherbrooke's to the right or south,
and Dunlop's to the left.   On reaching the summit of
the breach, a formidable ditch was found within, which
divided the outer from the inner rampart ; but a small
party of the Twelfth under Captain Goodall found
a means of crossing it, and, by following the inner
rampart in a parallel course with Dunlop's column,
did excellent service.   Dunlop himself was disabled by
a sword-cut on the wrist, but his men on the outer
rampart quickly cleared the north-west bastion and the
faussebraye beneath it, from which had come the dead-
liest of the fire in the breach.   This task accomplished,
they turned eastward along the northern rampart, for
the still grimmer work that lay before them.

Before they had proceeded three hundred yards they
were checked by a traverse, from behind which a large
body of the enemy, commanded by the Sultan in person,
maintained so steady a fire that the Europeans were
staggered.   Most of their leading officers had fallen in
the Cavery or in the breach, and the Grenadiers complained that their ammunition had been spoiled in passing the river.   With some difficulty, they were rallied
by Lieutenant Farquhar of the Seventy-fourth, an excellent and most gallant officer, who, among many other
dangerous services, had sounded and marked the ford
before the breach, and guided the storming party to the
breach itself.   He now led the Grenadiers forward, but
was instantly shot dead ; and the men were again
wavering when fortunately more troops came up.
Then with the help of Goodall's party, which flanked
the traverses on the outer rampart, the column quickly
swept everything before it.   The unhappy fugitives were
pent in between the outer and inner ditches, both of
them broad and deep, and the slaughter now became

terrible.   The blood of the British was up, and no
quarter was given.   The Sultan was borne back undis-
tinguished amid the press of the flying, though, being
still mounted, he was able to make for the gate on the
northern face of the works, which led to the interior fortress.   But here the terrified Mysoreans from without
were met by an equally strong current of the panic-
stricken from within; and the two parties of British on
the outer and inner ramparts, forming up in order,
poured in a regular fire by platoons upon the swaying
masses on each side of the archway.   The Sultan, twice
wounded before he reached the gateway, contrived to
pass within it ; but he received a third wound and his
horse was killed under him, as he emerged on the
interior side.   His attendants tried to remove him in
his palanquin, but were unable to do so owing to the
confused throng and the heaps of dead and dying
that choked the way.   Some English soldiers now
entered the gateway, and one of them seized the
Sultan by the belt.   Half fainting with loss of
blood, Tippoo seized a sword and aimed a wild
cut at his assailant, who, unable to distinguish
him from his fellows, instantly shot him through
the temple.   The Sultan fell dead, unknown and
unrecognised.   His body was presently covered by
many others through the slaughter at the gate, and the
left column of the British pressed on along the northern
ramparts to complete the victory.

Presently a mighty shout of triumph proclaimed
that the two attacking columns had caught sight of
each other, and were about to meet.   Sherbrooke's
troops, indeed, had encountered little resistance, though
there were strongholds which, in the hands of a few
resolute men, could have wrought great havoc among
them.   Many of the Mysorean troops who were
encamped outside the southern and eastern sides of
the fort fled by a ford towards Carighaut Hill, pursued
by the shot which the British directed upon them from
their own guns.   But a great crowd ran in abject

terror eastward, and, meeting the other stream of 1799. fugitives, which was flying before the British of the May 4. left attack, surged in upon it with all the hideous pressure of panic. A few had contrived to escape by the eastern or Bangalore Gateway ; but the leaves of the gate opened inward, and there was no unfolding them against the mass of struggling men who threw all their weight, in vain despair, upon them. The heat of the day was unusually oppressive, but the troops, and particularly the sepoys, were savage and did not weary of killing. In the midst of the carnage, the gateway from some unknown cause caught fire, and the dense multitude beneath the archway swayed to and fro in wild agony between the flames and the bayonets, finding mercy from neither. After two hours, all resistance had ceased, but the number of Mysoreans that perished in the storm was reckoned at ten thousand.[1]

Meanwhile, Baird, ignorant of Tippoo's fate, after making his dispositions for securing the southern rampart, sent a flag of truce to the palace to summon him to surrender. The flag was very reluctantly admitted, and two of the Sultan's sons, who were within, were afraid at first to take the responsibility of throwing open the gates. When after long hesitation they at last assented, Baird with the Twelfth and Thirty-third regiments was found to be waiting outside, both General and soldiers roused to the highest pitch of indignation by the discovery that all the British prisoners taken during the siege had been murdered in cold blood. In such circumstances it was hardly safe to admit the British troops within the palace, wherefore Baird entered with a small party only, disarmed the Mysoreans within, and sent away the two princes under an escort suited to their rank.

---

[1] Beatson, who accompanied the right attack, bears witness to the good discipline and humanity of the troops and, in particular, of their officers. Lieutenant Rowley's *Journal*, however, gives a different picture of the left attack, where the foremost troops, as commonly happens when an assault meets with serious resistance, passed for a time out of all control.

After searching the palace in vain for the Sultan, he went to the northern gateway, where among a vast heap of the dead a single man was found alive. He was one of the Sultan's faithful attendants, who had saved himself from suffocation by creeping beneath his palanquin, and now crawled out, faint and wounded, to show where his dead master lay. Corpse after corpse was lifted and passed out for examination under the ghastly torch-light until at last the body was found of a man, short-necked, broad-shouldered, and corpulent, with tiny hands and feet, which the attendants recognised to be that of Tippoo Sultan. On the following day it was buried by that of his father, under the fire of minute guns and under the escort of British Grenadiers ; and at the close of the ceremony a thunderstorm of a violence unusual even in those regions burst over Seringapatam, killing two officers and several men of the Bombay Army, and marking with terror the end of the dynasty of Hyder Ali.

So closed the last siege of Seringapatam, which, from beginning to end, cost the British just under nine hundred Europeans and six hundred and forty natives, killed, wounded, and missing,[1] the Seventy-fourth being the corps that suffered most heavily. It was no very heavy price to pay for the breaking of the most formidable power in the south of India ; and, indeed, had Tippoo been such a soldier as his father, it may well be doubted whether the siege could have been undertaken before the breaking of the monsoon rendered the Cavery impassable. The Sultan had pursued a wrong policy for the defence of his dominions by devoting most of his energy to the fortification of his capital. He had, it is true, made some improvements in his artillery and infantry, though

[1] Officers : killed 22, 45 wounded. Europeans : killed 181, missing 22, wounded 622. Natives : killed 119, missing 100, wounded 420. The casualties in the assault were 69 Europeans and 12 sepoys killed, 248 Europeans and 32 sepoys wounded, 4 Europeans and 2 sepoys missing.

he had marred them by constant changes, and by 1799. the promotion of undeserving officers. But he had suffered his cavalry to decay — the famous cavalry which was a better protection to Seringapatam than fifty ramparts and ditches. With judicious handling even of the troops which he possessed, the British force ought, in Colonel Wellesley's judgment, to have been still entangled among the jungles of Bangalore on the day when it reached Seringapatam.[1] That Tippoo was by no means wholly lacking in military talent is proved by his attack upon Stuart as well as by incidents in previous campaigns; but he failed to see that his true advantage against the British lay in his superior mobility. Against Cornwallis he had fought first what may be called a campaign of forage, and had won it, then a campaign of walls and ditches, and had lost it. Nevertheless, he had repeated a like campaign of improved walls and ditches against Harris, and had lost everything. Hyder had made every campaign against the British a campaign of bullocks, and thus had gained many great successes, while sustaining no decisive defeat. The cattle of Mysore were, and are, to other cattle in India what the Arab horse is to other horses, superior in blood, strength, energy, quickness of step, staying power, and endurance of privation; and Hyder knew how to use them for swift marches. Tippoo also had turned them to account on occasion, but he knew not their true value; and it is not too much to say that the transfer of his faith from bullocks to bastions was the principal reason for his fall.

AUTHORITIES.—Wilks' *Historical Sketches of the South of India*, Beatson's *View of the Origin and Conduct of the War with Tippoo Sultan* (the official history written by Mornington's order), Wilson's *History of the Madras Army*, Biddulph's *The Nineteenth and their Times*, Wellesley's *Despatches, Despatches and Supplementary Despatches of the Duke of Wellington*, Hook's *Life of Sir David Baird*, Lushington's *Life of Lord Harris*, Grant Duff's *History of the Mahrattas*.

---

[1] Wellington's *Suppl. Desp.*, i. 208.

CHAPTER XXVI

1799. On the night of the storm the troops broke loose and gave themselves up to the plunder of Seringapatam as their lawful right. Scarcely a house was left unpillaged, and bars of gold, jewels, and trinkets of great value were brought into camp for sale by private soldiers and sepoys. The treasure at the palace was saved, except one casket of jewels, said to have been worth £300,000, whereof it appears that at least one officer took his

May 5. share with the men. On the morning of the 5th, however, Wellesley took over the command of the city, and, by a few severe examples of hanging and flogging, restored order among the troops and confidence among the despoiled people. Within ten days all the subordinate officers of Tippoo surrendered, and on the

May 13. 13th General Floyd arrived with a gigantic convoy of nearly forty thousand cattle, chiefly draught and pack bullocks, and twenty-one thousand sheep, guarded by his own troops and two detachments under Lieutenant-colonels Read and Brown. Read's duty had been to cover the collection of supplies in Baramahal, for which purpose he had received a force of more than five thousand men, including only a handful of Europeans. After capturing one or two hill-forts to north of Rayacotta, he moved down to assemble the grain merchants at Caveriporam, whither he was followed on the 1st of May by Brown. This officer had marched from Trichinopoly on the 29th of March with over three thousand men, including eleven hundred of the Nineteenth and Hundred-and-second Regiments, and

had reduced Caroor, Erode, and Avaracoorchy, pre- 1799.
paratory to operations in the district of Coimbatore,
when he was summoned to assist Read.   Leaving
Caveriporam on the 23rd of April, Read was unable
to clear the pass until the 27th, when he met Floyd at
its head, while the convoy, accompanied by Brown's
force, took nine whole days to move from the plain to
the tableland.   Its arrival at Seringapatam set Harris's
mind at ease for the victualling of his army.

The next matter to be settled was the distribution
of the prize-property, of which the Governor-General
assigned the treasure and jewels, valued at over eleven
hundred thousand pounds, to the army, reserving the
destination of the captured ordnance, amounting to
nine hundred and twenty-nine pieces, besides other
military stores, for the decision of the Company.
Tippoo's own sword was made over by the Prize
Committee to Baird, and the gilded tiger's head from
the Sultan's throne has long adorned the treasures of
Windsor Castle.   This distribution of the prize-money,
however, gave rise to a long and acrimonious dispute,
which had serious consequences for Harris and, indeed,
for all the General Officers.   Harris had been recommended by Mornington for a peerage and a red riband.
Owing to the opposition of the East India Company,
he received nothing until 1815.   On the contrary, the
Company persecuted him with litigation over his share
of the prize-money for six years, until the Privy
Council, as the final Court of Appeal, confirmed it to
him.   Baird's claims to the Knighthood of the Bath
were most strongly urged by Mornington, and likewise
ignored.   We shall see that Floyd, Arthur Wellesley,
and Mornington himself, at a time when they had
doubled and tripled their services rendered in 1799, all
alike found cause to complain that the East India
Company was the worst of masters.

On the 22nd of June was signed the treaty for the June 22.
partition of Mysore itself.   Hereby the province of
Canara and the districts of Coimbatore and Wynaad

1799. passed to the East India Company; Gooty and Gur-
rumconda were made over to the Nizam; the small
district of Soonda and Harponhilly, on the north-west
was assigned to the Mahrattas; and the remainder was
restored to the representative of the old Hindoo
dynasty of Mysore, which was now re-established.
Tippoo's army was disbanded; and a treaty was made
with the new Maharaja for the defence of his country
by the Company's troops in return for an annual
subsidy. Harris, however, was particularly careful to
take over for the Madras Army Tippoo's establishment
of draft bullocks, which he had so often coveted during
his weary march upon Seringapatam. Meanwhile the
May 13. expeditionary force was broken up. On the 13th of
May Stuart and the troops from Bombay marched to
the west coast to occupy the province of Canara; on
May 17. the 17th Read's force was detached to take possession
of Savandroog, Nundydroog, and Bangalore; on the
May 22. 22nd Brown, leaving the Hundred-and-Second and
a native battalion behind him, retraced his steps to take
May 25. over the district of Coimbatore; and on the 25th two
subsidiary battalions of the Nizam's force were sent to
enforce the change of government in Gooty and Gur-
rumconda. The Thirty-third, the Scotch Brigade, and
three native battalions formed the garrison of Seringapatam itself, with Arthur Wellesley for commandant;
while Harris, with the remainder of the force, encamped
outside the town.

We enter now upon a long series of petty operations
which, though they may be tedious to the general reader,
must none the less be briefly chronicled as an essential
part of the history of the British Army and of British
India. The crushing of the Mohammedan dynasty
in Mysore signified something more than the mere
partition of Tippoo's territory; it was the first and
principal step towards the establishment of British
influence and authority as paramount in Southern India.
One great power, that of the Mahrattas, still remained
to be overcome; but the Nizam's dominions were

virtually dependent on the Company since Morning- 1799.
ton's last treaty.   Tanjore, to anticipate matters by
a few months, was made over to the administration
of the British upon the condition that a fixed subsidy
and one-fifth of the revenue of the province should be
paid to its native suzerain.   It remained to reduce to
order the lawless elements that might still linger in
Mysore itself, and the unruly tribes, independent and
semi-independent, that surrounded it on every side—
the Polygars on the east and south, the proud military
caste of the Nairs in Malabar, and the tribes of Arab
descent, bearing the name of Moplahs, that also claimed
independence on the western coast.   The period, as has
been well said, was the golden age of adventurers.
Only forty years had passed since Hyder Ali, a soldier
of fortune, had founded the dynasty just overthrown
by Harris.   In the far north Runjeet Singh, the
founder of the Sikh State in the Punjab, was rising to
eminence.   Between the Ganges and the Jumna Perron,
nominally in Scindia's service, was endeavouring to form
a province under French protection, only to find himself crossed by an Irish sailor, George Thomas, who in
his turn tried to set up an independent principality of
his own.   All these, to say nothing of lesser predatory
chiefs, were taking advantage of the anarchy which
prevailed everywhere without the sphere of British
authority.   Owing to the dissensions among the
Mahratta chiefs, any leader who could offer booty for
reward could assemble a band of brigands, which success
would quickly increase into an army, and a touch of
genius could convert into the conquerors of a kingdom.

The first trouble arose from the disbandment of
Tippoo's army, which threw a number of active and
discontented men upon the world without means of
subsistence.   These found a leader in one Doondia
Wao, who had once been in Hyder Ali's service but
had deserted during Cornwallis's campaigns, and, upon
conclusion of peace, had collected a gang of freebooters
which lived by depredation in the district of Darwar.

1799. Being driven out from thence by the Peishwa's troops, he in 1794 tried to make his peace with Tippoo, who, however, kept him in close confinement at Seringapatam. Escaping from prison upon the day of the storm, he at once gathered round him a number of the dismissed soldiers and made for the district of Bednore, where the general confusion enabled him to gain possession of many of the principal forts in the country. New adherents rapidly swarmed to him. He ravaged and plundered with merciless greed and cruelty, and having thus acquired artillery, arms, ammunition, and money, he claimed the province of Bednore as his own and proclaimed himself to be King of the Two Worlds.

By the beginning of July Doondia was recognised to be so formidable that two flying columns, each of two native battalions and one regiment of Native Cavalry were sent to suppress him, while the headquarters of the army also moved northward to their support. One of these columns under Lieutenant-colonel James

July 6. Dalrymple at once seized the hill-fort at Chitteldroog,
July 15. and on the 15th of July, after a forced march of forty miles in twenty-four hours, caught up a body of over six hundred of Doondia's followers and, attacking with cavalry only, destroyed the whole of them. Two days
July 17. later Dalrymple surprised another small detachment of the brigands ; and after further successes he presently turned westward towards the upper waters of the Toombudra to co-operate with the second column under Colonel Stevenson. The headquarters of the army had mean-
July 24. while reached Chitteldroog on the 24th, from whence it moved early in August to Hurryhur on the Toombudra, about forty miles west and north. The flank-companies of the Seventy-third and Seventy-fourth and a native battalion were then pushed northward for twenty-five
Aug. 16. miles to the fort of Hollal, which was carried by storm and its garrison destroyed. On the following day Dalrymple and Stevenson, having captured the strong-holds of Shimooga and Honelly, came up with twelve hundred horse and three hundred foot of Doondia's

force under the walls of Shikarpoor, stormed the fort 1799.
with their infantry, charged the troops in the open with
their cavalry and routed them with great slaughter.
Doondia fled to the Mahratta country, but was instantly
attacked by the Mahratta chief, Doonda Punt Gokla,
whereby the remainder of his following was dispersed.
The province of Bednore was then occupied by the
British without further opposition ; and it was fondly
supposed that there was an end of Doondia.

A few days later Harris returned to Madras, leaving Aug. 24.
Arthur Wellesley in command of all the troops above
the Ghauts, or, in other words, in full military and civil
charge of Mysore. The new commander at once set
out for the north of the province ; but almost immediately his plans for establishing the new ruler's authority
were upset by new orders from the Governor-General.
Mornington's treaty of 1798 with the Nizam had
caused great jealousy among the Mahrattas at Poona ;
but their plans for an alliance with Tippoo had been
disconcerted by the rapidity of the Governor-General's
action, and they were therefore the less disposed to
acquiesce in the Treaty of Partition, and to accept
Soonda as their share of the plunder. Mornington,
therefore, instructed his brother to take over Soonda for
the Maharaja of Mysore, and, since it was already
occupied by the Mahrattas under Doonda Punt Gokla,
Wellesley wrote a friendly letter to that chief, requesting him to evacuate it. At the same time he directed
a small force of native infantry under Major St. Leger
to move into the country from the south, while Sept. 10.
Stevenson crossed the river Wurda and entered it from
the east. St. Leger alone met with some opposition, Sept. 29.
being compelled to storm at some cost of life a fortified
village held by Mahrattas which barred his advance ;
but by the end of September the district was in British
possession. Wellesley, however, found in it so many
disadvantages through its proximity to Mahratta territory, its heavy jungles, and its unhealthiness that he
was by no means eager to retain it. "There is little

1799.   in it to govern," he wrote, " but trees and wild beasts ";
and the forest, being a harbour for freebooters, made
heavy demands upon his troops.[1]

Nov.   Wellesley returned to Seringapatam towards the
end of November, but there were still two troublesome
marauders on the Malabar Coast who defied all authority. The first was Kistnapah Naik, Rajah of Bullam,
who had taken possession of the Soobramy Pass,[2] leading from Mysore to Canara, and thus interrupted
communication with Mangalore. The second was an
individual known as the Pychy Rajah, who had seized
the district of Wynaad and other territory between the
Ghauts and the coast, at the south-western corner of
Mysore. Already in August a force had been sent
to seize Munserabad, a principal stronghold of Kistnapah Naik, and the place had surrendered without
1800.   resistance ; but this lesson proved to be insufficient,
March.   and on the 23rd of March 1800 Lieutenant-colonel
Tolfrey was detached with thirteen companies of Sepoys
and a body of Mysore troops to inflict severer punish-
April 2.   ment. On the 2nd of April he attacked the Rajah at
Arrakeera, a stockaded position in dense forest about
three miles south-east of Munserabad, and was beaten
off with a loss of nearly fifty killed and wounded.
Thereupon, the flank-companies of the Seventy-third and
April 30. Seventy-seventh together with four more companies of
Sepoys were added to his force, and on the 30th, in
spite of a stubborn resistance protracted by the enemy
along a mile and a half of obstacles, the position was
carried, at a loss to the assailants of one hundred and
forty killed and wounded. This defeat and the
destruction of several villages brought the refractory
chief to reason. Every preparation had been made
to mete out the like measure to his brother freebooter
in Wynaad, but circumstances gave him respite for a
year, when he too was compelled to cry for mercy.

[1] Wellington, *Suppl. Desp.*, i. 318-319, 341, 347-348, 355.
[2] Apparently the pass which was also known as the Bissly
Ghaut.

But, meanwhile, a far more troublesome enemy had   1800.
reappeared, with a following that threatened to become
really formidable.

This was Doondia Wao, to whom the intestine
quarrels of the Mahrattas had given the opportunity
of recruiting his bands to considerable strength. After
his defeat by Dalrymple he had for a time taken
service with the Rajah of Kolapore, who was at open
war with his suzerain the Peishwa. Then separating
from him he made a raid on the Carnatic, where he
plundered the territory both of the Company and the
Peishwa. He then returned to the neighbourhood of
Darwar, threatening the province of Soonda, but
thirsting above all for the blood of his old enemy
Doonda Punt Gokla. In the middle of April Wellesley
became anxious for the safety of his garrisons in the
north ; and on the 25th he ordered three regiments of
cavalry and a battalion of infantry to be concentrated
at Hurryhur for the protection of Bednore.[1] In the
first week in May came the news that Doondia had
completely defeated five thousand Mahratta horse,
which had been sent out against him ; and on the
2nd the Governor-General, having obtained from the
Mahrattas permission to enter their territory, gave
Wellesley orders to hunt down Doondia Wao and
to hang him on the first tree.

Accordingly, the Colonel marched on the 21st of May 21.
May from Seringapatam, and by the beginning of June
had concentrated at Chitteldroog the Seventy-third,
Seventy-seventh, and five battalions of Native Infantry,
the Nineteenth and Twenty-fifth Light Dragoons and
three regiments of Native Cavalry, besides pioneers and
artillery. Three more native battalions, a regiment of
Native Cavalry, and a thousand of the Nizam's horse
under Colonel Bowser were also ordered to co-operate
with him. The campaign was a peculiar one, having for
its object not the capture of territory nor the infliction
of the British will upon an enemy who declined to submit

[1] Wellington, *Suppl. Desp.*, i. 523, 539.

1800.
June.

to it, but the extirpation of a band of robbers, said to number forty thousand men, which, in Wellesley's words, increased as it advanced, like a snowball. Doondia, as the Colonel admitted, was a despicable enemy; but great preparations were needed to cope with him, for it was certain that the operations would take the form of a long and weary chase. Transport, therefore, was of the first importance, and the subject was one to which Wellesley had given much study. "In the wars which we may expect in India in future," he had written on the 16th of January 1800, "we must look to light and quick movements; and we ought always to be in that state to be able to strike a blow as soon as a war might become evidently necessary." With this object he urged the importance of keeping a sufficient number of bullocks for fifty field-guns always ready; but above all things he insisted on the need of maintaining a corps of bullock-drivers, even at the sacrifice of a regiment of sepoys, since without trained drivers the bullocks were no sooner collected than they perished from neglect. More than once he expatiated at some length on this theme, pleading in excuse that these bullocks were great favourites with him; but it does not appear from the sequel that any immediate notice was taken of his representations.[1]

June 16.

On the 16th of June Wellesley arrived at Hurryhur from Chitteldroog, hoping to cross the Toombudra, while it was still low; but he arrived one day too late. The monsoon burst, the river rose rapidly, and ten whole days were lost while the troops were passed over the river in boats. By the 24th all had crossed, and on

June 27.

the 27th he marched north-westward upon Ranee Bednore, from which fire was opened upon his advanced guard. Thereupon, the fort was at once stormed, and Doondia's garrison was put to the sword; for their atrocious cruelties forbade the granting of quarter to these robbers. Want of grain, due to the ten days lost at Hurryhur, now compelled Wellesley to halt for a

[1] Wellington, *Suppl. Desp.*, i. 432, 438.

week, when the bad news reached him that the force 1800.
of Doonda Punt Gokla had been caught in an ambus-
cade by Doondia, its leader killed, the whole of his
guns taken, and his levies utterly dispersed. Moving
still north-westward Wellesley arrived at Deogeri on
the 6th of July, and crossing the Wurda reached July 6.
Savanore on the 12th, where Doondia advanced to meet July 12.
him, but not daring to face a battle retired to Koondgul.
Wellesley at once followed him up, and reaching the
fort after a march of twenty-two miles, carried it there July 14.
and then by escalade, but found to his disappointment
that the place contained nothing but a garrison, Doondia
having continued his retreat with the bulk of his force.
On the following day the British force marched south- July 15.
eastward for seventeen miles to Lukmaisir, which was
found to be evacuated by the enemy, thence twelve July 16.
miles north-east to relieve Sirhitty, which was blockaded July 17.
by one of Doondia's adherents, and thence back to
Savanore to pick up baggage and stores.[1]

A halt of two days in that place cost him the loss of
half of his cattle. There was forage in abundance all
around, and such of the bullocks as possessed proper
drivers throve well enough ; but the men in charge of
the hired cattle refused to take their beasts out for two
or three miles to graze. Hence the unfortunate animals
were almost starved, and two days of very severe
weather sufficed to kill hundreds and thousands of them.
With great difficulty Wellesley crawled northward July 22.
again to Lukmaisir, a district full of cattle whereby
he was able to made good his losses. Advancing then
to Sirhitty he turned thence eastward upon Dummul, a
strong stone fort occupied by one thousand of Doondia's
men, which was at once attacked and carried by escalade. July 26.
Following up his success he turned next north-westward upon Gudduck, which was evacuated by the
enemy upon his approach. Thus the last of Doondia's
strongholds in the districts of Savanore and Darwar
was taken.

[1] Wellington, *Desp.*, i. 169, 181 ; *Suppl. Desp.* ii. 59.

1800.
July.
Wellesley was now inclined to await the arrival of Bowser for the execution of his final plan, namely, to drive Doondia into the angle formed by the Toombudra and Kistna, both of them unfordable during the monsoon, and so to render his escape impossible. Bowser, however, was still two days' march in rear ; and, since Doondia was known to be anxious to cross the Malpurba, which being in heavy flood barred his retreat to the north, Wellesley determined to allow him no rest. He had since the 19th been joined by two thousand Mahratta cavalry of Doonda Punt Gokla's force, and he hoped that these, though much frightened by their late defeat, might take heart when supported by the British. He therefore marched with all speed north-westward upon Soondooty, where Doondia was then encamped, but on arriving within fifteen miles of it heard that the robber-chief had parted his force into three divisions, sending one of them southward, another eastward, and a third northward to Manoli on the Malpurba. Making a rapid march of twenty-six miles, Wellesley surprised this last party, which was about five thousand strong, on the afternoon of the 30th, destroyed or drove into the river every soul in the camp, and captured the whole of the baggage and cattle besides six guns. After this severe blow Doondia's followers began to desert him, and Wellesley to think that his work was nearly done.[1]

July 30.

On the 1st of August Wellesley fell back to Soondooty, and thence, after three days' halt, moved southwestward by Bedkaira to Kitoor in order to prepare boats for the passage of the Malpurba. Doondia meanwhile had doubled back to westward along the river, crossed it by an extraordinary march through the jungle at its source, and again turned northward. But when he reached the river Ghatpurba all the native chiefs took arms and headed him back, and he was fain to turn eastward towards Cowdelghee. Wellesley therefore detached Colonel Stevenson and Bowser's

Aug. 5.

[1] Wellington, *Desp.*, i. 188, 191 ; *Suppl. Desp.*, ii. 61, 70.

column to cross the Upper Malpurba at Konapoor and 1800.
to follow in his track, while he himself passed the river
opposite Hoobly between the 16th and 18th and pur- Aug. 16-18.
sued a parallel course along the north bank.   At the
same time a detachment under Major Capper was
ordered to march likewise parallel with him on the
south bank, through Soondooty, Hooly, and Jellahal ;
and Colonel Bowser was detached by Stevenson to
Shapoor, about fifteen miles north-west of Konapoor,
apparently to check any attempt of Doondia to cross
the upper waters of the Ghatpurba and gain Kolapore.

The British columns now moved together eastward,
driving Doondia steadily towards the junction of the
Ghatpurba and Malpurba rivers.   There was but one
outlet to which he could possibly escape, namely, a ford
across the Malpurba a little above its junction with the
Kistna, and even this seemed likely to be closed by the
floods ; but Wellesley directed Capper to push on with
the Mahratta cavalry and hold the ford, in order to seal
up the passage beyond all doubt.   The Mahrattas,
however, had not forgotten their recent defeat, and
refused to move ; and Capper's main body had advanced
no further eastward than Jellahal when, on the 24th, the Aug. 24-25.
Malpurba suddenly fell.   Thus Doondia, by great good
luck, was able to cross the river twenty miles below him,
though at the sacrifice of five guns, a quantity of arms
and ammunition, and ten thousand draught-bullocks,
which fell into Wellesley's hands.[1]

Now Wellesley perceived his error.   He had
attempted to reduce by a stern chase an enemy who
lived on the country, whereas his own troops were
obliged constantly to wait for supplies, and who could
without distress march for a greater distance in twelve
hours than his own army with the utmost effort could
traverse in two days.   Such a method was hopeless,
and he resolved in future so to place his columns that
one should always be waiting to head the enemy while

[1] Wellington, *Suppl. Desp.* ii. 93, 95, 97, 102, 107 ; *Desp.*
i. 205.

1800.
Aug.
the rest pursued. For the present, however, he was obliged to halt the whole of his troops in order to replenish his supplies ; and meanwhile it was necessary to guard against the danger of Doondia's doubling back to destroy the British magazines at Savanore, or of his crossing the Toombudra, with the help of some native chiefs, and entering Mysore. Wellesley therefore, on

Aug. 29. the 29th, crossed to the south bank of the Malpurba by a very deep ford at Jellahal, turned eastward upon

Sept. 6. Hummunsagur, and thence marched on the 6th of September south-eastward upon Khanagerry so as to check any attempt of Doondia to escape to the south. Meanwhile Stevenson, continuing his march eastward,

Sept. 5. reached Hoonagoonda on the 5th, and pressed on towards Deodroog, rather ahead of the other columns ; while to south of him the contingents of the Nizam and the Mahrattas moved in a parallel course between

Sept. 8. him and Wellesley. On the 8th Wellesley left Kanagherry with his cavalry only, the infantry following in rear, and turning north-eastward by Buswapore and Chinoor reached Yepalparri on the following day. On

Sept. 9. that same day Doondia left his camp at Mudgheri, some twenty miles to the north-east of Yepalparri, heading northward for the Kistna ; but seeing Stevenson's camp he at once turned south again and encamped about nine miles to north-east of Yepalparri, within three miles of Conagul. Intelligence of this movement came early to Wellesley, but the weather was so bad and his horses were so weary that he could not move

Sept. 10. on that night. On the following morning he advanced, and after a march of six miles came upon Doondia at Conagul. The robber-chief was actually moving westward in the hope of slipping between Wellesley and the Mahrattas. Perceiving the British, Doondia halted and drew up his five thousand men in a strong position, whereupon Wellesley, forming his four regiments of cavalry into a single line, led them to the charge and dispersed the brigands in all directions. Doondia was killed and his camp captured ; another division of his

force was routed by Stevenson; his followers were 1800
hunted down by the Mahratta and Hyderabad Horse, Sept.
and his reign as King of the Two Worlds was ended
for ever.[1]

Thus brilliantly closed the first campaign fought by
Arthur Wellesley in independent command. In the
matter of mere fighting it furnished him with little
experience of any value; the simple rule being that the
cavalry should charge the enemy whenever they appeared
in the open, and that the infantry should storm the
strongest forts without hesitation. There was little
danger in either service, and the casualties in the campaign were absurdly few. But in the matter of making
rapid movements over execrable roads at the height of
the rainy season, and of overcoming the difficulties of
transport and supply, the experience to him was worth
very much. A great part of these difficulties arose
from the extremely cumbrous organisation for transport
which at the time prevailed in the Madras Army. It
appears that the draft bullocks were distributed among
the artillery-department, the grain-department, the
provision-department, and the camp-equipage-depart-
ment, besides which each regiment of cavalry possessed
a grain-department of its own, making from eight to
ten different departments for the transport of a force of
five thousand men.[2] He had, as has been told, fore-
seen the inconvenience of the system, and was in some
measure prepared for the disastrous loss of cattle which
overtook him at Savanore; but it was not in his power
greatly to amend matters, and hence it was really no
small feat that he should have continued to make from
time to time so many rapid marches and yet to keep
his troops supplied.

Shortly afterwards a part of Wellesley's force was

[1] Wellington, *Desp.* i. 214, 218, 223; *Suppl. Desp.* ii. 130.
There is a brief account of the campaign in Wilson's *History of the
Madras Army*, iii. 14 *sq.*, and Colonel Biddulph has told the story
clearly, fully, and tersely, as is his wont, in *The Nineteenth and their
Times*, pp. 116 *sqq.*

[2] Wellington, *Suppl. Desp.* ii. 89.

1800. placed under command of General Dugald Campbell to occupy the ceded districts of Bellary and Gooty, a duty which caused serious disturbances and kept the troops actively employed until September 1801, when the country was reported to be quiet. In November, however, the Polygar of Ternakul, a fort about seventeen miles east of Adoni, broke out into rebellion, and the Twenty-fifth Light Dragoons, with two regiments of Native Cavalry and three battalions of Native Infantry, were placed under command of Major

1801. Strachan to subdue him. Strachan attacked the fort

Dec. 14. on the 14th of December, and was repulsed with the loss of sixty killed and wounded. General Campbell then joined him with the Seventy-third, and a second

Dec. 20. attack was delivered on the 20th, which was again repulsed with the loss of over one hundred and seventy killed and wounded. The General then did what he ought to have done at first, and brought up siege-guns, after which the fort was carried by storm with the loss of four men wounded only.

Very similar were the difficulties that beset another campaign, which followed shortly afterwards in the extreme south of India. The Polygars of Madura and Tinnevelly had long given trouble by their refusal to pay their tribute, and by their predatory attacks not only upon each other but upon the territory of the Company. In 1792 an expedition under Colonel Maxwell had taught them a severe lesson, but this had been forgotten. In August 1799, therefore, a force of four hundred men of the Nineteenth Foot and thirteen companies of Native Infantry under Major John Bannerman was sent to reduce the fort of Panjalamcoorchy, which lies from twenty-five to thirty miles north-east of Tinnevelly and of Palamcottah, with orders further to capture the chief and disarm the whole of the southern Polygars. At the beginning of September Bannerman advanced from Palamcottah, and

Sept. 5. arriving before the fort on the 5th attempted to storm it immediately with his native troops only, the Nine-

teenth having not yet come up. He was repulsed, 1799.
owing to the misbehaviour of his troops, with the loss
of four European officers killed and two wounded and
of ninety-three Sepoys killed and wounded.   However,
on the arrival of the Nineteenth on the following day Sept. 6
the enemy evacuated the fort, and within six weeks the
Polygar was caught and executed, forty-four forts were
destroyed, several chiefs were imprisoned at Palamcottah,
and Bannerman's mission was declared to have been
accomplished.

In February 1801, however, the imprisoned Poly- 1801.
gars escaped from Palamcottah, and being joined near Feb.
Panjalamcoorchy by four thousand armed men broke
out again into rebellion. The moment was well chosen,
for at that very time operations were in progress against
the Pychy Rajah on the Malabar Coast, and against the
Polygars of Dindigul sixty miles south-west of Trichinopoly. Major Macaulay, who commanded in the
province, could collect no more than a battalion of
Native Infantry and two hundred irregulars, with which
he marched on the 6th of February against Panjalam- Feb. 6.
coorchy. After repelling several attacks of the enemy
on the march, he arrived before it on the 9th, when he Feb. 9.
found, to his great astonishment, that the fort which
had been destroyed in 1799 had been completely rebuilt
and was now much stronger than before. He therefore Feb. 10.
retreated, without further molestation than a single
attack on his rearguard, to Palamcottah, where he
remained, too weak for any but the pettiest operations,
until the end of March. Meanwhile the insurgents
captured the fort of Tuticorin, which was disgrace- March 2.
fully yielded up by its garrison of Sepoys in defiance
of their officer who, being a subaltern just arrived
from England, had no control over them. Altogether
there was every prospect of increasing trouble in the
south.

At length, after unavoidable delay, reinforcements of
nearly three thousand men, including two companies
of the Seventy-fourth and odd companies from six

1801. different native battalions, together with a few cavalry and heavy guns, were gathered together at Kytar, about
March 29. nineteen miles north of Palamcottah ; and on the 29th of March the whole advanced upon Panjalamcoorchy. On the march sixty troopers of the bodyguard charged and cut to pieces a body of two hundred Polygar pike-
March 31. men ; and on the 31st the entire force came before the fort. This was an irregular oblong structure, about five hundred feet long and three hundred broad, built of mud, with walls twelve feet high and a multitude of small square bastions, the whole being surrounded by a thick hedge of thorn.   Macaulay, having two heavy guns and two howitzers, prepared to batter a breach in the walls ; but after a few hours of futile cannonading with bad ammunition and shells that would not burst, he decided to storm without further delay.

The assault was led by two companies of the Seventy-fourth backed by the grenadier-companies of the Sepoys and one complete native battalion.   The men dashed forward gallantly under the heaviest possible fire, burst through the hedge, and made desperate efforts to sur-mount the breach, but in vain.   The bastions had been hollowed out by the enemy, so as to present no footing at the top ; and ingress was barred by a hedge of pikes, from eighteen to twenty feet long, held by invisible de-fenders below the level of the broken parapet ; while from an elevated spot behind them and from the bastions on each flank an incessant fire was poured upon the assailants.   Astonishing gallantry was shown by the officers, both native and European, but to no purpose. The assault was beaten back with heavy loss ; and the sounding of the retreat, as so often happens on such occasions, was the signal for a backward rush which greatly resembled a flight.   Instantly the enemy sprang to the breach in pursuit, some pausing to pierce with their pikes the bodies of the dying and the dead, others throwing themselves upon a howitzer, which was only rescued by the exertions of six officers and fifty Sepoys who had rallied on them.   The total number of casualties amounted to fourteen officers and three hundred and three men killed and wounded, but this figure only faintly represents the havoc wrought among the Europeans. Of the two companies of the Seventy-fourth, two officers and eighteen men were killed, three officers and fifty-three men wounded; and of one hundred and twenty British who formed the storming party only forty-six escaped unhurt. In short, on its own small scale, this was as murderous a fight as is recorded in the history of any British regiment. 1801.
March 31.

After the action Macaulay entrenched himself within fifteen hundred yards of the fort and awaited reinforcements. For three weeks he was little troubled except by occasional skirmishes, but on the 22nd of April the Polygars took advantage of a heavy thunderstorm to attack the camp, and actually carried off a gun. The Sepoys being unable to fire their muskets owing to the rain found a bayonet little defence against a long pike with a razor's edge. The gun was, however, rescued, and there was no further serious engagement until the 21st of May, when Colonel Agnew arrived with the Seventy-seventh Foot, seven companies of Sepoys, a regiment of Native Cavalry, a small party of Malays, and six pieces of heavy artillery. Regular batteries were then erected, which opened fire at dawn on the 23rd of May, and by noon had battered a practicable breach; but at Macaulay's entreaty Agnew continued the cannonade for another twenty hours. Then a storming party, formed of the two shattered companies of the Seventy-fourth, two more of the Seventy-seventh, and five companies of Sepoy grenadiers, made a rush for the breach. So stoutly did the enemy stand that it was half an hour before the British could obtain any footing upon the summit; but at length the defenders at the breach were all killed by hand-grenades, whereupon the whole body of the enemy gave way. The cavalry, with four galloping guns, was waiting to intercept them at the egress at the other end of the fort, but the Polygars formed themselves into two solid columns and presented April 22. May 21. May 23.

1801.
May 23.
a formidable phalanx against the charging horse. About six hundred of them were cut off and over four hundred more were found dead in the fort ; but the main body, about two thousand strong, made good its retreat. Nor was this the only evidence of the enemy's patient and enduring bravery. Thickly crowded into a miserably narrow space, they had dug burrows underground for shelter from shot and shell, which when seen by the British officers presented horrors beyond description. The casualties in the assault numbered one hundred and eighty-six killed and wounded, of whom eight were officers. The Seventy-fourth again lost two officers, and the two companies of the Seventy-seventh two officers and fifty-one men. The sense of their superiority to the native troops seems to have inspired the British regiments with a spirit which triumphed over the severest losses.

After the capture of the fort the rebel Polygars betook themselves about seventy miles northward to Shevagunga, then ruled by two chiefs named Vella Murdoo and Chinna Murdoo, who, having once been the principal officers of the Zemindar, had usurped his authority and now exercised supreme control over the district. Agnew called upon the Murdoos to give up their principal leaders, and, on their refusal to comply, began active operations against them. Accordingly, after leaving detachments to destroy the captured fort and to occupy Tuticorin, which had been evacuated by the rebels, Agnew, with the rest of the force,

May 26.
marched on the 26th north-eastward in order to relieve the garrison of Comery, over thirty miles west of Ramnad. From Comery he turned north-

June 2.
westward to Trippawannum, where he halted and sent his siege-artillery under escort to Madura. The escorting party was attacked on its way back to Trippawannum, but escaped with slight loss ; and on the

June 7.
7th of June the army turned south-eastward towards Ramnad, where Agnew hoped to find a friendly district in his rear while penetrating the jungles of Shevagunga

from the east. The march was of the most harassing   1801.
description, particularly after the third day, when the
road passed through a network of high banks, water-
courses, and jungle; for the enemy never ceased to
deliver petty attacks from every point of vantage, the
repulse of which on one day cost nearly one hundred
killed and wounded.

Arriving at Ramnad on the 14th, Agnew discovered June 14.
that the northern part of the district was in revolt and
could not be counted on to furnish him with provisions; and he was fain to march back to Madura,
which he reached on the 4th of July. Leaving it again July 4.
on the 22nd, he moved eastward to Trivatoor, where July 22.
he was joined on the 26th by a reinforcement of one
battalion and some detached companies of Native
Infantry, a detachment of the Twelfth Foot, the flank
companies of De Meuron's regiment, and apparently
a part of the Scotch Brigade under Colonel Innes.
The country was close and difficult; and Innes, incessantly attacked on all sides, made but slow progress
until Agnew sent out a detachment to help his advance,
when the junction was at last effected, after the two
divisions had lost nearly seventy killed and wounded.
The united force on the 28th moved south-eastward July 28.
to Ookoor, and on the following day eastward upon July 29.
Sherewele or Serruvial, a large village where stood the
palace of the Murdoos. The route on this day lay
through a maze of banks flanked by jungle, at every
one of which the enemy made a stand; and the march
in consequence consisted of a series of manœuvres for
turning the flanks of these obstacles. On the morrow, July 30.
as the force drew nearer to Sherewele, it was obstructed
by a battery of four guns in addition to the usual
obstacles, and six hours were needed to traverse a
distance of less than three miles. The enemy, however, made no effort to hold the village itself, which,
though eminently defensible, was occupied by Agnew
without opposition.

Now came the most difficult part of the work. Due

1801. south of Sherewele lay the fort of Caliarcoil,[1] the principal stronghold of the rebels, only five miles distant, but separated from it by some of the thickest and most impenetrable jungle in the Carnatic. Over two thousand pioneers and woodcutters had been collected to cut a road through the forest; and morning after

Aug. morning from the 31st of July to the 31st of August working parties were sent out for this purpose, covered by detachments of troops for their protection. At first the work went forward rapidly, but as the road drew nearer to Caliarcoil the jungle grew denser, and the enemy's harassing opposition more vigorous. Half

Aug. 9. of the distance had been penetrated by the 9th of August, when it was necessary to throw up a redoubt, close to a tree which was too gigantic to be felled, in order to cover further progress. Constantly repulsed, sometimes with heavy loss, the enemy persisted in their attacks, occasionally throwing up breastworks with cannon to fire down the road, more often plying the working parties and their escort with musketry from the forest. After a month of hard work only four out of the five miles of forest had been cut through, and the woodcutters were weary of their work. Dysentery also was playing havoc with the troops ; and the communications of the force were so effectually cut that it was practically impossible to pass even the smallest message through the circle of the

Sept. 2. enemy. On the 2nd of September, therefore, Agnew abandoned the enterprise, and returned to Ookoor. No roll of his casualties exists, but it seems certain that the losses of the force by sickness were very heavy.

At the end of the month, however, Agnew received information which gave him hope of surprising the rebels at Caliarcoil, and accordingly made arrangements to move upon it by three converging columns. The Seventy-seventh and a battalion of Sepoys under Lieutenant-colonel Spry marched from Ookoor on the

[1] In modern maps Kauliar Kovil.

night of the 30th to follow the road which had been
cut from Sherewele for some distance, and then to
leave it for a path, hitherto unknown to the British,
through the jungle.   Agnew himself, starting at dawn
of the 1st of October, took the main road leading to
Caliarcoil through Mootoor, and Colonel Innes, starting at the same time from Sholapooram, moved by
way of Kerranoor and Calangoody.   The operation
was completely successful.   By eight o'clock on the
1st of October Spry was in possession of Caliarcoil, and
Innes's column alone met with serious resistance, the
enemy leaving at one of their barriers one hundred
dead.   This success broke the back of the insurrection.
The rebels dispersed in every direction, and the leaders
were in a few weeks taken and executed or deported to
Penang.   By the end of March 1802 the population
had been disarmed, the forts destroyed, and the rebellion completely suppressed.

At about the same time, January 1802, Colonel
Wellesley undertook his first forest-campaign against the
Rajah of Bullum, advancing upon his principal stronghold in three converging columns, and forcing him to
abject submission in little more than a fortnight.   In
these operations the Seventh-seventh, only lately released from hard work about Caliarcoil, took a principal part, so heavy was the call upon British troops
for dangerous duty in India.

The operations above narrated may seem to many
not worth the chronicling; and yet such petty campaigns, of which no army has fought so many as the
British, tax the nerve and ability of officers and the
courage and endurance of their men as heavily as the
high-sounding wars of which alone history takes notice.
To ignore them would be to ignore some of the finest
work ever done by British soldiers, and some of the
grandest acts of individual heroism in the British or
any other army.   To give but one instance, in a skirmish on the march from Comery to Ramnad, Lieutenant
Parminter of the Madras Native Infantry with a small

1802. flanking party of Sepoys was overpowered by a large body of rebels in a patch of jungle. His men gave way, leaving him to fight his battle alone with a paltry regimental sword. Yet did he successfully hold the enemy at bay until by chance he stumbled, when he was instantly pierced in five places by pikes, one of which pinned him by the shoulder to the ground. A Polygar came up with musket and bayonet to despatch him, when Parminter with a desperate effort wrenched the weapon out of the ground, and rising to his feet with the blade still fast in his arm, renewed the fight and despatched his opponent. His men then ran up to rescue him, and the enemy, utterly amazed, turned and fled.[1] Such deeds of valour were common in those forgotten expeditions, when commanders relied upon fifty or one hundred British soldiers to make good the defects of two or three thousand Madras Sepoys, and never found them to fail.

Nor was the pacification of Southern India in itself a small thing, when such an adversary was in the field as Napoleon Bonaparte ; for these insurrections could easily have been turned into weighty and important diversions when some greater military enterprise was afoot. So far Bonaparte's plans and threats from Egypt had produced no effect in India, except the destruction of one of England's most dangerous enemies and the consolidation of her power on the Continent. It is now time to return to Europe, to take up again the thread of Bonaparte's career, and to trace to the end the history of his army in Egypt.

AUTHORITIES.—Wilson, Biddulph, Wellington's despatches, as at the end of preceding chapter ; Welsh, *Reminiscences in the East Indies.*

---

[1] Welsh, *Reminiscences in the East Indies,* i. 83.

CHAPTER XXVII

WHEN Bonaparte landed in France on his return 1799. from Egypt, the glamour of his enterprise in the East Oct. 9. covered all his failures and gained for him an enthusiastic welcome. He found the country crying out for a man who would put an end to the uncertainties and disorders that had harried her almost to death for ten long years. A group of malcontents soon rallied round him, and within a month the Directorial Constitution was swept out of existence by an armed conspiracy, which is commemorated in history by the date of the 18th Brumaire. Five weeks more sufficed to produce a Nov. 9. new Constitution, whereby three Consuls were nominally charged with the executive power, while an elaborate and extremely complex machinery of Senate, Tribunate, and Legislative Assembly dealt with the business of legislation. All this, however, was a mere matter of form, for, under the title of First Consul, Bonaparte became sole ruler of France, with autocratic powers far exceeding those enjoyed by Lewis the Fourteenth. He began to reign on Christmas Day, and the task Dec. 25. that lay before him was one of appalling difficulty. The local no less than the general government required to be reorganised ; the arrears caused by ten years of neglect in every department needed to be made good ; the Treasury was empty, and the financial situation more than ever confounded. Lastly, not only was France beset by enemies on every side, but the old sore of rebellion, inflamed by Royalist leaders, had broken out afresh in La Vendée.

1799.   Finance was the first object that occupied Bonaparte's attention; and he was driven unavoidably to very strange shifts to raise the funds that were so urgently necessary.   The armies of Holland and Switzerland supplied their needs by levying large contributions in those countries, and the army of the Rhine had done the like by exacting large sums from Swabia; but the army of Italy was absolutely destitute.   As a first step, he sent Moreau to take command on the Rhine and in Switzerland, despatched Masséna to save, if possible, the defeated and disheartened troops in Italy, and appointed Brune, the Jacobin, to restore order in La Vendée.   The army of Brune on the western coast was styled the army of England, as if still designed for an invasion of the British Isles; though Bonaparte on taking office had not omitted to write specious letters to King George and the Emperor Francis, setting forth his desire to put an end to the war.   Pitt, reckoning that the total exhaustion of France's military resources, so long expected, was come at last, rejected the overture with exaggerated energy; and in Austria also every one, with the solitary exception of Thugut, thought it impossible that the Republic could again take the offensive.   Nothing could better have suited Bonaparte's designs than this undervaluing of his strength, for he awaited only the favourable moment for dealing his enemies an unlooked for and fatal blow.

1800.   Meanwhile his wisdom, his energy, and his amazing power of work were framing and forwarding measure after measure for the reorganisation and restoration

Feb.   of France.   By the beginning of February a complete new scheme of local administration had been formulated which, being in essence no more than a revival of the intendants and sub-intendants of the monarchy, was calculated no less surely to turn the utmost powers of the country to account than to strengthen his authority as sole ruler.   Nor were his efforts to conciliate internal enemies in St. Domingo less remarkable, for on the day of his accession to power he wrote a

letter to the negroes there, insidiously promising to 1799.
them liberty and equality of rights with white men,
and urging them to be true to France.   A few days
later he took the first step towards making peace
between the French people and the Church ; and immediately afterwards he threw open his arms to receive
also the Emigrants and the Royalists.   By the end of
February, through a judicious blending of severity and
clemency, he had reduced La Vendée again to order ;
and the great work of uniting all France under one
banner had been well begun.   Never, perhaps, in his
whole career did Bonaparte show greater political
sagacity or higher statesmanship than in the first three
months of his rule.

Not so far-seeing were his adversaries, the Allies.
The campaign of 1799 had in fact ended with the
disruption of the Coalition.   The disasters in Switzerland had wholly alienated Russia from Austria ; and
the Tzar, in his first outburst of rage over Suvorof's
complaints, not only renounced all further co-operation
with the Emperor Francis, but called Prussia's attention
to the rapacity of Austria and proposed an alliance of
the Northern Powers to curb it.   Prussia, however,
clung fast to her neutrality ; and Grenville, when
sounded upon the subject, strove to reconcile the
injured Tsar with the Emperor.   His efforts were
seconded by a visit paid by Mr. Wickham, the British
Agent in Switzerland, to Suvorof in his temporary
winter - quarters at Augsburg ; when the veteran
General, always eager for action, proposed that during
the next campaign eighty thousand Russians should
act in concert with the Austrian forces in Switzerland and Italy.   Grenville approved this plan uncon-
ditionally, engaging that England would bear the cost
of augmenting the Russian Army ; and Paul was so far
mollified that he ordered Suvorof for the present to
suspend his retreating movement.

But Grenville's success was only momentary.   Falsely
conceiving that Austria was abashed by his august dis-

1799. favour, Paul demanded the dismissal of Thugut from the Emperor's councils. This request Francis contemptuously ignored; and Thugut, now elated to insolence, not only insisted upon Austria's most extravagant claims to territory in Italy, but rejected Suvorof's plan of campaign, and requested the immediate withdrawal of all Russian troops from within the bounds of the Empire. This in itself was sufficient to irritate the Tsar; but presently there came news from Italy which kindled his indignation against Austria to furious heat. Thanks to the energy of Nelson, Rome and Civita Vecchia had been yielded by their French garrisons, the former to the Neapolitan forces, the latter to the British; and

Sept. 20. some weeks later Ancona also was surrendered in like manner to the Russian Admiral. The Austrian troops had arrived too late to intervene in the fate of Rome; but they marched without hesitation into Ancona, expelled the Russian garrison, and hauled down the Russian colours. Paul, greatly exasperated, thereupon definitely recalled his troops to their own country, and pending reparation for the insult to his flag, broke off all diplomatic relations with Austria.

Thugut at first cared little for this, which was the more strange inasmuch as he had divined more truly than other men the danger which underlay Bonaparte's accession to power in France. He had, however, at last come to a satisfactory agreement with England, having signed, after two years' delay, the treaty for repayment of an English loan and thereby gained a fresh subsidy. He had also rid himself of Suvorof, who shortly afterwards died of a broken heart, and of the Archduke Charles, who in December had resigned his command on account of ill health; and, having thus driven the two ablest generals at his disposal from the field, he felt himself thoroughly at ease over the coming campaign. Meanwhile, the good understanding between Grenville and Thugut had decided Paul to break with England also. He had taken deep offence over the fancied ill treatment of his troops

during the campaign of the Helder; and his injured 1799.
feelings were not soothed either by Nelson's proceedings at Malta nor by a dispute with Grenville, wherein
he himself was in the wrong, over the payment of the
British subsidies.   Russia, therefore, retired from the
contest, to the great contentment of Thugut, who
reckoned that the money thereby saved to England
would be bestowed upon the Emperor.

For the coming campaign the Austrian Minister 1800.
calculated that, by means of increased contingents
from Bavaria, Würtemberg, and Mainz, which were
to be paid for by England, he could put into the field
two hundred and thirty thousand men.   Of these, one
hundred and four thousand were placed under the
command of General Kray, eighty thousand of them
being stationed along the Rhine from Schaffhausen to
Heildelberg, while twenty-four thousand, owing to a
superstitious solicitude for the hereditary dominions
of the Hapsburgs, were kept in the Grisons and Tyrol.
The ultimate task assigned to Kray was the conquest of
Switzerland, for which, however, he demanded at least
twenty-five thousand men from the army of Italy.
This latter force numbered rather over one hundred
thousand men under General Melas, of which about
thirty thousand men were required for garrisons and
seventy thousand were available for the field.   To
oppose them the French could for the present show
but thirty thousand men, holding a line of about a
hundred miles from the banks of the Var to Genoa;
and it was therefore vital to press them hard before
they could be reinforced.   The British Mediterranean
fleet under Lord Keith was at hand to cut off the
French communications by sea, and to hang upon
their westward flank along the whole length of the
coast.   On the 24th of February, therefore, orders Feb. 24.
were despatched to Melas to drive the French from
the Riviera and Genoa, which having been accomplished,
he was to send to Kray the detachment required by him
for the invasion of Switzerland from the north.

1799.   To a nation which, practically speaking, held un-
challenged the command of the sea, which possessed
one military base at Minorca and a second in Sicily,
this plan undoubtedly offered an opportunity of effective co-operation.   Moreover, England possessed a
striking force in the army which had lately returned
Oct. from Holland, and which a new Act of Parliament
had enabled Ministers to increase by drawing an unlimited number of recruits from the Militia.   Nor
was sound military advice wanting for the employment
Dec. of this force.   Charles Stuart in December 1799 laid
before Ministers a project for the concentration of
twenty thousand men at Minorca, from whence they
could move against the French at any point on the
coast between Toulon and Genoa.   It appears, further,
that some arrangements had been concerted for the
kindling of an insurrection at Marseilles by the
Emigrant General de Willot, who is described as
having possessed both talent and energy.   But, setting
all questions of insurrection aside, the fact that a
British force from Minorca could strike at the flank
and rear of the French in Italy while the Austrians
operated against their front, was sufficient to commend
the plan.   There was no other object in the Mediterranean to distract the troops from this service.   No
great number was needed for the blockade of Malta,
and the French army in Egypt was still imprisoned
1800. beyond hope of escape.   It is true that in January
Jan. 1800 Sidney Smith, who fondly conceived himself to
be a diplomatist, had, contrary to all his instructions,
concluded with Kléber the Convention of El Arish
for the evacuation of the country by the French,
and the safe conveyance of the army to French ports.
But the British Government had no idea of rati-
fying such a treaty ; and consequently the situation
remained unchanged.   From all of these considerations Stuart's plan seems at first to have found favour
with Dundas ; and the General thought the matter
Feb. so far settled, that in February he invited, and ob-

.tained, the services of John Moore for the projected 1800. operations.

With two such officers at its head this chosen corps would probably have effected much, and quite possibly might have altered the whole course of European history. But it was not to be. Abercromby, as we have seen, had entreated Huskisson that the army of the Helder might be kept together, trained and disciplined on its return to England; and Dundas had answered with big words. "Bring me back as many good troops as you can, and before next spring I will show you an army the country never saw before."[1] Nevertheless, no pains were taken to improve, nor even to preserve, the efficiency of this force. The regiments, to use Abercromby's expressive phrase, were allowed to "dance about" all over Great Britain. Officers were permitted to be absent as in time of peace; and when the various corps were finally collected, they were found to be deficient not only in discipline but in the equipment necessary for taking the field. Moreover, despite the new Recruiting Act, their number was found to be but ten thousand instead of fifteen thousand men, proving for the hundredth time the utter incapacity of the Minister for all military administration.[2]

Even ten thousand men, with five thousand more from the Mediterranean garrisons, might have turned the scale in the critical operations which were presently to go forward in Italy; but by the middle of March March. the Government had already another project in hand. During the winter of 1799 Dundas had become suddenly enamoured of an invasion of France upon a grand scale, and had urged a descent upon Brest with seventy thousand men. The enterprise was abandoned upon the discovery that the maritime resources of England were unequal to the transport of so large

[1] Dunfermline, *Life of Abercromby*, p. 208.
[2] Bunbury, *Great War with France*, pp. 57-66; *Diary of Sir John Moore*, i. 363-4.

1800. a body of men.   He therefore reverted with increased ardour to projects for a series of petty, useless raids upon the French coast.   "It shall not be my fault," he had written in May 1798, "if, with one expedition after another, the coast of France is allowed to sleep sound any one week during the summer."[1]   Windham also was convinced that no European coalition could succeed except by allying itself with the Royalists, in which term he included all that were opposed to Jacobin Government in France ; and the recrudescence of the Chouan insurrection in Brittany and La Vendée seemed to offer a favourable opportunity. The operation determined upon was the capture of Belleisle, less for its importance as a naval station than as a means for affording assistance to the insurgents. Four to five thousand troops were therefore detailed for this service ; a certain number more seem to have been destined for Portugal, owing to an alarm of a Spanish invasion ;[2] and the reinforcement for the Mediterranean was accordingly cut down to five thousand men, which were offered to Stuart in lieu of the fifteen thousand for which he had asked.   It does not appear, however, that the Ministers definitely came to this decision, or at all events communicated it to Stuart, until the middle of April—so dilatory were they in making up their minds at a time when every hour was precious.

Then, most unfortunately, a bitter quarrel deprived them of his services.   It has been written by one of his contemporaries that Stuart, a proud and hot-tempered man, on learning of the wreck of his wise and far-reaching plans, threw up the command in the Mediterranean in disgust and refused to have

[1] *Dropmore Papers*, iv. 224, 275.   The project for an attack on Brest is mentioned in several letters from Dundas to Grenville during the autumn of 1799, the last of these being of 2nd December.   *Dropmore MSS.*   It appears from the *Grey MSS.* that Sir Charles Grey was designated to command the expedition.

[2] *Life of Abercromby*, p. 219 ; Bunbury, *Great War with France*, p. 66.

more to do with it. But this seems to be incorrect. 1800. Stuart's real difference with Dundas arose from his refusal to accept instructions to restore the Knights of Malta and to subject the island to the despotism of Russia, which King George had bound himself by treaty to do. Events proved Stuart to be perfectly correct in regarding such instructions as ridiculous and impossible ; but the question was a political one and for the Cabinet, not for the General, to decide. " If our officers are to control our councils," wrote Dundas with perfect justice at this time, " there is an end of all Government." [1]   Stuart therefore resigned ; and this, lamentably enough, is our last sight of this exceedingly able officer. He died in May 1801 ; and if he be now remembered, it is as the subject of a fine portrait by Romney, who has handed down to us his noble features and dignified carriage, and as the father of the distinguished diplomatist who later became Lord Stuart de Rothsay.   Nevertheless, he seems to me to have been the greatest of all the British officers of this period—great enough, indeed, both as a man and a soldier to have done the work which afterwards fell . to Wellington in the Peninsula.

Since, therefore, according to the usual wisdom of Pitt's Cabinet, the small British striking force was broken up into fragments too small to accomplish any but trifling service, it will be convenient first to follow the detachment which was sent to Belleisle. This expedition was entrusted to Colonel Thomas Maitland, and may possibly have been suggested by him ; but there is no evidence, so far as I can discover, which gives any clue to its inception, though no doubt Windham was its chief advocate. The Government's knowledge concerning Belleisle was extremely vague ; and Maitland therefore began operations by sending Lieutenant-colonel Nightingale to Quiberon Bay to gain intelligence. Nightingale's orders were first to make a

[1] Bunbury, *Great War with France*, p. 66 ; Dundas to Grenville, 25th April, 1800. *Dropmore MSS.*

1800. few prisoners, and then to sail to the islands of Houat and Hedic, where he was to mark out large encampments, talk loudly about the disembarkation of a considerable force on the mainland, and meanwhile gather all possible information from all sources respecting Belleisle. He started accordingly in the first week of May with five hundred men of the Thirty-sixth foot;

May 18. and Maitland, following him on the 18th, cruised off Ushant until the 30th, when St. Vincent's fleet joined him and sailed with him to Quiberon Bay. There he learned from Georges, the Chouan leader, that the garrison of Belleisle was much stronger than had been supposed, amounting at the lowest estimate to four thousand men, and, according to the highest, to double that number. Maitland's own force, of which only a part had yet reached him, was to leave England in two divisions, the first nominally of four thousand men, which was supposed to effect a landing, and the second of two thousand more which was to reinforce him as soon as a footing on the island had been secured. He therefore sent Nightingale home to explain the situation, and meanwhile decided to attempt nothing until the whole of his six thousand men should have reached him.[1] His decision was the more easily taken since the want of flat-bottomed boats absolutely forbade him to essay a disembarkation.

Sir Edward Pellew, who was in charge of the squadron detached by St. Vincent to cover the operations, now instituted, without appearing to do so, a strict blockade of Belleisle; and Maitland, establishing his headquarters at Houat, made constant and careful reconnaissance of the island. He was almost convinced that the enemy's strength was exaggerated by the Chouans, though unable absolutely to satisfy himself;

June 17. and having by the 17th of June received the whole of

[1] Maitland to Huskisson, 28th March, 1st, 13th, 14th, 18th May; to Nightingale (instructions), 22nd April; to Dundas, 30th May, 6th June; Dundas to Maitland (instructions), 8th May 1800.

the first division of his troops[1] he completed all his   1800.
dispositions for an attack on the night of the 19th. June 19.
Bad weather caused him to defer the attempt for
twenty-four hours, when a confidential messenger came
to him from Georges to warn him that the enemy
were certainly seven thousand strong.   Though still
sceptical as to the truth of this statement, Maitland,
knowing that defeat would mean disaster, decided to
await the coming of his second division ; when, to his
surprise, there arrived on the next day instructions June 21.
from Dundas, dated on the 16th of June, to send the
whole of his troops at once to Minorca to join the
force in the Mediterranean.

Within twenty-eight hours of the receipt of the
despatch the six battalions were embarked, and the June 23
transports at sea ; and within forty-eight hours
afterwards came a second letter from Dundas to
say that, if a landing on Belleisle had been effected,
the troops were not to be sent away.   A few days
later arrived the second division of the troops,
numbering not two thousand men, as Dundas had
promised, but seventeen hundred only ;[2] and on the
4th of July Dundas instructed Maitland to leave these July 4.
at Quiberon Bay under command of the senior officer,
and to return home.   So ended the expedition to
Belleisle, eminently foolish, eminently mischievous,
eminently characteristic of Pitt's Government.   It is
difficult to see what good could have come of it even
if, according to the fond hope of Ministers, Lewis the
Eighteenth or some scion of his most unprofitable
house had hoisted the white standard at Palais.   In
1793 or 1794 the seizure of the island might have
produced great results.   Even in the winter of 1799,
when the Chouan insurrection was in full vigour, the
despatch of troops thither, though a mistake in military
policy, might have found some kind of justification.

[1] These were the 2nd Queens, 1/20th, 2/20th, 36th, 82nd,
92nd, 2 companies R.A.
[2] 23rd, 31st, 63rd Foot ; 1696 of all ranks.

1800.   But the expedition, as it was conducted, can only be termed a wanton and wicked waste of six thousand valuable soldiers during three most critical months.[1]

Meanwhile the Austrians had begun their advance upon the Riviera, not at the end of February, as had been ordained, but on the 5th of April. For the loss of these six precious weeks, which carried with it also the loss of Italy, a heavy fall of snow on the 13th of February was in part responsible ; but the chief reason is to be found in the fact that Melas was old and slow. He moved forward, however, in overwhelming strength, and by the middle of April succeeded in cutting the French forces in twain ; throwing back Masséna himself with some ten or twelve thousand soldiers into Genoa, and driving his left wing under General Suchet in isolation to the Var. Leaving General Ott to blockade Genoa in concert with the British fleet under Lord Keith, Melas set out on the 27th of April for the Var with the object of mastering the bridge and bridge-head over that river, in order, if possible, to paralyse Suchet's corps completely. For, until this was done, he could not consider his situation in the Maritime Alps to be secure, nor devote his whole attention to the reduction of Genoa and to the operations that were to follow upon it. Twenty thousand British soldiers would have been invaluable at this time to assist either in the attack on the Var or in the blockade of Genoa ; and the British Ministers in February had actually given the Court of Vienna to understand that such a force would be ready. But, for reasons which have already in part been explained, it was not forthcoming ; and it is now necessary to see what the British Government was actually doing in the Mediterranean.

Towards the end of August 1799, the garrison of Minorca was made up to more than six thou-

April 5.

April 27.

---

[1] Maitland to Huskisson, 13th, 21st, 24th June, 2nd, 6th July ; to Dundas, 21st, 24th June, 2nd, 6th July ; Dundas to Maitland, 16th June, 4th July 1800. The documents relating to the expedition are in *W.O. Orig. Corres.*, 28.

sand[1] men, a number sufficient not only to render   1800.
the island absolutely safe against attack, but even to
furnish a battalion or two for service elsewhere if required. In November General Fox, whom we last saw as
a brigadier under the Duke of York in the Netherlands,
arrived to take over the command, but with no instructions empowering him to furnish any troops to the
fleet either for the blockade of Malta or for any other
service. In January 1800 there arrived a reinforcement in the shape of the Ancient Irish Fencible Infantry, under Colonel Thomas Judkin Fitzgerald, an
Irish magistrate, who by extreme severity had kept
Tipperary from rebellion in 1798, and apparently had
been permitted to raise this corps for his reward.
Since the men were undisciplined and the Government
had not provided more than half of them with arms,
this regiment could not be regarded immediately as an
accession of strength ; though after a few months' training it might become sufficiently serviceable to release
some other regiment for work elsewhere. But at the
beginning of May Fox received advice that five thou-   May.
sand men were sailing from England to Minorca under
Major-general Pigot, that Sir Charles Stuart, who had
been nominated as Commander-in-chief, had been
" prevented by recent circumstances " from accompanying them, and that pending the appointment of his
successor the troops must be encamped. The first
division of Pigot's troops arrived on the 12th, and the May 12, 17.
remainder on the 17th of May,[2] by which latter date
there were in Minorca just under twelve thousand
men of all ranks fit for duty.[3]

[1] It amounted actually to 7000 men ; but the 28th Foot was
almost immediately withdrawn from it to Gibraltar.

[2] *1st division*, 1st and 2nd battalions of the 17th, 35th and 40th ;
2nd division, 18th and 48th ; 5548 of all ranks fit for duty ; 242
sick. The two regiments last named were from Gibraltar, where
two battalions from England had been dropped to relieve them.

[3] Erskine to Dundas, 22nd August 1799 ; Fox to Dundas, 3rd
November 1799, 20th January, 27th May 1800 ; Dundas to Fox,
25th April 1800.

1800.   Meanwhile, Sir Ralph Abercromby had been chosen to take Stuart's place in the Mediterranean. The Portuguese had asked for him to command their own army, but the old General declined to enter the service of another sovereign ;[1] and the idea of operations in Portugal appears to have been abandoned within a week in favour of wider schemes of aggression. On the 5th May 5. of May Abercromby received his instructions as Commander-in-chief of all the forces (including the troops at Gibraltar) in the Mediterranean. These prescribed to him four objects in succession. The first was to strengthen the British troops at Malta by two or three battalions, so as to hasten its surrender and liberate the blockading squadron ; and to this was subjoined the clause to which Stuart had objected, namely, that the island, after capture, should be garrisoned jointly by the forces of England, Naples and Russia, pending its restoration to the Knights of St. John. Secondly, after allowing three or four thousand men as the garrison of Minorca, he was to give every assistance to the Austrians which a light moveable force and a superior fleet could afford. Thirdly, he was to co-operate by the same means with any rising in the southern provinces of France, but to avoid pledging England to any further support to the Royalists ; and fourthly, in the improbable event of the Austrians being reduced to the defensive in Piedmont, he was to give assistance to Naples and Portugal, should their territory be threatened or invaded by the enemy.

This was an extensive programme for a force which, after providing for Malta and Minorca, could not have spared about five thousand men for other operations ; but Dundas, wishing to provide for every

---

[1] It was characteristic of Dundas that he none the less reported to the Cabinet that Abercromby was ready to accept the command of the Portuguese army. *Life of Abercromby*, p. 220. Abercromby's biographer uniformly describes Dundas as "sanguine" on such occasions. No doubt he was sanguine, but he was also consciously or unconsciously dishonest.

contingency, favoured Abercromby with a second set 1800.
of instructions. The purport of these was that, if the
position of the Austrians and the Royalists rendered
the former plans ineffectual or impracticable and if the
needs of Portugal were not pressing, Abercromby
should attack Teneriffe, "an acquisition not immaterial
in point of commerce and, by its position, of the
greatest importance to our navigation and the security
of our valuable distant possessions." For the capture
of this island, Dundas considered from three to five
thousand men sufficient, though he freely confessed
that he had no knowledge whatever of its means of
defence nor of the numbers of its garrison. However,
assistance to the Austrians and the Royalists was to
take precedence of this enterprise ; and only when his
presence in the Mediterranean was no longer desirable
nor likely to be needed, was Abercromby required to
sail for two thousand miles from Mahon into the
Atlantic against an island which, for aught he knew,
might be impregnable.[1]

The General left England in the King's ship *Seahorse* May 12.
on the 12th of May, in convoy of a few troop-ships and
store-ships; but he was driven back by a gale ; and on
the 19th he wrote that, with such heavy sailers as the
transports in company, it would be impossible for the
frigate to reach Minorca within any reasonable time.
Ultimately, he sailed again and arrived at Gibraltar
on the 6th of June ; but, meanwhile, the genius of June 6.
Bonaparte was rapidly altering the complexion of affairs
in Italy. Masséna, after a series of most skilful and
valiant sorties from Genoa, had been reduced after the
13th of May to a purely defensive attitude; but still he
held out, though terribly pressed by famine, and delayed
any decisive movement on the part of Melas by keeping Ott's corps tied to the blockade. And Melas's
time was running short, for by the 21st of May the May 21.
head of Bonaparte's main army of forty thousand men
had crossed the Alps by the pass of the Great St.

[1] Dundas to Abercromby, 5th May 1800.

1800. Bernard, and was debouching on to the plain of Lombardy. On his left fifteen thousand men under General Moncey were advancing southward by the pass of St. Gothard; on his right five thousand more were climbing Mont Cenis. On the 21st Melas heard of Bonaparte's advance, and leaving eighteen thousand men under General Elsnitz on the Var, where all his efforts had failed to capture the bridge, hurried with

May 31. the remainder to Turin. On the 31st he learned that Moncey was coming down upon Milan, across his line of communication; whereupon he hastily summoned all his troops to Alessandria, in order to fight his way back to Mantua. He recalled even Ott's detachment from before Genoa; but negotiations had already been opened with Masséna for the surrender of the city, and Keith insisted that the siege should be pressed.

June 4. Finally, on the 4th of June, the French garrison marched out with the honours of war.

But, meanwhile, Suchet had been reinforced on the Var, and, pursuing Elsnitz on his retreat from that river, not only inflicted upon him enormous loss, but forced him to take a circuitous route which greatly delayed his junction with his Commander-in-chief. Bonaparte also had entered Milan on the 2nd of June; and, in these

June 5. circumstances, Melas wrote on the 5th to Keith that, in consequence of Elsnitz's mishap, he must withdraw the whole of Ott's corps, excepting a feeble garrison, from Genoa. He therefore entreated him, if possible, to reinforce both Genoa and Savona with troops from Minorca. Keith at once forwarded this letter to Fox with a quotation from Abercromby's instructions, which had been communicated to him, as to the detachment of a force to the assistance of the Austrians. He subjoined an expression of his own opinion that an English garrison thrown into Italy would be the saving of all Italy; and he added the intelligence that the French from the Var were in full march upon Genoa, and that Ott on his own responsibility had left five thousand men in that city. Keith's letter seems to have reached Fox

very speedily and to have caused him much anxiety; 1800.
but the General could only answer that his instructions
were to encamp his force at Minorca until Abercromby's arrival, and that he had but one transport
ready to embark troops.   On the 12th Keith again June 12.
wrote to him more urgently, giving still worse news
of the French successes in Italy, and announcing the
despatch of transports to Minorca; whereupon Fox,
though in mortal dread of deranging Abercromby's
plans, made all preparations to embark the troops if
Keith should repeat his request.   But on the 14th of June 14.
June Melas was completely defeated at Marengo; and
the favourable moment had passed away for ever.[1]

On the 22nd Abercromby arrived at Mahon, June 22.
where he found letters both from Keith and Melas
pressing him to hasten to Genoa with every man that
he could spare.   He decided to sail thither at once;
and so perfect were Fox's arrangements that five
thousand men were embarked within twenty-four
hours.   The whole put to sea on the 23rd, but only June 23.
to learn a few days later that the Austrians had
evacuated Genoa, and that Keith had sailed to Leghorn.
Pursuing the Admiral thither, Abercromby learned
from him on the 1st of July that Melas, after his July 1.
crushing reverse at Marengo, had concluded with
Bonaparte the convention of Alessandria, under which
all the Imperial troops, except the garrisons of
Peschiera and Mantua, were to retire to the east of
the Mincio.   All chance of co-operation with the
Austrians being thus at an end, the greater number of
the transports was ordered back to Mahon before they
were arrived at Leghorn, and the remainder returned
on the evening of the 5th.   This, however, was not July 5.
accomplished without a struggle; for Nelson, the
Queen of Naples, and Sir William and Lady Hamilton
were all at Leghorn, uniting to put pressure on
Abercromby to land his troops for the defence of

[1] Fox to Dundas, 15th and 21st June, enclosing correspondence
with Keith.

1800.
July.
Naples. But Keith and Abercromby were obdurate alike against the royal tears and the royal reproaches. The General therefore sailed for Malta, and the Queen with her retinue, including Nelson, made her way to Vienna.

Upon his arrival at Malta, to which he had previously detached General Pigot with two battalions of the Thirty - fifth, Abercromby found another letter from Melas, written from Villafranca on the 5th of July, wherein the Austrian commander begged that the British might be disembarked at Leghorn to undertake the defence of Tuscany and Naples. He replied that, in circumstances so changed, he felt himself no longer authorised to act in Italy, and that five thousand men were too few for the task required of him. Considering that the French had already spread as far south as Modena and Bologna, is it not easy to see what other answer he could have given. Since there was nothing further to be done at Malta, which was amply provided with troops, Abercromby left it at the end of the month for Mahon.[1]

On arriving there on the 2nd of August, he was surprised to learn that now six new battalions were lying in the harbour under the command of Lord Dalhousie. They were those which had been so suddenly removed from Maitland's command in June. Also he found a fresh letter of instructions from Dundas, dated the 16th of June, recommending him to employ the whole of his troops in the defence of the coast of the Riviera, so as to liberate the entire force of Melas for service in the field. Three months earlier such instructions would have gone near to fulfil the wishes of Stuart, and would probably have saved Italy ; but written, as they were, two days after the battle of Marengo, they were a cruel mockery. Abercromby, however, at once sent Brigadier John Hope to Melas with a message that he would hold his troops ready to sail at the shortest notice, and was prepared to

[1] Abercromby to Dundas, 5th and 23rd July 1800.

co-operate with him in any specific plan which might be 1800.
profitable to the common cause.

The project suggested by Melas was, that the British
should occupy the port and fortress of Leghorn, and
countenance a rising of the Tuscan peasantry against
the French.   The Neapolitans at this time occupied
Rome in force; the Austrians held Ancona; and bands
of armed peasants, under the direction of an Austrian
officer, were swarming in the Apennines along a line of
some fifty miles from the borders of Lucca to the borders
of Ancona.   These last were thoroughly in earnest, and,
indeed, later in the year those about Arezzo offered
a determined resistance to the advance of the French;
but at this moment the French troops were fully
occupied with an equal force of Austrians on the
Mincio, and could have spared not a man for Tuscany.
Moreover, Bonaparte had quitted Italy for Paris on
the 25th of June, leaving the command first to
Masséna and later to Brune, so that the master's hand
had actually been withdrawn.   Abercromby, however,
appears to have regarded Melas's plan as neither feasible
nor valuable; and he spoke of Hope's mission as a
failure which no efforts of his own could have converted into success.   At the root of his unwillingness,
possibly, were a sense of the impotence of so small a
body as ten thousand men, a recollection of Austrian
trickery in 1794, and a just conviction of the utter
incompetence of the British Cabinet.[1]

Meanwhile, Bonaparte, upon reaching Paris on the
3rd of July, had, with his usual activity, thrown himself into the work of reaping, by diplomatic means, the
fruits of his great victory.   It was not only in Italy
that the French arms had triumphed.   In Germany
also, Moreau, after a series of successes, had forced
Kray back first to Ulm, and thence behind the Inn; July 7.
and on the 15th of July the truce concluded at July 15.

---

[1] Dundas to Abercromby, 16th June; Abercromby to Dundas,
4th and 16th August 1800; Bunbury's *Great War with France*,
pp. 69-70, *note*.

1800. Alessandria was extended to Germany under the name of the Armistice of Parsdorf. Immediately after Marengo, Bonaparte had renewed his appeals to the Emperor Francis to conclude peace ; but, since the treaty between England and Austria, signed so recently as on the 20th of June, bound the Emperor not to come to terms with France before February 1801, his overtures could only be answered vaguely so as to gain time. Russia the astute First Consul gained by undertaking to make over Malta to the Tsar, as Grand Master of the Order of St. John, and by releasing, clothing, and equipping seven thousand Russian prisoners to form its garrison. It was true that Malta was then closely blockaded by the British, and almost at the last gasp from famine ; but Paul in his simplicity overlooked this ; and thus Bonaparte gained his point of turning him into an enemy of July 22. England. Lastly, the First Consul set on foot a negotiation [1] with Spain, offering to grant a small kingdom in Italy to the Duke of Parma, who was a brother of the Spanish Queen, in return for the cession of Louisiana and six ships of war to France ; his principal object being to force Spain at once into war with Portugal, and so to drive the British fleet from Lisbon. Under the influence of Godoy, who was eager to be on good terms with the victor of Marengo, the Court of Madrid was inclined to go more than half way to meet him, and made little secret of its willingness to bend itself to his service.

In these circumstances, Dundas, judging that there was no longer employment for the British troops in Aug. 1. Italy, on the 1st of August issued to Abercromby two new sets of instructions. The first of these reversed his previous orders that Russian troops should share in the occupation of Malta after its surrender, bidding the General do his best, without coming to actual hostilities, to dissuade her commanders "for their own safety and comfort" from attempting to land their

[1] *Corres. de Napoléon,* vi. 415.

troops in the island.   At the same time Abercromby was 1800.
to encourage and complete the native regiments raising
in Malta, and to impress upon the inhabitants the
advantage of the British connection.   It is difficult to
see how the Russians could be alarmed for their safety
and comfort without the menace of hostilities, though,
as usual, Dundas tried to shroud this characteristic
evasion of responsibility in a mist of words.   It is
easy to read between the lines of these instructions
that the Government wished the Russians to be
excluded from Malta at any cost, but had not the
courage to give the General definite commands to do
so.   This, however, was, comparatively speaking, a
subordinate matter.   The second batch of instructions
set forth a new military policy to be executed by
Abercromby's troops, namely, the destruction of the
Spanish naval forces and arsenals by attacks upon
Ferrol, Vigo, and Cadiz.·   For this purpose the General
was to sail immediately with his striking force from
Minorca to Gibraltar, where it would be joined by
reinforcements sufficient to raise its strength to twenty
thousand men.[1]

The reinforcements in question consisted of about
eleven thousand men, namely, five companies of artillery and fifteen battalions of infantry, four of which
last had for a month past been unprofitably kept at
the island of Houat.[2]   They were to be assembled
first at Quiberon Bay, there to be met by a detachment
of Lord St. Vincent's fleet, after which they were to

[1] Dundas to Abercromby, 1st August 1800.
[2] The four battalions at Houat were the 23rd, 31st, 1/52nd,
63rd.   The remainder of the force consisted of 1/ Coldstream
Guards, 1/3rd Guards, 2/1st, 3 batts. 9th, 13th, 2 batts. 27th,
2/52nd, 2 batts. 54th, 79th, 3 companies of the Rifle Brigade.
A brigade from Ireland, 2500 strong, was to have made the
numbers of the force up to 13,663, but I cannot discover that
any part of this brigade was forthcoming, and the two battalions
of Guards (which are not in the list first sent to Pulteney) appear
to have been substituted for it.   They certainly came from
Ireland.   Pulteney in the House of Commons called his force
13,000 men.

1800. proceed to Ferrol, to disembark there, and, if possible, to destroy the arsenal, dockyards, and fortifications. This service effected, they were to proceed to Vigo, in order to work the like destruction in that place also. The command was entrusted to Sir James Pulteney, who had retrieved and enhanced his reputation by the skill and resource which he had displayed in the campaign of the Helder. He made his way accordingly to Quiberon Bay, whither St. Vincent had detached for him

Aug. 25. a squadron under Sir John Warren; and on the 25th of August the entire armament appeared before Ferrol.

On the same night the disembarkation began in a neighbouring bay, and by five o'clock on the follow-

Aug. 26. ing morning the whole army was ashore, when after a brisk skirmish the enemy were driven from the heights that overlook the town and harbour. Pulteney then examined the works with his brigadiers, and came to the conclusion that to carry the place by *coup-de-main* or escalade was out of the question. It was surrounded on three sides by the sea, and the landward side was regularly defended along its whole length of two thousand yards by formidable fortifications of masonry, including a high wall upon the curtain, with seven bastions of considerable elevation and other flank-defences. The garrison numbered seven thousand men, or over two thousand more than were necessary to man the works; cannon could be seen mounted on the ramparts; and everything (as was afterwards ascertained by accounts from Madrid) was ready to meet an attack. A siege also was out of the question. It must have been lengthy; and meanwhile the fleet was lying insecure in an open roadstead. But, even if the works covering the harbour had been taken and the fleet admitted to a safe anchorage, no more than eight thousand men could have been spared from the protection of the communications for the double duty of conducting the siege and shielding the besiegers against any army that the united forces of all Spain could despatch for relief of the town. The

operation would in fact have been not only foolhardy 1800.
but foolish ; and with the full assent of his brigadiers
Pulteney ordered the army to be re-embarked. He
had lost in the skirmish of the morning eighty-four
killed and wounded : the Spaniards had lost as many,
besides thirty or forty prisoners. The chief military
interest of the action was that it brought under fire for
the first time three companies of a regiment whose
origin has yet to be described, and whose ranks were
still not wholly filled—the Ninety-fifth, now better
known as the Rifle Brigade.[1]

Upon the order to re-embark there arose a howl
from the Navy, which was taken up by the Army and
reverberated a few months later from within the walls
of Parliament. Pulteney seems to have entered upon
his task with high hopes of success, and very imprudently to have communicated them to Dundas. The
Minister confessed to a sense of severe disappointment ;
but it was the naval officers above all who clamoured
loud against the General, and talked of the storming
of Ferrol as though it were child's play ; the most
powerful cause of their discontent being that they had
counted upon large prize-money and gained none.
The malcontents of both services found a spokesman
in a Mr. Sturt, who, on the 19th of February 1800,
brought forward in the House of Commons a motion
for inquiry into the expedition to Ferrol, and as a
matter of course censured the General. Pulteney then
rose and adduced the facts above enumerated as to the
fortifications of the place ; adding that only one naval
officer had ever seen Ferrol, or even approached it,
from the side of the land, and that junior military
officers were not universally judges either of the
management of a large body of troops, or of the
nature of the attack or defence of fortified places. Nor
did he fail to insist upon the undoubted fact that such
enterprises were of greater difficulty and hazard than

[1] Dundas to Pulteney, 31st July ; Pulteney to Dundas, 27th
August 1800.

1800. ordinary military operations, and that it was for the commander to decide whether the object to be attained were worth the risk to be run.

This of course brought Dundas and Pitt to their feet, both of whom urged that the destruction of a naval arsenal and of eleven Spanish ships of the line, the consequent weakening of the confederacy which Bonaparte was forming against England, and the distraction of Spain from the invasion of Portugal, constituted very sufficient objects. Neither of them, however, said a word about the risk, nor attempted to meet Pulteney's arguments concerning it. Pitt indeed announced that Lord St. Vincent had approved the plan; but St. Vincent, great man though he was, had never seen the place from the shore. Moreover he had equally approved a similar attempt upon Carthagena, against which Charles Stuart, his favourite general, had given the Government a most emphatic warning. Thomas Maitland, who was with Pulteney, was entirely of his opinion as to the impracticability of an assault; and John Moore, who reconnoitred Ferrol by stealth in 1804, came to the same conclusion.[1] The end of the whole matter, therefore, seems to be that Pulteney was right, and that the Ministers alone were to blame for selecting, upon imperfect information, an impossible enterprise for their forces.[2]

After re-embarking his troops Pulteney proceeded to Vigo, whence, finding that there was no object worth gaining by an attack, he proceeded after some delay Sept. 19. to Gibraltar, where he arrived on the 19th of September. Meanwhile, Abercromby, having received Dundas's new instructions on the 24th of August, had sailed with ten

---

[1] *Diary of Sir John Moore*, i. 373. Bunbury, *Great War with France*, p. 73.

[2] The original papers respecting Ferrol I have unfortunately been unable to discover beyond the letters already quoted from Dundas to Pulteney of 31st July, and a second of 30th October, in *W.O. Sec. of State's Letter Books*, 19. Pulteney's despatch of 27th August is taken from the *Gazette*: his speech in the Commons from *Parl. Hist.*, xxxv. pp. 973 *sqq.*

thousand men from Minorca on the 31st, and reached 1800.
Gibraltar on the 11th of September.　Upon the advent Sept. 11.
of Pulteney, Lord Keith was called into consultation
for the attack on Cadiz ; and upon the 3rd of October
the entire armament passed through the Straits, anchor-
ing within sight of the city on the next day.　Aber- Oct. 4.
cromby had little intelligence as to the condition of the
enemy at Cadiz, being able to discover for certain only
that the Spaniards had been expecting a descent for
some time, and that the plague was raging with peculiar
malignity.　He had therefore been for abandoning the
enterprise, but Keith had given him to understand that
he considered his orders to attack to be peremptory.
The plan preconcerted before sailing had been to land
a force a little to the north of the northern shore of the
Bay of Cadiz, capture the batteries and a strong fort
which commanded the haven from that side, and so
gain a secure anchorage for the fleet.　Keith, however,
on consulting some of his officers who were better
acquainted with the coast than himself, became doubtful whether this anchorage would be safe in all conditions of weather ; but though pressed by Abercromby
to give an opinion on one side or the other he for long
hesitated to do so.　On the 7th three thousand soldiers Oct. 7.
were actually embarked in the flat-boats to be landed ;
but Abercromby, on learning that these men must be
left ashore unsupported for several hours before the
boats could return and land another division, summarily
cancelled all orders and decided to abandon the expedition altogether.

In his report to Dundas he enclosed a letter from
Keith, dated the 6th of October, wherein the Admiral
at last advised him definitely not to land the troops,
since he could not undertake that the fleet would not
be blown off the coast and might possibly be unable to
return for weeks.　Official reports therefore very rightly
gave no sign of the friction between the General and
the Admiral, though Abercromby appears to have
resented not a little Keith's attempt to evade his re-

1800.   sponsibility.   As to the wisdom and propriety of Abercromby's decision there can be no question whatever.   The naval arrangements for the dis-embarkation seem to have been of the crudest.   To have landed twenty thousand men on a hostile shore without the certainty of being in constant communication with the fleet would have been madness : to have done so when the plague was raging in their appointed destination would have been criminal madness.   Here, therefore, was another of the Government's great schemes gone to wreck, because no trouble had been taken to ascertain first if it were feasible at all, and secondly whether, if it were feasible, the season of the equinoctial gales was not likely to be most unfavourable to it.   In a word, the project was thoroughly characteristic of Pitt's military administration.[1]

Sept. 5.   Meanwhile, on the 5th of September Malta had fallen, after a blockade of nearly twelve months ; and this was the sole fruit of the British campaign in the Mediterranean during the year 1800.   It is difficult to speak with patience of the conduct of the British Ministers during this year.   Already in 1799 they had been guilty of the egregious blunder of sending their troops to a most hazardous campaign at the Helder, though Stuart had pointed out to them that Sicily was the true point of concentration for operations either in Italy or in Egypt.   On the evacuation of Holland Abercromby had pressed them to train and equip the army carefully so that it should be ready for service in the spring ; but they had taken no pains to do so.   In December 1799 Stuart in person had urged upon them for the second time the vital importance of sending twenty thousand to Minorca, from whence it could strike at any point in Italy ; but, though apparently they had accepted the suggestion for a time, they had presently abandoned it.   Had twenty thousand men

[1] Abercromby to Dundas, 7th October 1800.   *Diary of Sir John Moore*, i. 373-379.   Bunbury, *Great War with France*, pp. 74-78.

been collected at Minorca, as Stuart had urged, by the 1800. end of March, they might have landed at Nice or Ventimiglia, and, falling on the flank and rear of Suchet's corps while the Austrians assailed it in front, could have utterly destroyed it.

Far from this, the Government actually kept a force of nearly ten thousand men inactive for nearly two months before it could make up its mind to do anything at all. Pigot's troops were detained for weeks on board their transports before they were finally despatched to Minorca; and the first division of Maitland's detachment did not sail upon its idiotic errand against Belleisle until the third week in May. Had even these seven or eight thousand men reached Minorca by the end of April or the beginning of May, they might have shortened the blockade of Genoa or at all events have liberated that number of Austrians to capture the bridge-head at the Var, so as to have thrust Suchet altogether out of the field of action. Had they been landed at Savona even in the first week of June, they must have checked Suchet's pursuit of Elsnitz, and, by enabling that general to join Melas by the shortest route and with numbers little diminished, might have given the Austrians a decisive superiority at Marengo. And Melas, it must be remembered, had beaten Bonaparte himself at Marengo, and was only deprived of his victory by the arrival of Desaix at five o'clock in the evening. In fact on a dozen occasions a very little must have turned the scale against the French, and that little it had been in the power of the British Ministers to bestow. Yet, even after a most capable and far-seeing soldier had for months striven to show them how to wield their tiny force to the best purpose, they had not the sense to take his advice.

Even more futile were the enterprises prescribed to the Generals after the belated arrival of Abercromby at Minorca. Had every possible man been sent out with him, he would have been in a position to hearten

1800. Melas to future efforts, to countenance the insurrection of the peasants in Tuscany, and by an advance from the south to bring serious pressure to bear against the right flank of Brune, who was a very incompetent commander. This would have marred the effect of Bonaparte's victory, would have weakened his diplomacy and might well have recalled him from Paris to Italy once more. As things were, a renewal of the suspension of arms in September enabled Brune to detach a force which suppressed the rising of the peasantry and occupied Tuscany. Meanwhile, the British army was divided in order to make useless displays of weakness around the Spanish ports, nominally for the object of distracting the Spaniards from the invasion of Portugal, but in reality to save the Navy from the trouble of blockading them, though in truth there was nothing but this tedious duty left for the Navy to do.

This was the true secret of these foolish expeditions against Ferrol and Cadiz, and probably also for the ridiculous project, which appears to have been tacitly ignored, of an attack upon Teneriffe. One and all had their origin in the counsels of naval officers, which were not wholly uninfluenced by the question of prize-money. No doubt the destruction of the Spanish fleets and naval arsenals was, on general grounds, desirable ; but, if the object were worth the employment of ten thousand troops, it was also worth some effort to obtain intelligence and information. On the other hand, it must be remembered, in justice to the Navy, that the work of a blockading squadron was weary, harassing, and thankless in the extreme both to officers and men. The life at sea, at a time when ships sometimes did not drop anchor for months and even years together, was one of such continual hardship and peril as to claim great rewards. Bitter feelings were excited during this war among the crews of the line-of-battle-ships, which cruised before the enemy's ports, towards the frigates which roamed at large over

the seas, picking up prizes in all directions. It was 1800.
not easy for an Admiral to keep his officers and crews
in good humour in such circumstances ; and hence we
find St. Vincent detaching Nelson and his squadron to
Teneriffe in July 1797, to give him and his men, as it
were, a holiday. On that occasion both of these great
Admirals tried hard to persuade first General de Burgh
at Elba and afterwards General O'Hara at Gibraltar,
to spare them a thousand or fifteen hundred men for
their raid ; but the two soldiers shook their heads, and
Nelson thereupon proceeded to pass sweeping judgment upon the whole of their service. " Soldiers," he
wrote, " have not the same boldness in undertaking a
political measure that we have ; we look to the benefit
of our country, and risk our own fame every day to save
her : a soldier obeys his orders and no more." [1]

The political measure in question was the anticipated
capture of six millions sterling of Spanish treasure, the
circulation of which would doubtless have given untold
relief to England at that moment, when cash-payments
had recently been suspended. But the Navy's share
of prize-money would also have been enormous ; and,
though we may freely grant that this was very far
from being the first consideration to Nelson, it would
be absurd to suppose that it did not count in his own
mind for something,[2] and in the minds of his officers
and men for a great deal. It may be remarked, moreover, that though his reproach against the soldiers
generally of unwillingness to take responsibility was
not altogether without justice, the Commander-in-
chief of the Mediterranean fleet was in a very different
position to a humble Major-general in charge of three
or four thousand men and wholly under the orders of
ignorant Ministers. It may be noted further that
Colonel Maitland's convention upon the evacuation

[1] Mahan, *Life of Nelson*, pp. 254 *sqq.*
[2] Hood gained £50,000 as his share of prize-money by the
capture of a single ship laden with bullion and specie in 1793.
Brenton's *Naval History*, i. 100.

1800. of St. Domingo was a far bolder, greater, and more successful political measure than any of Nelson's.

But, to return from this digression, Nelson, as is well known, sailed to Teneriffe, knowing nothing whatever about the defences of the place, and was completely and disastrously defeated. His landing-party numbered a thousand men : had O'Hara complied with his requisition it might have been twenty-five hundred men. The Spaniards had eight thousand men in strongly fortified positions, and were quite prepared to meet them. Here was a warning, and it was not the first. Hood had utterly misconceived the position both at Toulon and at Bastia, in the former case with disastrous results ; and the fall of Calvi had been due solely to the soldier, Stuart. St. Vincent, again on insufficient information, had given his sanction to an attempt on Carthagena, which had only been averted by Stuart's adjuration to Dundas not to trust the light-hearted advice of naval officers upon such operations. Nevertheless, the raids upon Ferrol, Vigo, and Cadiz were deliberately ordered by the Government ; and this although there were in Egypt a French force waiting to be captured and a British squadron pining to be relieved from a blockade. The conclusion of the whole matter cannot be better summed up than in the words of Cornwallis. " What a disgraceful and what an expensive campaign have we made ! Twenty-two thousand men, a large proportion not soldiers, floating round the greater part of Europe, the scorn and laughing-stock of friends and foes ! The infatuation of Ministers is so great that I have no hopes of amendment ; and if the means of forming another army should fall as unexpectedly again into their hands, they would in a few months and in like manner bring it to ruin and disgrace." [1]

[1] *Cornwallis Corres.*, iii. 300-301.

CHAPTER XXVIII

Upon his return to Gibraltar Abercromby received on the 24th of October yet another batch of instructions. Bonaparte's diplomacy had begun to bear fruit. On the 1st of October the Court of Madrid concluded with the First Consul the preliminary Treaty of San Ildefonso. Hereby Spain yielded to France six ships of war and Louisiana in return for the cession of a kingdom in Italy for the Duke of Parma; though for the present she continued to evade an express stipulation that she should declare war upon Portugal. On the 30th of September France also agreed upon a treaty with the United States whereby both parties renounced the right of search, and the rupture created by the folly of the Directory was healed. Finally the Tsar Paul had been definitely alienated from England by his exclusion from Malta and was working with France towards a revival of the Armed Neutrality of 1780, with good hope of persuading Sweden, Denmark, and Prussia to accede to it. In fact, though France and Austria were still held apart by a suspension of arms only, there seemed to be every prospect that England would shortly be left to deal with Bonaparte single-handed.

The first of Dundas's new instructions related to Portugal, which, rightly anticipating a Spanish invasion, had begged that the British auxiliary force should be raised to fifteen thousand men with Pulteney in command. Abercromby was therefore directed to send eight thousand men under Pulteney to Lisbon,

1800. where five thousand Dutch troops were to join them
from England. The next orders concerned Malta,
from which the commandant was now directed absolutely to exclude Russian troops by every measure
short of actual hostilities, and upon no account to
admit them to any of the principal fortresses or works.
This last sentence was meaningless unless it signified
that, in case of need, the Russians should be debarred
from access to the works by force ; but the Ministry,
as usual, had not the courage to speak its mind outright.

Finally a third batch of instructions ordered Abercromby to embark fifteen thousand infantry, take them
to some suitable port at Cyprus, Crete, Rhodes, or
the coast of Asia Minor for the purchase of supplies,
and there to concert operations with the Sultan's
officers for a landing in Egypt and the reduction of
Alexandria. The French force in Egypt Dundas
calculated at thirteen thousand men, of which three
thousand men formed the garrison of Alexandria, while
most of the remainder were tied (as he conceived) to
different posts in Upper Egypt and Syria. The
defences of Alexandria itself were, as he had been
correctly informed, so incomplete that the place would
be easily reducible ; nor was it possible, in his opinion,
that the enemy could oppose to the British such a
force as could disturb them in the prosecution of a
siege. The French army was known to be very
anxious to return home ; wherefore Abercromby was
authorised to offer to transport the troops in Alexandria, and later on those in the other posts also,
direct to France. If this offer were rejected by the
French Commander-in-chief, he was to take care that
it should become known to the French rank and file.
Any advance up the country after the capture of
Alexandria and the sea-ports, though not absolutely
forbidden, was to be deprecated except with the object
of facilitating a passage to the Turkish army ; and
Dundas added that, in order to straiten the resources

of the enemy to the utmost, five thousand troops had 1800. been ordered to sail from India for the capture of all posts occupied by the French army on the Red Sea. Finally the Minister gave Abercromby to understand that he had been so urgent in pressing this expedition upon the Cabinet that he held himself solely responsible for it ; that he had long been deterred from insisting upon it by reports of the difficulties of navigation in the Levant, but that his misgivings upon this head had been set at rest by a report from Sir Thomas Troubridge, which was the chief authority upon which he had acted in advising the expedition. This report, which was so brief, vague, and meagre as to be practically worthless, he carefully enclosed. For the rest he left Abercromby full discretion to act contrary to these instructions, if on further enquiry he should think fit ; and he concluded by a series of compliments which, reading between the lines, I can interpret only to mean that he threw himself upon the General's mercy to deliver him from his troubles by a great success. Considering how many and how shameful had been Dundas's failures in the conduct of the war, it is not surprising that he should have trembled over the issue of this, his last adventure.[1]

The explanation of this sudden attention to Egypt is explained by a variety of causes. In the first place a number of letters from French officers, both before and after the departure of Bonaparte from Alexandria, had been intercepted and published in England, all of which, including one in particular from Kléber, painted the condition and prospects of the French army in the gloomiest colours. These accounts the Government accepted without further enquiry, being always content with the baldest intelligence. Next, though Colonel Koehler and a small party of officers and non-commissioned officers had for some months been attached to the Turkish army at Jaffa in order to improve its

[1] Dundas to Abercromby and Pulteney, 6th October (4 letters), to Abercromby, 13th October 1800.

1800. training and discipline, the Grand Vizier had asked for five thousand British troops to join them. Indeed both Koehler and Sidney Smith declared that, without such support, the Turks could never drive the French from Egypt. Moreover, it was plain that Bonaparte was excessively anxious about his troops in Egypt and longed to rescue them if he could. He had tried to do so by inviting England to accede to the suspension of arms which had been initiated by Austria ; but Grenville insisted upon excepting Malta and Egypt from such a truce, and the negotiations in consequence had fallen to the ground.

Most important of all was the fact that the conversion of the Tsar to friendship with France had altered the entire situation. If the First Consul should succeed in forming a hostile confederacy of the Northern powers against England, then it might be necessary to withdraw part of the British fleet from the Mediterranean ; and Bonaparte was not likely to miss such an opportunity of reinforcing the troops in Egypt. Nor was it possible to foresee what arrangement the autocrats of France and Russia, the one absolutely unprincipled and the other insane, might not concert for the partition of Turkey and possibly for attack upon the eastern possessions of Britain. Some of these contingencies might have been considered by the Government before the Convention of El Arish was annulled. It is true that at the beginning of 1800 it was most undesirable to restore a body of French veteran troops to France ; and this indeed had been the principal ground for the repudiation of that treaty. But Sidney Smith, according to his own account, had provided against that difficulty. He had stipulated not to transport the French army from Egypt in a mass to any particular port, but to take every man to his home clear of the army ; and he had intended to scatter the transports among all the ports of France, where they would have been kept in quarantine owing to the plague, so that the troops could not

easily have been collected nor trained to good con- 1800.
dition for a campaign.   However, it was now too late
to think of such matters; and the only remedy
was to hurry Abercromby to Alexandria as quickly as
possible.[1]

The design of bringing troops from India to Egypt
seems to have occurred to several people, but to
Dundas himself first of all, very soon after he had
heard the news of the battle of the Nile.   Sidney
Smith had also thought of it; and Lord Elgin, the
Ambassador at Constantinople, either took the idea from
him or conceived it independently.   Both of them
wrote to consult Lord Wellesley in India as to the
feasibility of the plan, and Sidney Smith at any rate
received an answer that lack of troops rather than of
good-will prevented the Governor-general from entertaining it.[2]   However, Dundas lost no time in writing
to Wellesley for a thousand European troops and two
thousand Sepoys, boldly predicting that Abercromby
would arrive in Egypt by December, and the Indian
contingent by the following April.   We shall presently
see how utterly false these and all other of Dundas's
calculations proved to be.   But in truth the man
looked upon the coming Egyptian campaign as a very
trifling affair.   On the 13th of October, a week after
the date of his first instructions, he wrote to Abercromby that he need give Pulteney only five thousand
instead of eight thousand men for Portugal.   He was
sanguine, he said, that, with such an addition to the
force for Egypt, the General would perform the whole
service expected of him without serious resistance
or loss, and would be able to send home the whole

---

[1] *Letters from General Bonaparte's army in Egypt.* London,
1798-99.   Koehler to Grenville, 2nd August, enclosing a letter
from Sidney Smith of 27th July; Abercromby to Dundas, 11th
September (with enclosures from Koehler); Sidney Smith to
Keith, 27th September 1800.

[2] *Dropmore Papers*, iv. 423.   Elgin to Mornington (undated),
1799; Sidney Smith to Keith (enclosing letter from Wellesley of
26th April), 29th September 1800.

1800. of his troops, excepting the garrison of Alexandria, in the course of the ensuing summer.[1]

Abercromby, when these letters reached him, was not in the happiest temper. Anticipating some distant expedition, he had been engaged in sorting out the regiments enlisted for general service from those enlisted for service in Europe only, and embarking the former on the old half-armed two-deckers which in those days were termed troop-ships.[2] For some days, however, the wind had blown hard from the east, which made all repairs impossible, prevented the ships from lying in Gibraltar, and, worse still, forbade them to proceed to Tetuan, where alone they could obtain the water necessary for their voyage to Minorca. Moreover, Dundas had, as usual, utterly miscalculated the number of men at his disposal. Instead of eight thousand men, as originally ordered, Abercromby could only spare to Pulteney fewer than five thousand men "of the worst species," and even then he reserved to himself something less than the prescribed force of fifteen thousand infantry. In addition to this difficulty, the troops were growing sickly from long confinement on board ship, more particularly such regiments as had drawn recruits from the Irish Militia, whose men paid as little attention to cleanliness as their officers to duty. Matters were not improved by the enormous price of fresh meat at Gibraltar, though fortunately vegetables were procurable in sufficient quantity to check the scurvy which had already made its appearance.[3] Clothing and necessaries again were so deficient and so urgently required, there being no means of procuring either at Gibraltar, that Abercromby was obliged to ask that these articles might be provided at once by special convoy. Lastly, many of the transports were in great need of repairs, which could not be effected in those days at Gibraltar ; and it was therefore

[1] Dundas to Abercromby, 13th October 1800.
[2] Bunbury, p. 93.
[3] Anderson's *Journal of the Forces*, etc., pp. 62, 97.

imperative that they should be overhauled at Malta 1800.
or Minorca before they could proceed to the final
rendezvous on the coast of Asia Minor.   All these
little things Dundas had of course left out of calculation; and the casual fashion in which he spoke already
of the return of the troops to England after the com-
pletion of their work in Egypt irritated even the
gentle Abercromby into something greatly resembling
sarcasm.[1]

The first division of the troops weighed anchor for
Minorca in the last week of October; but the second, Oct.
which was much the larger, was so long prevented by
inclement weather from taking in water that it did not
sail for Malta until the second week in November. Nov.
Both the divisions united at Malta at the end of that
month; and several regiments were stationed permanently ashore while the transports were under
survey and repair.   At least one of the vessels, which
had carried John Moore among other passengers, was
condemned as unfit for sea, and many of the troop-
ships were in little better plight.   From this and from
various other causes it was the 17th of December
before the troops could be re-embarked, and the 20th Dec. 20.
before the wind enabled them to put to sea.   The
entire force on the 15th of December numbered sixteen
thousand non-commissioned officers and men fit for
duty, and twelve hundred and seventy sick.   Of this
total the cavalry and artillery claimed from seven to
eight hundred men, the whole of the remainder being
infantry; but it must be remarked that among the
infantry of the line were two battalions of the Fifty-
fourth and four flank-companies of the Fortieth, both
of which regiments were composed of militiamen,
engaged for service in Europe only.   The men of
these two battalions and four companies numbered
fifteen hundred; and, had not they volunteered for
service beyond the limits fixed by their agreement,
Abercromby could not have collected the fifteen

[1] Abercromby to Dundas, 28th October 1800.

1800. thousand infantry ordained by Dundas for the expedition. Hence it was only through the public spirit of the British soldier that the armament was able to start at all from Malta for the appointed rendezvous on the coast of Asia Minor ; and even then at a date when the sanguine ignorance of Dundas had reckoned that they would already have reached the coast of Egypt.[1]

Meanwhile, under the pressure of the French armies and of Bonaparte's diplomacy, events had moved rapidly upon the Continent of Europe ; and the difficulties of the British Government were increased by the failure of the harvest for the second year in succession, and consequently by general distress and discontent at home. On the 17th of November Dundas informed Pulteney not only that no reinforcements could be spared to him, but that nearly all of his troops were imperatively needed to preserve order in England and Ireland. He was therefore directed to send one of his six battalions to Minorca, to embark the remaining five for England immediately, and to despatch five hundred men of the Twelfth and Twenty-sixth Light Dragoons to join Abercromby. Thus all British troops were withdrawn from Portugal, and the three foreign regiments of Mortemar, Castries, and Le Chastre alone remained ; the British Government having now made up its mind, erroneously, that the country was no longer in any danger from the menaces of France and Spain. To Pulteney himself Dundas gave the option either to join Abercromby or to return home, a proceeding which was nothing short of monstrous. Pulteney was the officer next in seniority to Abercromby in the Mediterranean, and was therefore bound to succeed him in the chief command in the event of that General's death. For this position he was either fit or unfit ; and, in fairness to himself and to Abercromby, he should have received definite instructions either to assume it or to return to England.

[1] Abercromby to Dundas, 10th December 1800, enclosing return of troops of 15th December.

Being probably aware that Abercromby had selected 1800
Hutchinson for his second in command, Pulteney, with
great tact and good taste, elected not to join the army ;
but the whole incident affords another proof of
Dundas's incurable negligence even of the most
elementary military arrangements.[1]

But the affairs of Portugal were those of least
moment in the great change which Bonaparte had
brought about in Europe.   The hostility of Russia
towards Britain was becoming more strongly marked ;
and Dundas's letter to Pulteney was accompanied by
another of the same date to General Pigot, repeating Nov. 17
his former instructions to exclude Russian troops and
officers from Malta.   He ordered him, moreover, to
increase the militia of the island and to assure the inhabitants that they should not be allowed to fall into
the hands of Russia nor of the Knights of St. John—
the very measure that Charles Stuart had pressed for
in vain six months before.   A few days later the Tsar,
without any declaration of war, laid an embargo on all
British shipping in Russian ports.   Thereupon Dundas,
on the 2nd of December, wrote to warn Abercromby Dec. 2.
that he and Keith must be prepared to repel an attack
by Russia from the side of the Dardanelles, though
they were to confine themselves to observation only of
the Russian forces until war should be actually declared
or some hostile act committed.   The Minister, however, added that these new duties called for increased
diligence in the campaign against Egypt, so as to liberate a large portion of the fleet for service in the Baltic.
This comment proves how ludicrous was his mis-
conception of the true state of affairs in the Mediterranean.   His anticipation of the need of a fleet in
the Baltic was, however, only too just.   After fruitless
negotiation at Paris the Austrians decided to try the
fortune of war once more, and on the 1st December
they reopened the campaign in Germany by an attack
upon General Moreau.   Two days later they sustained Dec. 3.

---

[1] Dundas to Pulteney, 17th November 1800.

1800. a crushing defeat at Hohenlinden, and from that moment they abandoned all hope. Thugut, who had threatened to resign from the moment when the Emperor had favoured a pacific policy, now finally withdrew from office ; and Austria sued for peace at

Dec. 16. any price.   Finally, on the 16th of December, the revival of the Armed Neutrality became an accomplished fact, and England was left alone with many enemies but without a friend in Europe.

Ignorant of all these matters but with sufficient anxiety for his own task, Abercromby sailed eastward

Dec. 29. from Malta ; and on the 29th and 30th of December the fleet and transports anchored in Marmaras or Marmorice Bay, on the coast of Asia Minor, about forty miles north of Rhodes.   Immediately upon receiving his orders for the Egyptian expedition the General had sent his Quartermaster-general and two more officers to Rhodes, in order to obtain supplies and to concert operations with the army of the Grand Vizir at Jaffa ; but in spite of these precautions and of the British Government's instructions to the Ambassador at Constantinople, there was no sign of the slightest preparation on the part of the Turks.   No small craft had been collected ; the Turkish gunboats at Rhodes were not manned ; no provisions had been procured ; no horses had been sent from Constantinople, and no supplies, except a little barley, had been amassed.   It was not that either Lord Elgin or the British officers had failed in their duty.   The Porte had been lavish of promises and decrees, but it had done nothing, and, whether from natural apathy or from fear of Russia, showed every sign of persistence in doing nothing.   The Turkish army at Jaffa was without magazines or the means of advancing.   The Capitan Pasha, who had taken the Turkish fleet to Constantinople with solemn assurances of an immediate return, now declared that he could not come back for forty days.   It was very evident that the British must trust to their own exertions alone.

Abercromby did not shrink from the prospect, but 1801. there was little to reassure him. He had been unable anywhere to obtain any trustworthy information as to the numbers of the French in Egypt, and could learn only that they had twelve thousand regular troops besides auxiliaries. Accepting this figure, which as a matter of fact underestimated the strength of the enemy by one half, he could at best hope to meet them only with equal numbers. His officers and men had been patient in the extreme of the long confinement on board ship, and of the insolence of the officers, naturally not the choicest in the King's Navy, of the troopships ; but the upper works of those vessels were in such disrepair that the men were often wet for days together ; and, from this cause added to deficient clothing, the number of the sick had been greatly increased. The army, in fact, notwithstanding the addition of five hundred Maltese pioneers, had already shrunk from seventeen thousand to fifteen thousand five hundred effective men.[1] Moreover, from intelligence supplied by the intercepted letters from the French army—intelligence which had lain before Dundas long before it was forwarded to Abercromby — it appeared that, until Alexandria should be captured, every drop of water for the British force must be landed from the ships. Troubridge had hinted at this difficulty by stating that both troopships and men-of-war " must be filled chock full of water " ; but it never struck Dundas that it was anything unusual to launch fifteen thousand men into a semi-tropical campaign against a force of unknown strength, with no more water than they could draw from the fleet, and with no prospect of a regular supply until they should have carried a fortified city by siege or assault. It never occurred to him that if the fleet should be forced to sea by a gale the army would die of thirst. Nevertheless Abercromby knew

[1] Exclusive of officers, the actual number was 15,526 N.C.O.s and men : 932 sick present, 800 sick left at Minorca, Malta, and Gibraltar. Return of 11th January 1801.

1801. British Ministers of War too well to be surprised. He was too loyal a servant to be deterred even by such difficulties as these ; and his hidden indignation revealed itself only in one stinging sentence : " There are risks in a British warfare unknown in any other service." [1]

To ascertain the truth about the Turkish army, Moore was sent to Jaffa to inspect it ; but his report only confirmed those already received as to its inefficiency and unreadiness. Unfortunately, too, Koehler had died just when his influence with the Grand Vizir would have been most valuable. There was no resource, therefore, but to wait and hope that in due time the Turks would fulfil their promises, and meantime to train the army most carefully for the coming disembarkation. Abercromby remembered the confusion of the landing at the Helder, and was determined to have no more of it. Full instructions were issued for the officers of both Army and Navy, presenting a curious but most effective combination of naval and military tactics. The advance of the flotilla was to be made in three lines : the first line consisting exclusively of flat-boats at intervals of fifty feet, the second line of cutters, to stand by the flat-boats and render any assistance that might be required, the third line of cutters to tow the launches which carried the artillery. The flat-boats in which each grenadier-company was embarked were to hoist the camp-colours of their regiment for distinction, and the boats with the remaining companies were to fall in upon their left according to the order in which the troops were to stand when landed. The dressing of the line of flat-boats was to be carefully kept, and the intervals most accurately preserved, so as to allow the cutters and launches from the second and third lines to reach the shore between them. The men were positively forbidden to speak, stand up, or load their muskets in the

[1] Abercromby to Dundas, 11th and 15th January 1801. *Life of Abercromby*, pp. 265-66.

boats ; they were to sit absolutely still and silent until 1801. they reached the shore, and then form up in line opposite to the point at which they had landed. These manœuvres were practised again and again by the troops appointed to lead the disembarkation, and simultaneously the whole army was trained ashore continually in the tactics best suited to foil the French in Egypt.

Nevertheless the long delay was intolerably irksome and disappointing to the Commander-in-chief. The arrival of the Twelfth and Twenty-sixth Light Dragoons from Portugal had raised his force of cavalry to eleven hundred men, but he had not the means of mounting them.   A few horses were indeed furnished by Lord Elgin, but they were so poor that most of them were given to the artillery ; and indeed the whole number supplied did not exceed five hundred and fifty.   Transport-ships for these animals had been hired from Smyrna, but did not arrive before the middle of February ; and without them it was impossible to move.   The news from Egypt also was not reassuring.   Sidney Smith, who had joined the expedition from before Toulon, gave the numbers of the French and their auxiliaries at thirty thousand effective men.   This figure, though it proved to be not far from correct, Abercromby thought an exaggeration, reckoning that the enemy could not bring more than at most ten thousand men to oppose him in the field.   But, even so, the number of his boats did not permit him to land more than six thousand men together ; and, even if the disembarkation were successfully accomplished, he had neither waggons nor draft-animals for purposes of transport.   Everything therefore, even water, would require to be dragged by the seamen and soldiers under a burning sun from the ships to the camp.   It was, therefore, practically certain that many men would be driven to hospital, and that friction would arise with the fleet from the natural, and indeed laudable, solicitude of the naval officers for the health of their

1801. ships' companies. However, it was idle to think of waiting until these defects should be made good. His army at least was in good order and good spirits, though sickness had reduced its numbers to little more than sixteen thousand effective men.[1] He decided therefore to sail on the 18th of February, but being delayed by foul winds did not finally put to sea until

Feb. 22. the 22nd. "We are now on the point of sailing for Egypt," he wrote to the Military Secretary on the 16th, "with very slender means for executing the orders we have received. I never went on any service entertaining greater doubts of success, at the same time with more determination to conquer difficulties."[2]

Meanwhile Bonaparte's anxiety and activity on behalf of his army in Egypt had long been extreme. He was eager above all to prove to the French nation that, under its new ruler, victory signified peace;[3] and he saw that, in the negotiations which he was pressing forward for a general cessation of arms, the nation that occupied Egypt would possess an enormous advantage in the driving of a bargain. The British Ministers were fully alive to this fact; and Dundas was prepared to maintain, for diplomatic purposes, that the possession of Egypt was in dispute from the moment when Abercromby's force was assembled at its final rendezvous. As far back as in February 1800 Bonaparte had issued orders for a French fleet to raise the blockade of Malta and send relief to Egypt; while constant references to these places occur in his correspondence until he left Paris to lead his army over the Alps, and reappear

[1] Infantry, 14,555; cavalry, 1125, of whom 400 mounted; artillery (including drivers), 667. Total, 16,347 N.C.O.s and men fit for duty; 1098 sick present; 794 sick at Malta, Minorca, etc. Return of 14th February 1801. The increase in numbers over the last return was due to the arrival of the 12th and 26th Light Dragoons and of recovered invalids from Malta and Minorca.

[2] Abercromby to Dundas, 15th and 21st January; 16th February 1801. *Life of Abercromby*, p. 267.

[3] For a curious instance of his methods for the propagation or this idea, see *Corres. de Napoléon*, vi. 160, letter to Lucien Bonaparte of 3rd March 1800.

within a week after the battle of Marengo.[1]   In October   1801.
he again issued orders for the despatch of a fleet to
Egypt, but it was not until the 23rd of January 1801 Jan. 23.
that a heavy gale drove the British blockading squadron
from before Brest and enabled Admiral Ganteaume to
slip out with seven ships of war, carrying on board them
four thousand troops.

Ganteaume passed the Straits of Gibraltar in safety,
but, being followed by four British ships under Admiral
Warren, took fright and put back into Toulon.   Of March 25.
four frigates, however, that started from Toulon and
Rochefort at about the same time, three successfully
evaded the blockading squadron before Alexandria,
bringing to the garrison ordnance stores and from six to
eight hundred troops.   The fourth was taken off Ceuta
by the British frigate *Phœbe* on the 19th of February.
This vessel, the *Africaine*, a frigate of forty-four guns,
carried four hundred troops besides her ship's company
of three hundred sailors ; and when, after a most gallant
fight of two hours, she at last hauled down her colours,
the number of her dead was two hundred, and of her
wounded one hundred and fifty.   The *Phœbe*, of about
the same weight of metal but with a crew of only two
hundred and thirty, lost but one killed and twelve
wounded.   From this example we may gather what
would have happened if Nelson's squadron had met
that of Bonaparte on its way out to Egypt.[2]

Thus by means of single frigates Bonaparte contrived to add a few men to his army in Egypt ; but
there were—perhaps there always had been—influences
at work which had tended to undermine its efficiency.
The troops had formed part, it is true, of Bonaparte's
army of Italy in 1796 ; but though under the magic of
his leadership they had done great things, yet they
were not in the first instance particularly good material,
nor had they ever been properly disciplined.   They

---

[1] *Corres. de Napoléon*, vi. 142, 146, etc. ; Letter to Carnot, 20th
June 1800, *ibid.* 379.

[2] *Corres. de Napoléon*, vi. 529 ; James, *Naval History*, iii. 239.

1801 had beaten the Austrians again and again; but the composition and spirit of the Austrian armies opposed to them had been lamentable beyond description. Four hundred of their officers had at one time been found skulking in a single town, having deserted their regiments; and they had been led by Generals always of incapacity and sometimes of downright stupidity.[1] Triumph over such adversaries was not very difficult; and hence, though the training of the French troops in Italy had made them terrible in attack and even more terrible in victory, the plunder of Lombardy had taught them bad lessons in self-indulgence and insubordination. The hardships of heat and thirst in Egypt had found out their weak points very early; and though Bonaparte had compelled them to obedience he had failed to constrain them to content. " They are the most intrepid troops in the world," wrote one of their officers from Egypt in July 1798, "but they are not formed for distant expeditions. A word dropped at random will dishearten them. They are lazy, capricious, and a law unto themselves. They have been heard to say, 'Here come our butchers,'[2] with a thousand like expressions, when their generals pass by."

This quotation has been selected from the most moderate and thoughtful of the letters intercepted from the French army in Egypt. There are many others, which have been very freely quoted by every description of writer, depicting the soldiers as committing suicide in Bonaparte's presence, with other details, which give the impression of an army in open mutiny.[3] These documents, however, are in

[1] Delavoye, *Life of Lord Lynedoch*, p. 117; and see the whole of Graham's letters from Italy, pp. 111-152.

[2] " Voilà les bourreaux des Français," *Intercepted Letters*, i. 161.

[3] Count Yorck von Wartenburg has collected a large assortment of these quotations in *Napoleon as a General*, and from that source General Maurice has borrowed specimens (apparently without recollection that the originals were first published in England) in *Diary of Sir John Moore*, ii. 37-39. Even Sybel quotes the passages about the suicide of the men, which, judging from the general tone of the

many cases evidently the work of confirmed grumblers, 1801. and full of exaggeration ; and I believe it to be quite a mistake to rate the military value of these troops so low. The men were beyond doubt miserably homesick, not only because Frenchmen abroad always are homesick, but because they were wholly cut off from the food, the wine, and the brandy to which they were accustomed. But they had become acclimatised to a hot sun, mosquitoes, fleas, flies, and other plagues, over which, upon first landing, they had howled like children ; and they had settled down, though not with the best grace, to make the best of things in the hope of deliverance. They had suffered severe trials, first when Nelson won the battle of the Nile, and later when Bonaparte deserted them ; but though they had never been really well-disciplined troops, they were kept well in hand by Kléber, and under his leadership were quite ready to give a good account of themselves. Granted success, they were as formidable as ever ; but they were not, nor ever had been, well fitted to struggle with failure or adversity.

Kléber, however, was assassinated by a fanatic in May 1800, and the command devolved upon General Menou. French writers have conspired to write this man down as utterly incapable either for civil or military purposes ; and it seems certain that, whatever his capacity, he was vain, flighty, short-sighted, and self-seeking. Thinking, apparently, that Egypt was safe from an invasion, he boldly proclaimed it a French colony, upset the existing civil administration to make way for a new scheme of his own, and, having already

two letters which mention it (*Intercepted Letters*, ii. 50, 220), are gross exaggerations. That one or two men, probably confirmed drinkers, mad with thirst or through the approach of sunstroke, may have used violent language to the General and even have blown out their brains, is quite possible. But discontented officers, perhaps deservedly under their General's displeasure, do not inquire strictly into these matters before reporting them in the hope of injuring him with the public, particularly under such a government as the Directory.

1801. embraced Mohammedanism, showed particular partiality
to those who were of his new faith.   This quickly
brought him into conflict with his divisional Generals,
and in particular with Reynier, who, though he had
indeed seen more service than his chief, possessed no
less vanity and no greater military talent.[1]   One and
all of these divisional Generals were intensely jealous of
their chief, and Menou, finding that they would not
work with him, ignored them and corresponded direct
with the brigadiers.   This injuriously affected discipline,
and the army became full of feuds and parties, thoroughly
unhappy, and as a natural consequence discontented
and quarrelsome.   Its numbers in March 1801 were
slightly over twenty-five thousand, or, excluding auxiliaries, twenty-four thousand of all ranks.   Of these,
from six to seven thousand were either unfit for active
service or fixed permanently in garrison, so that the
force at disposal for the field amounted to about seventeen thousand of all ranks, of which about seventeen
hundred were excellent cavalry.[2]   With this force, which
was certainly superior to Abercromby's, Menou judged
himself so secure that, though amply warned of the
danger that threatened him, he took no precautions to
throw up additional defences nor even to victual the
fortresses which he actually possessed.   In fact he despised
his enemy, as very reasonably he might ; for the English
military enterprises since the beginning of the war had
almost invariably failed with ignominy ; and, judging
them to have been projected by military men, he had
naturally formed a low opinion of the English military

[1] I judge this by the fact that the British beat him in fair fight
with inferior numbers both at Maida and at Sabugal.

[2] The returns given by Jomini and Reynier do not exactly agree,
Jomini giving the cavalry at 1250 and Reynier at 1661, exclusive
of officers.   I have preferred Reynier's figures for this detail.   For
the force at large the two returns are in substantial accord.   Bunbury
gives the numbers of the French at from 27,000 to 28,000 veterans,
and Wilson, apparently from authentic returns, puts the figures, in-
clusive of auxiliaries, at 32,000.—*Expedition to Egypt*, p. 255.   To
avoid all semblance of favour to the English side, I accept the
French figures throughout.

service. Better testimony could not be found to the 1801.
contempt into which Pitt's Ministry had brought the
British Army.

On the afternoon of the 1st of March the British March 1
fleet arrived off Alexandria, when Keith, for some reason,
stood in close enough to distinguish the signals of the
vessels in the harbour, but stood off again in consequence
of boisterous weather, finally coming to anchor at nine
o'clock on the following morning in the Bay of Aboukir. March 2.
Abercromby had sent forward from Asia Minor two
officers of the Engineers to reconnoitre the shore; but
he now found that they had ventured in too close, and
that one of them had been killed and the other taken.
The General therefore rowed off in a cutter with Moore
to look for himself, the men-of-war being moored from
five to seven miles from the beach owing to the shallowness of the water. They duly selected the point for
disembarkation ; but, as they returned, a French armed
vessel ran through the lines of the fleet and anchored
under the Castle of Aboukir in a position to rake the
appointed extent of beach from end to end. Lord
Keith, however, declared that he could not spare a
vessel to look after her, and the matter proved to be of
small importance ; for, though Abercromby gave orders
to land upon the following morning, the wind freshened
into a regular gale which blew persistently for four
days, raising a heavy sea and rendering disembarkation
absolutely impossible.

Menou at this time was at Cairo, in and about
which city there were eight thousand of his troops.
He had heard of the arrival of the British on the
4th, so that by undeserved good fortune he had still March 4.
time to move a formidable body to Alexandria by
the 9th. His Generals urged him to concentrate
his troops to oppose the British landing, but he nevertheless remained at Cairo, merely sending Reynier
with about fifteen hundred men about thirty miles
northward to Belbeis, detaching five hundred more to
Damietta, and ordering General Lanusse at Ramanieh

1801.   to reinforce Alexandria with a bare six hundred men. General Friant, who commanded at the port last named, had with him about two thousand effective soldiers, and about the same number of seamen and invalids. Of these he stationed one small detachment at Rosetta and another about ten miles to south-west of it, while he himself with sixteen hundred infantry,[1] two hundred cavalry and fifteen guns, took up a position at Aboukir.

March 7.   On the 7th of March the gale abated, and in the afternoon Abercromby gave orders for the landing to be attempted on the morrow. The anxiety of the veteran must have been trying almost beyond endurance, for he had not the slightest information as to the enemy's strength or movements. The place selected for the disembarkation was the eastern front of the peninsula of Aboukir, in a bay measuring about two miles from north to south. Upon the northern horn of this bay stood the Castle of Aboukir, mounting, besides smaller guns, eight twenty-four pounders and two twelve-inch mortars, which enfiladed the beach to southward up to a range of eighteen hundred yards. Upon the southern horn stood a block-house with at least one heavy gun. At about the centre of the bay rose a high sand-hill, of which the seaward face was partially flanked by the guns of the Castle ; and to the south of it the ground was simply a confusion of lower sand-hills, rising in tiers one behind the other, and dotted with patches of scrub. The French General thus possessed every means of concealing his troops ; but Moore, after reconnoitring the ground carefully, could perceive no entrenchments whatever, though the visible presence of picquets along the whole length of the line showed that the enemy was there in unknown force. The guns of the fort of Aboukir forbade any attempt at a landing to north of the high central sand-hill ; and Moore resolved that

---

[1] Two battalions of the 61st and 75th demibrigades, half a battalion of the 51st and a detachment of the 25th demibrigades, 18th Dragoons, detachment of 20th Dragoons.

this hill should be the objective of the right of the British attack.   From its situation it could not but form either the left or the centre of the French position, and in either case the possession of ground so commanding was important.   The attack was therefore to be limited to a front of about a mile along the beach from this sand-hill southward ; and the troops appointed for the service were, counting from right to left, the Reserve under Moore, the Guards, and the Royals and Fifty-fourth from Cavan's brigade.[1]

On the evening of the 7th two boats were moored in advance to mark the points upon which the line of flat-boats was to be formed.   The naval officers received and issued their orders ; the troops of the second disembarkation were transferred to vessels of light draught so as to be closer to the shore ; and all was ready for the morrow.

At two o'clock on the morning of the 8th of March the darkness was broken for a moment by a rocket which flew aloft from the flagship ; and upon this signal all the boats of the fleet repaired to their appointed

1801.
March 7.

March 8.

[1] The Army was brigaded as follows :—

Guards' Brigade.—Major-general Ludlow—1/ Coldstream, 1/3rd Guards.

1st Brigade.—Major-general Coote—2/1st, 54th (2 batts.), 92nd.

2nd Brigade.—Major-general Craddock—8th, 13th, 18th, 90th.

3rd Brigade.—Major-general Lord Cavan—50th, 79th.

4th Brigade.—Brigadier-general Doyle—2nd, 30th, 44th, 89th.

5th Brigade.—Brigadier-general John Stuart—Minorca Regiment, De Roll's, Dillon's.

Reserve—Major-general Moore, Brigadier-general Oakes—23rd, 28th, 42nd, 58th, 4 companies /40th, Corsican Rangers.

Cavalry Brigade.—Brigadier-general Finch—1 troop 11th L.D., 12th, 26th, and Hompesch's L.D.

Artillery.—About 700 of all ranks.

Field-pieces.—24 light 6-prs., 4 light 12-prs., 12 medium 12-prs., 6 $5\frac{1}{2}$-inch howitzers.

Siege-pieces.—4 iron 12-prs., 20 24-prs., 2 10-inch, 10 8-inch howitzers, 18 $5\frac{1}{2}$-inch, 10 8-inch, 12 10-inch mortars.

ships. By half-past three the whole of them were filled and moving in dead silence, broken only by the monotonous plash of oars, over the five miles that separated them from the rendezvous. By daylight most of them had reached the appointed alignment, but much time was consumed before Captain Cochrane,[1] who was in charge of the naval arrangements, and Moore could draw them up in their proper order. The first line consisted of fifty-eight flat-boats, each packed to its utmost capacity with about fifty soldiers, who, burdened with three days' provisions and sixty rounds of ammunition, sat patiently with their firelocks between their knees, blinking at the fierce glare of the low morning sun. In rear of them, ready to slip into the intervals, came the cutters, eighty-four in number, also packed with men. Then in third line were thirty-seven launches, and in rear of all fourteen launches, containing nearly five hundred seamen and gunners with fourteen field-guns, these last being under the orders of Sidney Smith. On each flank of the flotilla were three armed vessels—two gunboats and a bomb ship— and three more ships of light draught were moored as close in as possible with their broadsides to the shore. At last the regiments were sorted out into their several stations. The place of honour on the right was held by the militiamen of the flank-companies of the Fortieth, and then in succession from right to left came the Twenty-third, Twenty-eighth, Forty-second, Fifty-eighth, Corsican Rangers, Coldstream Guards, Third Guards, Royals, and Fifty-fourth. A little before nine o'clock all was ready. The gunboats and bomb ships opened fire, and Cochrane gave the signal to advance.

The boats then pulled slowly and steadily forward; and the enemy, who had for some hours been visible watching the preparations, disappeared from view. Closer and closer the flotilla crept in, until it passed

[1] This was not Lord Cochrane, more famous in later days as Lord Dundonald, as has been represented by some writers.

within range of the French cannon; and then from the
Castle of Aboukir, from the central sand-hill, from
four different points to right and left of it, and from
the blockhouse there rained upon it a furious cross-fire
of shot and shell.   The water seethed under the tempest of iron, and the men were drenched to the skin,
but little damage was done.   The boats moved implac-
ably on till they drew near to the shore, and then
instead of round-shot there poured upon them a stream
of grape and langridge which churned up the water
like hail and struck down seamen and soldiers right
and left.   The fiercest of the fire naturally fell about
the centre, where one shell burst in the midst of a
flat-boat which carried some of the Coldstream Guards,
killing and wounding many men and sending the rest
to the bottom.   This part of the line appears in consequence to have swerved somewhat to its left,[1] but
still the bluejackets rowed coolly and steadily on, the
soldiers joining them in an occasional cheer.   Grape
and langridge were now supplemented by musketry,
but still the boats advanced; and on the right of the
line, where the order had never been broken, Moore's
eyes were fixed steadily upon the great sand-hill.   At
last the boats touched bottom, and during their last
moments of immunity the enemy poured in a savage fire
and even thrust down the soldiers as they landed, with
the bayonet.   But the British quickly sprang ashore and
formed; and Moore, drawing up the Fortieth, Twenty-
third and Twenty-eighth in line, led them straight
upon the central sand-hill.   It was so steep as to
seem inaccessible; but the men, without a thought of
loading their muskets, scrambled after him, some in
perfect order as if on parade, some on their hands and
knees, but all close upon their leader.   On the summit
stood the Sixty-first French demibrigade, but did not
stand there long.   Suddenly and unexpectedly the red-
coats appeared at the head of the steep ascent, as though
they had sprung out of the ground, swept them head-

[1] Wilson, *Expedition to Egypt*, p. 14.

long down with the bayonet, captured their four guns, and hunted them from the sand-hills into the plain beyond. There Moore halted them, to see how the army was faring elsewhere.

On Moore's left Oakes with the remainder of the Reserve had been not less successful. Landing a few minutes later than his commander, he had found the French prepared to meet him not only with infantry but with cavalry ; but the Forty-second, which was the first to land, formed under heavy fire as if on parade and repulsed the horsemen by their volleys. The Highlanders then advanced, with the Fifty-eighth in support, drove the infantry opposed to them also out of the sand-hills, and captured three guns. On the left of Oakes the brigade of Guards, having been thrown into confusion by the sinking of two of their boats, reached the shoal water in disorder, some part of it in rear of Oakes's brigade. The men were therefore thrown ashore intermingled and in small parties, which prevented them from forming readily ; and the French cavalry, observing their plight, seized the moment to deliver a second attack. With the help of the Fifty-eighth, however, the horsemen were again hurled back ; and Ludlow, quickly setting his two battalions in order, advanced to his appointed place in the line. The Fifty-fourth and Royals landed shortly afterwards upon the left of the Guards, just in time to drive away a battalion of French infantry which was marching along a hollow upon Ludlow's left flank. Coote by this time had formed the whole of the troops which had landed on the left of the Reserve ; and, after another hour and a half of petty work against the French sharpshooters in the inner sand-hills, the enemy's entire force was thrust back into the plain, with a total loss of eight guns. From the moment when the British first set foot ashore to the carrying of the high sand-hill by Moore, the time did not exceed twenty minutes ; and the action was practically won by the twenty-five hundred men of the Reserve.

Thus was gained the landing in Egypt, perhaps the most skilful and daring operation of its kind that was ever attempted.   Tactically, the advance of the flotilla into the concave of the beach was equivalent to an assault upon a re-entrant angle of a fortress, in which the hands of the assailants were tied until they reached the counterscarp; and the patient endurance of the troops as they sat, powerless for resistance, between the peril of a furious fire above and the peril of drowning below, was beyond all praise.   Undoubtedly the storming of the high sand-hill was the most brilliant as it was the decisive movement of the day; for the French, who held that ground, seem to have given way instantly before Moore's battalions, as if panic-stricken by their mere appearance on the summit.   At the last moment before the advance Abercromby had sent a message to ask Moore if he would not direct his boats a little to the south of it instead of straight upon it; but Moore answered that the steepness of the hill was in favour of his men rather than the contrary, and events proved him to be right.   Nevertheless the finest performance of the day was that of the Forty-second Highlanders, who, after suffering heavily in the boats, were so steady and so perfectly formed upon landing that they beat off the attack of the French cavalry.   Their losses amounted to twenty-one men killed, and one hundred and fifty-six, including eight officers, wounded.   Next to them the heaviest sufferers were the Coldstream Guards, with six officers and ninety-one men killed, wounded, and missing.   Altogether the casualties of the Army in this action amounted to thirty-one officers and six hundred and twenty-one men killed, wounded, and missing, of whom a Corsican officer and twelve men were prisoners.   The losses of the Navy, which had played a most noble though thankless part in the advance without the satisfaction of a fight ashore, were seven officers and ninety men killed and wounded, raising the total of casualties to over seven hundred.   The loss of the French was from three to four hundred men.

1801.
March 8.

While the fight was still proceeding the boats returned to bring off the rest of the troops, and before evening the entire force had been disembarked, when Abercromby advanced for a couple of miles and halted for the night. The army stood now upon a narrow strip of land which stretches for some forty miles from Aboukir in the east to the Arab Tower on the west, and divides Lake Mareotis from the sea. Abercromby's front faced to westward, his right flank resting on the open sea, his left upon the salt lake of Maadieh or Aboukir; and the average width of the peninsula for the eleven miles that separated his position from the city of Alexandria was between three and four thousand yards. The ground consisted merely of sand of irregular surface dotted with palm trees; and by digging near these trees, in obedience to Sidney Smith, the men found water, to the intense relief of Abercromby, upon whom the thought of dependence upon the fleet for water had lain inexpressibly heavy. In theory it seems strange that he did not follow up his beaten enemy, but in practice his halt is easily explained. The men had been afoot since two o'clock in the morning; they had been mewed up on board ship for many months before; the sand made marching very laborious even for soldiers in the best of condition, and finally no stores and but few horses had yet been landed. Friant meanwhile drew in all his detachments except a small party at Rosetta and the garrison at the Castle of Aboukir, which last had been blockaded by two British brigades, and stationed himself in advance of Alexandria so as to cover the city. There on the following morning he was joined by General Lanusse, who had hastened with his division towards the sound of the cannon. This raised his force to about five thousand of all ranks with twenty-one guns.

March 9.

On the 9th and 10th the wind blew too hard to permit the landing of supplies and stores, and the main body of the British army remained stationary. The Reserve, however, was moved forward for a short

distance to a point where the width of the peninsula
shrank to less than a mile; and the Second Queen's,
with four hundred dragoons, liberated the two brigades
from the blockade of the Castle of Aboukir.   On the
11th calmer weather allowed the horses and supplies March 11.
to be disembarked, and fortunately Lake Maadieh
furnished a means of transport by water; otherwise,
for want of animals, it would have been impossible
for the army to advance.   The British gunboats had
already entered the lake, where by a strange over-
sight the French had no gunboats to oppose them, and
thus both the left flank and the line of supply were
secured.   On the 12th the force moved forward about March 12.
four miles through deep sand, the French cavalry retiring before it and gradually revealing the main body of
their army, which seemed to be advancing for a general
action.   Presently, however, the French halted and
took up a position upon some heights a little beyond
the western end of Lake Maadieh.   Friant, in anxiety
lest his communications with Lower Egypt should be
severed, had determined to guard the dyke which
divided Lake Mareotis from Lake Maadieh, and which
adjoined the canal that bore the waters of the Nile to
Alexandria.   For, though Lake Mareotis was dry,
the French General conceived that at that season it
would be impassable, and that consequently the dyke
was the only route by which Menou could lead his main
body to the city.   Abercromby upon the first sight of
the march of the French had deployed his troops, but
he halted on perceiving their true object, and resolved
to attack on the morrow.   The French position, which
was known as the Roman Camp, was commanding.
The heights occupied by Friant afforded a perfect
glacis for the play of his numerous artillery, and his
line was extended obliquely across the peninsula, the
right being in advance, and the left thrown back to
some old ruined buildings that abutted upon the sea.
Bivouacking therefore for the night at a distance of
about a mile and a half from the enemy, Abercromby

1801

gave his orders to march at five o'clock on the morrow morning, and laid his plans to turn Friant's right flank.

March 13. From some untoward circumstances it was half-past six before the British army was able to move forward, as ordained, in three parallel columns. The Reserve under Moore formed the right column, next to the sea; Craddock's, Coote's, and the Guards brigades the central column; Cavan's brigade, strengthened by a battalion of Marines, Stuart's foreign brigade and Doyle's brigade, the left column. The paltry little body of mounted dragoons was disposed between the right and central columns; the guns, apparently about sixteen pieces in all, were painfully dragged by the seamen at the heads of the several brigades; and the advanced guard was formed by the Ninetieth Foot and the Ninety-second Highlanders, the former before the central, the latter, with a field gun and a light howitzer, before the left column. In this order the army, now about fourteen thousand strong, struggled slowly and painfully through the heavy sand, halting frequently to enable the guns to keep their place and enduring heavy loss through the fire of the French artillery. The result was that the Ninetieth and Ninety-second pressed on too far in advance, and appeared in full view of the French at a point where, by chance, the central column was invisible owing to some rising ground. Supposing them to be unsupported, Friant, upon Lanusse's suggestion, left about eighteen hundred men with a few guns to contain Moore's column by the sea, and brought forward the rest of his force to crush not only the two advanced battalions, but also, as he imagined, the isolated left column of the British.

The French cavalry were the first to come into action, the Twenty-second Mounted Chasseurs swooping suddenly down with the greatest impetuosity upon the Ninetieth. The latter regiment was in the act of deployment from column into line, and the rear sections, having no time to complete the movement, massed themselves six or eight deep upon the left.

In this order the Ninetieth awaited the shock, reserving
its fire until the sabres were close to the bayonets, when
it poured in a crushing volley which shattered the
French horsemen to pieces. Immediately afterwards
the French infantry and artillery came up, and for a
short time the Ninetieth and Ninety-second bore their
attack single-handed, suffering very heavily both from
musketry and artillery, but standing with a steadfastness beyond all praise.[1]   But now Abercromby's central
and left columns began to deploy, pursuant to their
orders, in two lines, under a heavy fire from the French
guns ; and the action became general, though the
Reserve on the right and the Fourth Brigade on the
extreme left still retained their formation in column.
The pressure upon the Ninetieth and Ninety-second
was relieved ; the French began to fall back all along
the line ; and the Highlanders, pressing forward against
the French position, captured three guns.   The general
advance of the British was, however, very slow ; and
the French horse-artillery took advantage of Abercromby's weakness in cavalry and gun-teams to make
a running fight for every yard of ground, unlimbering
at every opportunity to pour in a destructive fire, and
galloping off to take up a new position before the
British guns could come forward to silence them.
None the less the British moved steadily onward in
most perfect order; the Reserve and Craddock's
brigade, on the right, being somewhat in advance of
the rest of the line, since the weakening of the French
in their front enabled them to make sure of turning
the enemy's left.   As the Reserve gained the heights
of the Roman Camp the French abandoned the position; and Moore and Craddock halted their men until
the rest of the army should come up.   Meanwhile on

---

[1] The Ninety-second was extremely well handled, being disposed in echelon of half-battalions, with the left half-battalion
refused and well sheltered among a patch of scrub, so as to meet
any attempt to outflank it upon that side. *Narrative of a private
soldier of the 92nd.*

the extreme left Dillon's regiment most gallantly stormed a French field-work, in which two guns were mounted, upon the Alexandria canal ; and, delivered from this menace on its flank, the left of the British came level with the right, and the whole again moved forward for about half a mile into the plain on the west of the Roman Camp. There Abercromby suddenly ordered the entire line to halt, and summoned Hutchinson and Moore to him for consultation.

The French had now fallen back to their main position on a chain of fortified heights, known as the heights of Nicopolis, about thirteen hundred yards east of Alexandria ; and Abercromby, who was extremely short-sighted, had apparently failed to realise immediately how formidable it was. He now decided to turn it by both flanks, to which end Hutchinson with the Third, Fourth, and Fifth brigades was ordered to attack upon the left, while Moore, conforming his movements with Hutchinson's, was simultaneously to assault from the right, the rest of the troops lying down where they had been halted on the plain. Hutchinson accordingly made for a bridge close to the southern end of the French position, by which to cross the canal on to Lake Mareotis ; hoping to march round the right of the French position upon the dried mud at its edge, and from thence to storm. The bridge, though defended by a strong party of French with a howitzer, was gallantly carried by the Forty-fourth ; but the main column was saluted by a tremendous fire from the artillery on the heights of Nicopolis. Thereupon Hutchinson, perceiving that this position was very strong, and moreover commanded by the guns of Alexandria, hesitated to commit his troops further without orders. Meanwhile the French, finding themselves untroubled, brought forward the guns along their front and opened a murderous cannonade upon the British troops in the plain, which, since it could not be silenced, was passively endured. In due course Hutchinson's messenger reached Abercromby ; and the General despatched John Hope from his staff

to examine the French right and report to him.　But
all these matters took time, and the rain of shot from
the French guns never ceased to pour upon the unlucky British infantry.　The day was now wearing
towards evening.　Abercromby resolved to abandon
the projected attack, and drew back his troops to the
position from which he had driven the French in the
morning.

The loss of the French in this action was about five
hundred ; that of the British, including the casualties
of the seamen in the gunboats, was just over thirteen
hundred killed and wounded, of whom seventy-nine
were officers.[1]　Of these over two hundred and forty
belonged to the Ninetieth and one hundred and forty
to the Ninety-second ; and, as a reward for their
gallant behaviour, these two corps still enjoy the
exclusive privilege of carrying the name Mandora
upon their colours and appointments, the engagement having taken place near the Mandora redoubt.
But the action was both costly and unsatisfactory,
and does not show Abercromby at his best.　Either
he should have halted the army after carrying the
first position of the French, until he had made up
his mind whether or not to assault their second
position upon the heights of Nicopolis ; or, having
brought his troops into the plain within range of the
French cannon, he should have made his attack upon
the second position forthwith.　As matters were conducted, a great many of his battalions were exposed
for hours to a destructive cannonade, and suffered very
heavy loss for no object whatever.　It seems too that,
if Hutchinson had continued his flanking movement
further to the west, he might have attacked the
southern front of Alexandria itself with every prospect
of success.　But Hutchinson's eyesight, like Abercromby's, was extremely defective ; he had no informa-

---

[1] *Army*, 6 officers, 150 men killed ; 66 officers, 1016 men
wounded.　*Navy and Marines*, 3 officers and 27 men killed, 4
officers and 50 men wounded.

tion as to the safety of the bed of Lake Mareotis for the passage of infantry and artillery; and it is extremely probable that both he, and indeed all the officers of the army, were misled by mirage. The country was new to every man in the force except Sidney Smith and a few naval officers; and it is well known that, in an atmosphere so clear as that of Egypt, some time is needed for strangers to train their eyes to the judgment of distances and elevations. In fact, the advance of Abercromby beyond the Roman Camp rather suggests the error of a man who, having begun by mistaking a mile of distance for half a mile, has run to the opposite extreme of misjudging half a mile to be a mile.

Apart from this, Abercromby appears to have been precipitate in not endeavouring to make some reconnaissance of the heights of Nicropolis before moving his men within the range of the French cannon. That he could have carried the position, there can, I think, be no doubt; but he does not seem to have asked himself until too late whether he could hold it as well as capture it. He had forced the enemy back from the Roman Camp practically without artillery and without cavalry,—indeed if he had possessed either he could have destroyed Friant's force,—but his losses for this very reason had been extremely heavy; and he might well have doubted whether, without entrenching tools and with at best a very few barely mobile guns, he could maintain himself within cannon-shot of the forts of Alexandria. Again, after passing the head of Lake Maadieh he possessed no longer the means of water-transport; and, since he had no land-transport, he must have been reduced to his own men's backs to bring up supplies and stores from the waterside. Chilly bivouacs, foul camping-grounds, and bad water had already caused much sickness among his troops, and the additional fatigue of acting as beasts of burden must inevitably have broken many of them down. Yet, after seeing his soldiers maltreated, through no

fault of his or their own, in the most exasperating 1801.
fashion by the French horse-artillery, it is hardly March.
surprising that he should have been loth to stop
them when the enemy was in full retreat, and that he
should have thought of all the objections to an advance
just an hour too late.   The only satisfaction, therefore,
to be found in the day's work lay in the admirable
behaviour of the troops under a very severe trial, and
in the five captured guns which bore witness to their
valour.

Still in complete ignorance of the enemy's numbers,
Abercromby now set himself to assure his position
upon the peninsula.   Heavy guns were landed for the
siege of the Castle of Aboukir, and the men were
busily employed in entrenching the new position.   It
was by nature strong.   The peninsula at this point is
about a mile and a half wide, of which distance five
hundred yards on the southern extremity adjoining the
Alexandria canal is level plain.   To this level margin
succeeds a ridge, which runs from north to south for
three-quarters of a mile, and is bounded on the north
by another six hundred yards of level ground, beyond
which rises a second ridge of considerable height running parallel to the sea and descending in gradual slopes
from east to west.   The summit of this ridge was
crowned by the ruins of a large building, dating from
the days of Roman rule, which gave to the hill its
name of the Roman Camp.   The position thus presented the features of a central ridge with a level space
on each flank, that on the left hand being unprotected,
but that on the right covered by the natural bastion of
the Roman Camp.   This bastion or salient angle was
the key of the whole, and was accordingly strengthened
first by a small redan on the lowest slopes, next by an
unclosed redoubt on one of the intermediate acclivities,
and finally by the ruined building on the summit.   Its
defence was entrusted to the Reserve under Moore,
who quickly arranged every detail so that each man
should know his duty in case of attack.   Flêches and

1801.
March.

field-works were thrown up also on the central ridge, more particularly at the southern end, so as to command the margin of plain to the south. Two twenty-four pounders and thirty-four field-guns in all were mounted along the whole length of the position ; and on the left of Moore the Guards' and Coote's brigades carried the first line of defence to the southern end of the central ridge, from which Craddock's brigade was thrown back to the head of Lake Maadieh. The general formation of the British was therefore an echelon with the right advanced. In second line stood in succession from right to left the brigades of Stuart, Doyle, Finch, and Cavan, the last being now made up to three battalions by the arrival of the second battalion of the Twenty-seventh from Minorca.[1]

The duties of entrenching, of dragging up guns, and above all of bringing forward supplies and stores from the magazines now fell very heavily on the men ; and the sick-list increased rapidly.[2] Fuel also was scarce, there being none except the trunks of date-palms, which were only to be found at a distance and burned ill with an exceedingly pungent smoke. On the 18th of March the sick-list had reached the figure of twenty-four hundred on the spot and eleven hundred shipped away to the Mediterranean stations. Horses were still unobtainable, and the few already in the hands of the cavalry

March 18.

had been diminished by an unlucky affair with a small French party of hussars and chasseurs, in which the Twenty - sixth Light Dragoons, from too rash an advance, lost five officers, twenty-five men and forty-two horses killed, wounded, and taken. However, on the same day Abercromby was somewhat compensated by the surrender of the Castle of Aboukir with its garrison of two hundred men. But he was still most

[1] I have been unable to discover when this battalion joined the army. Abercromby sent most of it to Pulteney in November as unfit for active service ; but seven companies arrived at Minorca early in February. Abercromby to Dundas, 2nd November 1800 ; Fox to Dundas, 19th February 1801.

[2] Wilson, p. 25.

uneasy about his situation, for he was now aware of his 1801. inferiority in numbers to the French.   He thought it March. his duty to bring up some heavy cannon and attempt by a night attack to drive the French from the heights of Nicopolis ; but, even if he succeeded, he did not know how far his success would forward the siege of Alexandria, while, if he failed, he could see no alternative but to re-embark.   It went to his heart that so fine an army as his own should be thrown away ; but, since the Government persisted in despatching inadequate forces upon imperfect information, no other result was to be expected.[1]

Meanwhile Friant worked indefatigably to strengthen the fortifications of Alexandria, and Menou began to concentrate a part of his troops, though still only a part instead of the whole, at Ramanieh.   A way practicable for artillery was found across Lake Mareotis, and on the 19th the French Commander-in-chief March 19. arrived at Alexandria with his reinforcements, raising the strength of his army to ten thousand men, including fourteen hundred cavalry, with forty-six guns. Being aware that both the Turkish Army and Baird's force from India were shortly expected, he determined to take the initiative ; and to this end he adopted a plan suggested by Lanusse for an attack upon the British.   According to this scheme Lanusse's division of infantry, twenty-seven hundred strong, was to storm the redoubts and the Roman ruins on the British right. Rampon's division of two thousand men, with Reynier's in support, was to fall upon the British centre as soon as Lanusse had made good his footing ; and to Reynier likewise, whose division was thirty-five hundred strong, was assigned the duty of holding the British left in check and of sending a detachment, strengthened by three hundred cavalry, between Lakes Maadieh and Mareotis to close the road to Alexandria. Finally, the rest of the cavalry, about nine hundred sabres, under General Roize, was to remain in reserve

[1] *Diary of Sir John Moore,* ii. 12.

1801   in rear of the centre. The general idea was to force the right and centre of the British in succession under cover of a feint upon their left, and by a final charge of cavalry to sweep them into Lake Maadieh. It was arranged that the first attack should be delivered before daylight, so that the advancing columns should not be exposed to the fire of the cannon in the redoubts nor of the gunboats which guarded the British right flank ; and it was reasonably reckoned that the assault might come as a surprise, since Abercromby had no intelli-

March 20. gence of Menou's arrival at Alexandria. On the 20th of March, however, Abercromby in a general order warned the troops of the possibility of a night-attack ; giving directions that they should sleep fully accoutred in their appointed positions, and that the entire force should be always under arms half an hour before daylight.

On the 20th it happened that Moore was Major-general of the day, and consequently charged with the duty of visiting the picquets during the night. The first hours of darkness had passed quietly enough ; and in going his rounds from right to left of the line he had reached the left-hand picquet of the Guards, when,

March 21. at a little after five o'clock, he heard a dropping fire from the picquets of the extreme left. He trotted forward in that direction ; and Brigadier Stuart, whose brigade formed the reserve far away in the rear, was actually setting his battalions in motion towards it when suddenly a sound of heavy firing was heard on the extreme right. "This is the real attack," exclaimed Moore, and striking spurs into his horse he galloped instantly to the Roman Camp. There he found all the picquets falling back. The light had not yet broken, and the darkness was increased by the smoke of guns and small arms. Shot and bullets were flying in all directions ; and in front there was a confused hubbub of drums beating the charge, and hoarse voices shouting "Vive la France ! Vive la République !" but it was as yet impossible to discover what the

enemy was actually doing.   Nevertheless Moore's
battalions were already taking up their assigned
positions quietly and in order.   Edward Paget was
manning the redoubt with his men of the Twenty-
eighth, throwing back two companies on his left to
guard against an attack from the rear.   The Fifty-
eighth was lining the ruins in rear of the redoubt.
Brigadier Oakes had already brought up the left wing
of the Forty-second to the left of the redoubt, and
Moore at once sent his aide-de-camp to summon the
right wing also, and to bring the Twenty-third and
Fortieth to reinforce the Fifty-eighth in the ruins.
Moore's horse was shot under him in the redoubt
itself, and Paget, who was talking to him, was knocked
out of his saddle by a bullet in the neck.   He fell,
crying out that he was killed, but presently recovered
and remounted his horse ; for it had been ordained
that he was yet to be Moore's right hand on the retreat
to Coruña.   And so the two men waited, watching for
the moment when they should see clearly enough to
enable them to act.

They did not wait long.   The French advance upon
the extreme left had been, as Moore had divined, a
feint.   A small party on that side had successfully
surprised an advanced redan, capturing the gun and the
twenty men that were in it, but had been immediately
driven out by the fire from a flêche immediately in
rear of it, and had retired carrying off their prisoners
and wounded.   Meanwhile Lanusse's division had
advanced upon the Román camp in two columns,
Valentin's brigade following the sea-shore, and Silly's
moving straight upon the redoubt.   Silly's leading
battalion carried the flêche in advance of the redoubt,
but was unable to pass the ditch of the redoubt itself
under the fire of the Twenty-eighth, and swerved to
its left.   Meanwhile Valentin's brigade was attempting
to ascend the height from the sea, its right battalion
towards the north-western face of the redoubt, its left
battalion in the re-entrant angle between the redoubt

and the buildings. The former encountering a terrible fire of grape began to waver, and Lanusse, galloping to its head to rally it, was presently struck down with a mortal wound. This completed its discomfiture; and the left battalion also gave way, being unable to stand against the cross-fire of the Twenty-eighth and Fifty-eighth.

Meanwhile Rampon's division likewise came into action, but his left brigade in the darkness moved too far to its left, and thus, becoming entangled with Silly's brigade about the salient angle of the redoubt, interposed itself between its leading and rear battalions. Rampon's right brigade meanwhile advanced towards the hollow between the Roman camp and the central ridge, where its leading battalion ascended the hill, apparently unnoticed in the tumult and the darkness, and came up between the rear of the redoubt and the ruins just as the right wing of the Forty-second appeared in answer to Moore's summons. Moore instantly ordered the Forty-second and some of the Twenty-eighth to face about, and drove this hapless battalion into the building, where the Twenty-third and Fifty-eighth gave it such a welcome that every man was killed, wounded, or taken. Without delay Moore then re-formed the Forty-second and led them back to the left flank of the redoubt, just in time to meet Silly's rear battalion, which had extricated itself and was now advancing. He instantly attacked and repulsed it, receiving a wound in the leg in the course of the fight; and some of the Forty-second and Twenty-eighth followed them for some distance in pursuit. Whether for this or for some other reason, Menou now ordered the first line of his cavalry to charge. The horsemen, galloping impetuously past the flank of the redoubt, quickly overthrew the rash pursuers, but presently were floundering in all directions among a number of holes, which the Twenty-eighth had dug for shelter before the arrival of their tents. The Highlanders rallied immediately, and the two

gallant French regiments were driven back with very   1801.
heavy loss.

The light was now improving ; and the various March 21.
corps that encircled the redoubt made a second attack
upon it in front and both flanks, Silly's leading battalion
having apparently moved round to the northern face
in order to hearten the shattered remnants of Valentin's
brigade.   These brave men fared no better than their
comrades.   The British gunboats off the northern
coast now came into action with great gallantry ; and
the Fifty-eighth, holding their fire till their assailants
were within sixty yards of them, gave them a volley
which sent them staggering back.   At about the same
time Rampon, having recalled what was left of his
division,[1] advanced against the front of the Guards'
brigade, but, being driven back by steady and
destructive volleys, changed his tactics and sought to
turn its left flank.   This manœuvre Ludlow met by
throwing back some companies of the Third Guards,
which for a time appear to have been very severely
engaged, until the Royals from Coote's brigade came
forward to take the pressure from them.   Then, completely baffled and disheartened by failure and heavy
losses, Rampon drew off his division and gave up the
attack.

Meanwhile Menou had shot his last bolt.   Undismayed by the rout of his first line of cavalry, he now
ordered General Roize to lead his second line also to the
charge, while Reynier set a part of his division in motion
to support them.   With a desperation that heightened
their natural gallantry, Roize's three regiments, barely
five hundred sabres, galloped furiously up the southern
slope of the Roman camp and towards the central ridge.
Some of the squadrons of their left broke through the
Highlanders on the flank of the redoubt and came in
upon its rear, where Moore had to gallop hard to keep

[1] English accounts appear to indicate that a battalion or two of
Reynier's division took part in this attack, and I hardly see how the
Guards could otherwise have been so hardly pressed as they were.

clear of them. Abercromby, who also stood in this part of the field, was actually taken prisoner, but was immediately delivered by a soldier of the Forty-second, though not before he had received a severe contusion in the breast. But, though broken and disordered as a regiment, the Highlanders stood fast as individuals, each man fighting desperately for himself. The Twenty-eighth faced about and killed such of the dragoons as were in rear of the redoubt; and the mass of horsemen mingled with the Highlanders then surged along the side of the ruins, from which the Fortieth poured upon them two volleys which crushed them out of existence. Simultaneously the right-hand squadrons of Roize's brigade dashed headlong into the valley between the Roman camp and the central ridge, where Stuart's Minorca Regiment, opening out to let them pass, poured a shattering fire upon them as they galloped by, and, intercepting them as readily when they tried to return, practically destroyed them.

This was the last effort of the French. Every one of their attacks had been repulsed with heavy loss. The divisions of Lanusse and Rampon were dispersed among the sand-hills at the foot of the slope, some of them keeping up a scattered fire; some, whose ammunition was spent, engaging the Twenty-eighth with volleys of stones, one of which killed a sergeant dead on the spot. The Twenty-eighth returned these missiles with all possible vigour, for the ammunition both for the muskets and the guns of the Reserve was completely exhausted. This was the result of sending troops to active service without land transport. Reynier, however, though his division was still intact, thought it hopeless to attempt to renew the engagement; and there was a long lull, during which the French, training their guns at great elevation, poured in a heavy fire which wrought some havoc on the British second line in rear of the two ridges. Abercromby, meanwhile, rode to a field-work at the north end of the central

ridge from which he could see the whole field, and
there paced up and down amid a storm of cannon-shot,
complaining of the pain from the contusion on his
breast, but betraying neither by word, manner, nor
gesture that he had been struck by a bullet in his
thigh.   At length fresh ammunition was brought up,
and the British guns again opened fire with great
effect upon the French on the plain ; but still Menou
hesitated to retire, until a couple of his ammunition-
waggons had been exploded by the British shells,
when, at about nine o'clock, he drew off his maltreated
army in good order and unpursued.

This was a hard and well-fought battle.   The
numbers on both sides seem to have been as nearly as
may be equal, though it is impossible to arrive at any
certainty upon this point ; for General Reynier, whose
returns furnish the authority for the strength of the
French, was not a man of scrupulous veracity in details.
But in any case it was only a part of each army that
was engaged.   On the French side Reynier's division
hardly came into action ; and on the British side the
brigades of Cavan, Doyle, Craddock, and (excepting
one battalion) of Coote took as little share in the
fight as Reynier's men.   It is probable therefore that,
in the numbers actually engaged, the French had the
superiority, though the British on the other hand
enjoyed a decided advantage of position.   Menou's plan
of attack was not without the merit of audacity and
even of a certain skill ; but considering that he staked
so much upon the capture of the Roman camp, which
he knew to be the key of the position, it is surprising
that he did not stake his all, and throw half of Reynier's
division in addition to those of Lanusse and Rampon
against the British right.   It is, however, unlikely
even so that he would have succeeded.   The darkness
enabled Lanusse to approach close to Moore's position
with very little loss, but the French infantry never
really obtained any footing upon it.   The one battalion
that contrived to penetrate to the rear of the redoubt

was annihilated, and the remainder were beaten back with comparatively little difficulty.

Nor was the loss of Moore's regiments, the Forty-second excepted, very heavy; for Moore was careful to keep them as far as possible under the shelter of the redoubt and the ruins, with the result that the Twenty-eighth escaped with only four officers and seventy men killed and wounded, while the Twenty-third, Fifty-eighth, and Fortieth had not fifty casualties between them. But, on the other hand, the battalions that were exposed to the attack of the French cavalry suffered terribly. Among these the Forty-second stands pre-eminent for a gallantry and steadfastness which would be difficult to match in the history of any army. The battalion had embarked about eight hundred strong. It lost eight officers and one hundred and sixty-nine men in the disembarkation of the 8th of March; three officers and thirteen men on the 13th; and four officers and forty-eight men killed, eight officers and two hundred and fifty-three men wounded on the 21st. And these losses were not those of rout and demoralisation, but of persistent and victorious fighting; for the regiment repulsed two attacks of infantry and, though broken by two furious charges of Roize's cavalry, took a principal part in the annihilation of those rash and daring horse-men. John Stuart's Minorca Regiment, which was chiefly concerned in the repulse of Roize's second charge, lost thirteen officers and just over two hundred men killed, wounded, and missing; and the casualties of the two remaining regiments of the foreign brigade amounted to over one hundred and forty. In fact this little band of Minorquins, Germans, French, and Swiss, which Charles Stuart had taken over in the worst possible condition, behaved themselves, thanks to his training, most admirably. When such was the spirit that animated even the poorest troops on the British right, not even Napoleon's veterans of the Army of Italy could have hoped for success. Even the failure of ammunition found Moore undaunted and

confident. "We were for an hour without a cartridge,"
he wrote ; "the enemy during this time were pounding
us with shot and shell and distant musketry.   Our
artillery could not return a shot, and had their infantry
advanced again we must have repelled them with the
bayonet. Our fellows would have done it ; I never
saw men more determined to do their duty." [1]

Next to the Reserve the brigade of Guards, which
lay immediately to its left, endured a trial little less
severe. Few details or none are to be found respecting
Rampon's advance upon this part of the field, except
that the Third Guards were thrown back to meet an
attempt at a flanking attack, and that it cost them
nearly two hundred officers and men to repel it. The
Royals, who were detached from the right of Coote's
brigade to their assistance, lost over eighty officers and
men ; the Coldstream, who to a great extent were
covered by redans, lost more than sixty ; but the
havoc wrought among the Third Guards, who were
not cut up by cavalry like the Forty-second and
Minorquins, points to a very arduous struggle in
the centre as well as on the right. The casualties of
the remainder of Coote's brigade were about one
hundred, and of Cavan's brigade about seventy,
numbers which would be unworthy of comment but
for the fact that these battalions hardly fired a shot.
It should seem indeed that the hour of passive endurance, during which Abercromby's guns were silent
for want of ammunition, added some hundreds to the
list of British killed and disabled ; and it is impossible
to banish a suspicion that the brigadiers of the second
line took less care than Moore to keep their men
under shelter. But still more significant is it that the
French infantry, when broken up by their defeat, kept
up an incessant fire as skirmishers at long range, and
that the British made no attempt to silence them by
similar tactics. Hence the British casualties were
more numerous than they should have been, reaching

[1] *Diary of Sir John Moore*, ii. 16.

...nd fourteen hundred

...British was as nothing
...nch, who actually left
... dead and over six
...t two hundred un-
... the usual proportion
...can have fallen little
... it is therefore small
...ly a man of Lanusse's
...is own to renew the
...th whom was captured
... others) of the Bridge
...rk in Italy had been
...e actions of the 8th,
...at they had never yet
...obably this was true;
...gypt had been similar
...est Indies, they would
... veterans of Italy as
...hese battalions of 1801
...nd their fire, as the
...st time, was the most
...less the enemy might
... withdrawn his men
...British had been re-
...de he kept them still
...bility of a successful
... unfortunate soldiers
...hen the British guns
...to me, was his most
...though it is possible
...e paralysed for a
...s. Of Lanusse's
...of his two
...d; in Ram-
...d'Estin, were
...men wounded;

843

1801.
March 21.

...dot was
...General
...severely
..., though
...ly of the
...action
...son, who
...djutant-
...ief.
...ercromby
...thin the
...ground.
...ainst the
...ly drawn
...should be
...advised
...out delay.
...lieutenant
...blanket
...you are
..."Only
..."Only a
...soldier's
...send me
..., that it
...ast order
...it was
...the field
...him with
...hose rude
...ich to a
...sovereign
...son, who
...each, and
...ty under
...command.
...of his
...the bone
...ptoms of

tand on the 28th of
the expired.
ta, where its resting-
nscription. In Eng-
were granted to his
to his memory in St.
l Order of the Duke
up, in no unworthy
he imitation of the
doubted whether by
ce was done to the
Though delighting
Cæsar and Tacitus,
t was best in con-
y was essentially a
opinions were based
y; and the quality
e men who served
ically he was a Liberal,
n opinion nor in the
l for this reason he de-
America. Moreover
ch Republic banished
s against France, he
br ng the monarchy of
ccepted service in
iderations aside; and
hims lf absolutely to
nmen might impose
d without complaint.
f age when he went
dier under the Duke
d after the disastrous
he became the com-
nt resorted in all its

ne and unapproached
ity; for Moira and
qual if not superior

to him. It was not that Ministers set any great 1801.
store by his counsel; for his advice was sought only
for the execution, not for the choice, of enterprises,
and even then was invariably unheeded. It · was
simply that, no matter what impossibilities Ministers
might require of him, no matter how distasteful
their projects to his feelings or how repugnant to his
judgment, he was always ready to take their orders
and to do his best. He did not lack the courage
to point out the fatuity of their plans, nor to protest
against them, undismayed even by positive rudeness
from Pitt; but, when once the decision of the Cabinet
was taken, he accepted it with unswerving loyalty as
the will of the country, communicated through its
chosen rulers. Thenceforward it remained for him
only to wrest, if he could, from their folly both welfare
to the nation and credit to the Army. Hence, though
with deep inward disgust and misgiving, he led his
rabble of raw recruits to the Windward Islands and
Porto Rico, accepted the command in Ireland, threw
his unformed militia ashore at the Helder, devised a
serious plan for the ridiculous attack upon Cadiz, and
finally, in the face of risks which no General should
have been called upon to encounter, invaded Egypt
with an inferior force.

There is something very touching in the patient
submission of this wise, upright, and sagacious soldier
to a master so blind, ignorant, and disingenuous as
Dundas. The struggle was often difficult, for Abercromby loved his men as well as his country, and
it must have gone to his heart to lead them again
and again to destruction and failure. The trial was
indeed too hard for high-spirited men like Moira and
Charles Stuart. Moira, who addressed himself almost
exclusively to Huskisson, revealed his feelings by
occasional irony, of which dry humour only sharpened
the sting. Stuart, hot-tempered, imperious, and
tingling with nervous energy, treated Dundas in
public correspondence with scarcely disguised con-

1801. tempt. It must be added also, to the eternal dishonour of Dundas, that he succeeded in exhausting the patience even of Abercromby. The old General never forgot how the Government had treated him in Ireland; he could not overlook its neglect of his counsel respecting North Holland; he was deeply distressed over Stuart's resignation of the command in the Mediterranean; and the vague and haphazard instructions for the expedition to Egypt were the last straw that made his burden intolerable. Like a desperate gambler Dundas had staked all the reputation that remained to him upon the success of the enterprise. Its failure would have meant his ruin; and he threw it upon the General to succeed, no matter by what shift, and to save him.

The cowardice and unfairness of this proceeding appear to have affected Abercromby deeply. In previous expeditions he had pointed out negligence and shortcomings in the matter of preparation with plainness enough; but in his last campaign there runs through his letters an under-current of indignation and even bitterness which occasionally comes to the surface. He was as determined as ever to do his best, but he thought ill of the whole adventure, and was tormented by anxiety and apprehension to the end. Moore noticed that the General, who was always inclined to expose himself overmuch in action, never courted personal danger so persistently as in Egypt; and it is difficult to believe that death, which followed so quickly upon his wound, was unwelcome to him. He did not know that Menou's blunders had crowned Dundas's last campaign with unexpected success. He did not know that his own last battle was really decisive, that it had irremediably disheartened the French for further resistance, and that his work was practically done. It was not given to him to say like Wolfe, " Now God be praised, I can die in peace," for to the very end he had no certain intelligence of the numbers of the French except that they were superior.   He could not reckon 1801. that the British would receive reinforcements, and that Menou would not.   He could form no plans that were not haunted by visions of an army reduced to impotence by plague, fatigue, and sickness, of a difficult retreat, and of a humiliating re-embarkation. He could find no comfort except in the cheerful courage which had borne him through so many diffi- culties, in the devotion which, not less through his care and gentleness than through his bravery and his skill, he had won from his soldiers, and above all in the consciousness that he had done his best.   The Duke of York did right to hold him up as a pattern to the Army.   Ministers come and Ministers go ; politicians of Dundas's type are always among us, and from time to time still find their way to the War Office ;. but Ralph Abercromby stands forth as an example to British Generals that by serving even a Dundas faith- fully they may serve their country well.

CHAPTER XXIX

1801. THROUGHOUT the first months of 1801 Bonaparte had pressed foward his diplomatic schemes with astonishing
Feb. 9. success.   By the Treaty of Lunéville Austria had accepted the line of the Adige for her boundary in Italy, and had guaranteed the independence of the Cisalpine, Ligurian, Helvetian, and Batavian Republics. In Germany France had gained the left bank of the Rhine, and practical control of such interior redistribution as should be necessary.   Naples abjectly accepted peace on condition that she should evacuate the States of the Church, close her ports to the British, and pay for the maintenance, at Taranto, of a French corps which was designed for the reinforcement of Egypt. Spain signed a new treaty, whereby she engaged herself to declare war upon Portugal, unless the Portuguese Government should place territory in her hand in pledge for the evacuation of Malta, Minorca, and Trinidad by the British.' The Armed Neutrality was assembling its forces ; and the Tsar was, in addition, preparing an expedition to march upon India by way of Khiva and Herat.   England was isolated in Europe ; and even there Pitt, the protagonist so greatly dreaded
Feb. 10. by France, had resigned office on account of a difference with the King concerning the removal of the disabilities of Catholics.   His successor was William Addington, Speaker of the House of Commons, who possessed the sober mediocrity which qualifies men for that office.   All in fact was going prosperously for Bonaparte when the luck suddenly changed.   On the

21st of March Abercromby won his decisive action ; on the 23rd the Tsar Paul was assassinated, and on the 1st of April Nelson's naval victory at Copenhagen dealt a heavy blow at the Armed Neutrality. By the time, therefore, when the news of the third engagement at Aboukir reached London, the British Government had every encouragement to continue the struggle against France.

In Egypt, however, there presented itself an unforeseen difficulty. Hutchinson, who succeeded to the command upon Abercromby's death, was little known to the army, and outwardly had little to commend himself to it. His features were harsh and jaundiced by ill-health ; his eyesight was extremely defective, his figure awkward and stooping, his dress slovenly, his manners ungracious, and his temper violent. Withal he was well read and well informed ; he had closely studied his profession, and his bravery was unquestioned ; but the troops knew him only by his appearance, which was by no means to their taste. During the first days of his command he busied himself in fortifying his position to great strength, so as to blockade Alexandria with a part of his force and with the rest to deal with the enemy's detachments in detail ; and he did not fail at the same time to write to Minorca for reinforcements. On the 25th, to his great March 25. relief, the Capitan Pasha arrived with six ships of the line, a few frigates, and some four thousand Turkish troops, twelve hundred of which had been partly trained and in appearance were agreeably superior to the British expectations. Hutchinson therefore resolved first to possess himself of Rosetta, and, by opening that branch of the Nile to the British gunboats, to master the navigation of the river. Accordingly on the 6th of April Colonel Brent Spencer with the Queen's, the flank- April 6. companies of the Fortieth, the Fifty-eighth and some Turkish troops marched upon the town of Rosetta, which the French evacuated upon his approach, leaving three hundred men to hold Fort St. Julien at the mouth of the Nile. Batteries were erected against this strong-

1801. hold, which after three days' firing surrendered; and
April 19. thus the entrance to the Nile was secured.

April. 13. Meanwhile after much hesitation Hutchinson had taken the momentous step of cutting through the dyke of the Alexandra canal and admitting the sea to inundate Lake Mareotis, thereby isolating Alexandria more completely than before and opening a communication by water with the Arabs to westward. The measure had been much dreaded by the French for many reasons, and not least because it destroyed the regular channel which carried fresh water to Alexandria; but there were still wells and cisterns in the city which furnished a sufficient supply. The fortifications of his position being now improved and its flanks secured by the inundation, Hutchinson was able to detach in succession ten more battalions to Spencer, who had taken up a strong position at El Hamed, five or six miles south of Rosetta. The reinforcement was necessary, for a few miles up the stream, at El Aft, was a force of about five thousand men under General Lagrange, which had been gradually detached by
April 26. Menou from Alexandria. On the 26th Hutchinson left Coote with six thousand men in the position before Alexandria, and himself took personal command of the troops which had been assembled at El Hamed. These amounted to about five thousand British[1] besides the Turks, whose indiscipline made them rather an encumbrance than a help. It was Hutchinson's object if possible to capture Rahmanieh, the main French position about eight miles south of El Aft, for this was the point from which both the road from Cairo and the canal from the river branched off to Alexandria, and through which the French carried on all their communication between the Delta, Cairo, and Upper Egypt. He did not doubt that Lagrange would fall back from El Aft as soon as he himself moved forward, but he looked with reason for a sharp action at Rahmanieh.

[1] 11th L.D., 12th L.D. 1st, 2nd, 8th, 18th, 30th, 40th, 58th, 79th, 89th, 90th, Corsican Rangers.

After a week of further delay, due apparently to the   1801.
deficiency in land-transport for guns and ammunition,
the British moved forward from El Hamed on the 5th May 5.
of May, the main body being upon the western bank,
and about twelve hundred men (half of the Eighty-
ninth regiment and half irregulars) upon the eastern
bank.   A flotilla of gunboats and transport-boats moved
up the river between these two divisions.   The advance
was exceedingly slow ; but on the morning of the 7th May 7.
it was discovered that the French had evacuated El
Aft, and on the morning of the 9th the British came May 9.
up to the enemy's position at Rahmanieh.   A desul-
tory action followed, which lasted till nightfall, when
the French retired southward, after a very feeble resistance, leaving a few prisoners behind them.   Thus the
communication between the French forces at Alexandria
and at Cairo was severed ; and Hutchinson prepared to
march upon the capital.   The day of the occupation of
Rahmanieh was one of good fortune on every side, for
it brought not only the first reinforcements from Malta
to Aboukir,[1] but the news of the advance of the main
Turkish army under the Grand Vizir over the eastern
desert, and a vague report of the arrival of the East
Indian contingent in the Red Sea.

No sooner, however, did Hutchinson announce to his
principal officers his intention to move straight upon Cairo
than they broke out into protests which were almost muti-
nous in their violence.   They urged the risk to the troops
of a campaign during the hot season, the want of magazines and hospitals, the prevalence of plague, the superior
force that must be encountered at Cairo, and the im-
possibility of besieging the citadel ; all of which was
little more than a cloak to disguise their personal dis-
like and distrust of the General.   In their infatuation
these officers actually invited the concurrence of Coote

---

[1] 1/27th and recovered invalids of other regiments, in all about
1200 men.   Bunbury (p. 124) says that they came from England,
but this is incorrect.   Pigot to Fox, 16th April (enclosed in Fox to
Dundas of 22nd April) 1801.

1801. and Moore in a plan to deprive Hutchinson of his command, with the only result of calling down from Moore, who was still at Rosetta disabled by his wound, a rebuke so stern as effectually to silence them. This conspiracy was the more wicked since it was precisely such a cabal, headed by Reynier against Menou, that was paralysing the energy of the French army.

This trouble being ended, Hutchinson summoned two more battalions from Aboukir, and continued his advance
May 11. up the river on the 11th. On the 12th arrived intelligence that General Belliard was about to march from Cairo to crush the Grand Vizir ; upon which Hutchinson sent urgent messages to the latter not upon any account to risk an engagement with the French, feeling assured that his own movements would speedily compel them to return to Cairo. At the same time came definite but disheartening news that only one man-of-war and two companies of infantry had yet arrived at Suez from India. None the less Hutchinson pushed on, though slowly, for the bar at Rosetta had fallen so low that boats with provisions from the fleet could only with the greatest difficulty pass over it. The hot wind also blew fiercely from the sun-baked desert of the south, choking the men, retarding the boats on the river, and forbidding any but short marches. The French at Cairo were nine thousand strong, or nearly half as numerous again as the British ; but Hutchinson knew that they were demoralised by internal divisions and by Abercromby's victories, and was determined to pursue his advantage.
May 14.   On the 14th a large convoy of supplies and stores was captured in the canal of Menouf, together with
May 17. its escort ; and, on the 17th, a small party of one hundred and fifty British dragoons, wide upon Hutchinson's western flank, came upon a French convoy with five hundred camels, which had been sent out from Alexandria to collect supplies. The French force numbered five hundred and seventy men composed of cavalry, infantry, and a dromedary corps, with

one gun; and the nearest support to the British dragoons   1801.
was Doyle's brigade, which was still toiling over the May 17.
sand three miles away. With great readiness Major
Robert Wilson, of Hompesch's dragoons, galloped
forward waving a white handkerchief, and summoned
the French to surrender ; loudly offering the condition
that, on laying down their arms, they should be sent
back to France. Colonel Cavalier, who was in command of the convoy, indignantly refused ; but his
troops had caught the word France, and showed signs
of unsteadiness.   Before Wilson could return to his
own men, a French aide-de-camp came galloping up to
recall him, when, after a short parley, the terms were
accepted. Cavalier's detachment marched to Hutchinson's headquarters and laid down its arms ; and thus
the number of French prisoners taken in various petty
affairs since the 21st of March was raised to fifteen
hundred. Home-sickness had become irresistibly
strong in Bonaparte's veterans, since their three defeats
on the peninsula of Aboukir.

On the same day came news which testified more
than ever to the demoralisation of the French. Despite
Hutchinson's recommendations, the Vizir had been
unable to restrain his army from advancing upon Cairo ;
and on the 16th its advanced guard encountered some May 16.
five or six thousand men under Belliard, about twenty
miles north of the city. The Turkish commander,
however, while declining to come to close action, man-
œuvred his cavalry so skilfully against Belliard's flanks
and communications that, after a prolonged and desul-
tory skirmish, the French General retired to Cairo.
The true reason of his retreat was that Hutchinson
was preparing to cross the river and fall upon his rear,
but it was of course given out that the redoubtable
French had been beaten by the Turks.[1] Thus Hutchinson's communications with the Grand Vizir were
assured ; and he now halted for several days at Algam,
some forty miles north of Cairo, to permit the two

[1] Hutchinson to Hobart, 9th January 1802.

1801.
May.

armies to form their junction, and to allow transport to be collected for the Indian contingent. This last was now reported to have arrived at Cosseir on the 14th; but further intelligence showed that the ships had been dispersed, and that many of them were still missing. At the same time there came from the Mediterranean disquieting intelligence that Admiral Ganteaume's squadron with a large force of troops was off the African coast to westward of Alexandria, and that one of his corvettes had actually entered the port. Moreover, ophthalmia, dysentery, and other diseases had reduced Coote's force to four thousand men, while Hutchinson himself had sent nearly a thousand invalids down the Nile from his own column. The party of mutiny and discontent again raised its head, and unfortunately Moore had not yet rejoined the army from Rosetta to crush it.

June 1.

The advance, however, was none the less resumed on the 1st of June, and the junction of twelve hundred Mamelukes on the 3rd supplied one of Hutchinson's chief wants in the field—a large and efficient body of horsemen. The united force now moved southward in three columns: the Turks on the left, the British in the centre, and the Mamelukes, who loathed and distrusted the Turks, wide on the right. In a few days came the news that Ganteaume's squadron had disappeared. The unfortunate Admiral had, in fact, tried to execute a mad scheme of Bonaparte to land his troops at Derna on the north coast of Africa, that they might march thence over four hundred miles of desert upon Alexandria; but being frightened by the appearance of strange sails in the offing he had returned to Toulon.[1] This was an immense relief to Hutchinson, who, on the 15th, sent a summons to General Belliard to capitulate.

[1] Egypt by this time stank in the nostrils of the French soldier. Hutchinson reported (letter to Hobart, 16th August 1801) that even the Generals on board Ganteaume's squadron believed themselves to be bound to St. Domingo, otherwise it would have been impossible to embark the troops.

The message was defiantly rejected ; but on the 21st 1801.
the British army came before Gizeh and the Turkish June 21.
before the walls of Cairo, on both banks of the Nile,
and on the 22nd Belliard sent a flag of truce to open June 22.
negotiations.   The parleying lasted for some days, but
on the 27th a convention was signed for the surrender June 27.
of all places occupied by the French in Egypt, and for
the shipping of the troops themselves, with their arms
and artillery, to France.   The numbers of the French
in Cairo were nearly thirteen thousand, of which eight
thousand men were fit for duty ; whereas Hutchinson's British were, by this time, reduced to four thousand.   In ordinary circumstances any officer trained by
Bonaparte would have scattered the rabble of the Turks
first, and overwhelmed the British afterwards ; but now
the red coats came as deliverers, for only on their ships,
which commanded the sea, could the exiled Frenchmen return home.   It was a curious comment upon
Bonaparte's dream of an Oriental empire.

Shortly afterwards Hutchinson and Craddock fell so
sick that the command of the army devolved upon
Moore, who, with Hope, had returned to the front on
the 29th of June.   To Moore, therefore, fell the delicate June 29.
duty of escorting eight thousand French, besides their
arms, artillery, and ammunition, some two hundred
miles to Rosetta, with a division of undisciplined Turks,
a few hundred Mamelukes, and but thirty-five hundred
British ; but his arrangements were so skilful, and the
French so delighted at the prospect of returning to
France, that no difficulty of any kind occurred during
a fortnight's march.   The whole body, French and
English, marched on the 15th of July, leaving five July 15.
hundred British soldiers to guard the sick French
officers, but otherwise making over the occupation of
Cairo wholly to the Turks.   On the 30th they reached July 30
Rosetta, and within another fortnight the French were
embarked and on their way to France.

There now remained to be driven from Egypt only
the four or five thousand men in Alexandria under

1801. Menou, who had rejected the capitulation accepted by
Belliard ; and their chance was the worse since large
reinforcements had recently reached Hutchinson from
various quarters. At Minorca General Fox had been
much embarrassed by Hutchinson's appeal for troops,
since nearly all of his battalions were enlisted from the
militia for service in Europe only—a point which Dundas, with his usual carelessness, had overlooked in the
planning of the campaign. However, one and all of
the regiments volunteered to serve in Egypt, whereby
Fox was enabled to spare not only the Ancient Irish
Fencibles, whose sphere of service was unlimited, but
also the two battalions of the Twentieth. In addition
to these there arrived from England, besides drafts,
the Twenty-fourth, Twenty-fifth, and Twenty-sixth,
and from different quarters the three foreign regiments
known as Watteville's, the Chasseurs Britanniques, and
Löwenstein's Rifle Corps.[1] Hereby the losses of the
campaign were nearly, if not quite, made good ; and
the only difficulty which remained was that of money,
the pay of the troops being five months in arrear.
Abercromby had begged for £250,000 in October 1800 :
it was now July 1801, and no money had been sent,
nor even an answer to his letter.[2] The new administration in England was evidently as ignorant as the old
of the nature of war.

Meanwhile the Indian contingent, after long delay,
also appeared upon the scene ; and it is now necessary
briefly to trace its fortunes. When Dundas's letter,
ordering the shipment of a force from India to Egypt,
arrived at Calcutta, Lord Wellesley had already pre-

[1] Watteville's was composed of Swiss, who had enlisted from
the disbanded men of the old Swiss regiments in the French
service, and had served in British pay with the Austrian army.
The Chasseurs Britanniques were formed from the remains of the
Prince of Condé's Royalist army, which had at different times been
in the pay of England, Austria, and Russia. It was dissolved at
the peace of Lunéville, and such individuals as cared to re-enlist
were embodied into this new corps.
[2] Hutchinson to Hobart, 29th June 1801.

pared a force of four British battalions[1] and a few
native troops for the capture first of Java, and afterwards of Mauritius.   In the former enterprise Major-
general David Baird was to hold the chief command,
with Arthur Wellesley for his second ; of the latter,
as a minor expedition, the supreme direction was to be
entrusted to Wellesley.   This force was assembled at
Trincomalee, where Wellesley held temporary command of it ; and Baird was on the point of sailing to
join it from Calcutta, when the Governor - general
intimated to him the change in its destination, re-
appointing, however, both officers to their former posts
as chief and second in command.   But the new instructions had already been communicated to Arthur
Wellesley also, who, taking note of the lateness of the
season, sailed at once with the troops to Bombay, without waiting for his Commander-in-chief, in order that
provisions might be taken in and the transports despatched to the Red Sea without further delay.   Baird
followed him, but Wellesley would have started in
advance of his chief had he not been prevented by a
severe attack of fever.   On the 31st of March Baird
arrived at Bombay ; the last of his troops sailed a day
or two later ; and he himself followed on the 6th of
April, leaving his second in command behind.   Wellesley was then recalled to his government of Mysore,
not unwillingly, for, though his illness was genuine,
and at the last moment his regret at not accompanying
the expedition was sincere, yet his reluctance to serve
as second to Baird was unquestionable.[2]

Then came a long train of mishaps.   On reaching

1801.
Feb. 6.

March 31.

April 6.

---

[1] 10th, 19th, 80th Regiments, with detachments of the 86th
and 88th.

[2] Wellington. *Despatches*, i. 287, 289, 299, 306, 309 ; *Suppl.
Desp.* ii. 324-6, 333, 345, 347-8.   The nominal strength of the
force despatched was 3170 Europeans (10th, 19th, 80th, 86th,
detachment of 36th), besides which the 61st was expected from
the Cape.   The native troops were 1 battalion of Bengal and 2
battalions of Bombay Native Infantry.   The Artillery numbered 230.

1801.
April 25. Mocha on the 25th of April, Baird learned that two divisions of his army had left the place not many days earlier, the one for Jeddah, the other for he knew not whither; whereas the rendezvous which he had fixed

April 28. upon was Cosseir. On the 28th the third division of the army came in to Mocha; and, after some days spent in taking in water, the General sailed with it to Jeddah on his way to Cosseir. On arriving at Jeddah

May 18. on the 18th of May, he found that the two advanced divisions, not having received the orders which he had endeavoured to convey to them, had proceeded up the Gulf for Suez. Meanwhile Rear-admiral Blankett, who had no concern with the expedition, had arrived at that port already with a detachment of the Eightieth on board his flagship, thus inspiring Hutchinson with false hopes that the Indian contingent would shortly be able to co-operate with him. A few days later Sir Home Popham came into Jeddah with two ships of war, having sailed from the Cape with the Sixty-first, some of the Eighth Light Dragoons, and a company of field artillery in convoy. He reported that he had called at Mocha, but had heard nothing there of the fourth division of the army nor of the provision ships which were expected from India. However, on the 26th

May 26. of May, Baird sailed with Popham for Cosseir, which

June 8. he reached on the 8th of June, and there found that two divisions of troops had been waiting for him for six weeks, and by the care of the Quartermaster-general, Colonel John Murray, had already been provided with

June 15. a certain number of camels. A week later Blankett arrived, bearing a letter dated the 13th of May from Hutchinson, to welcome him and to assure him that he would not leave the vicinity of Cairo until the Indian contingent had passed safely across the desert.

Learning from the Admiral that it was hopeless to think at that season of sailing to Suez, Baird prepared to conduct his column across one hundred long miles of arid sand to the Nile at Keneh. Colonel Murray went forward to Keneh itself to forward supplies of water and provisions from thence to different stations on the route ; and parties of Sepoys were employed from the side of Cosseir in searching for springs and digging wells at different points. The whole journey was thus cut up into seven stages, at the first, third, and fifth of which water was to be obtained, while the seventh ended at the Nile itself.[1] Baird's plan was to pass his army over the whole distance in small divisions, of which the first, on reaching Keneh, was to send back its camels and water-bags to the fifth stage ; the second, on reaching the fifth stage, was likewise to send its camels back to the third stage ; and the third division, on reaching the third stage, was to send back its camels to the first stage, enabling the remaining divisions to come forward in succession after the same principle.

The first division, consisting of the Eighty-eighth under Lieutenant-colonel Beresford, later better known as Marshal Beresford, marched accordingly on the 19th of June, accompanied for the first stage by Baird himself. The skins or *mussucks* containing the water, however, almost emptied themselves from leakage, so that when the first division reached the third stage, Baird was obliged to forward to them the water and camels of the second division. It seemed, indeed, as if the passage of the desert must have been abandoned as impracticable, had not additional water fortunately been found by digging midway between the third and fourth stages ; but by the 8th of July Baird had brought the Tenth, Eighty-eighth, and a few companies of Sepoys to Keneh, where

1801. June.

July 8.

---

[1] The stages from Cosseir were :—

1.	To the New Wells .	11 miles.	Water.
2.	Half-way to Moilah .	17 miles.	No water.
3.	Moilah . .	17 miles.	Water and provisions.
4.	Advanced Wells .	9 miles.	Water.
5.	Half-way to Segeta .	19 miles.	No water.
6.	Baromba . .	18 miles.	Water.
7.	Keneh . .	10 miles.	The Nile.

101 miles.

1801.
July.

he halted to await orders from Hutchinson. For several days he could obtain no news of him whatever, and remained in painful doubt whether to advance or to retreat ; but at length he learned through a circuitous channel of the fall of Cairo, and later he received a letter from Hutchinson himself. From this it appears that nothing but the very vaguest information had been furnished to the Commander-in-chief as to the strength of the Indian contingent·or the time and place of its disembarkation, and that Abercromby had never believed in its existence. However, Hutchinson was now able to give Baird definite instructions to move down to Gizeh ; and the latter therefore summoned the rest of his force to join him from Cosseir. Additional troops had arrived there since his departure, raising the whole force disembarked from India to six thousand men ; but several transports and storeships were yet wanting, and more than one vessel had been lost or compelled to return owing to the perils which, in those days of imperfect charts and surveys, beset the navigation of the Red Sea. Ultimately the whole force from Cosseir arrived at Keneh with the loss of only three men.[1]

Far more terrible was the march of the three companies of the Eighty-sixth, which had been carried to Suez on Admiral Blankett's flagship, over seventy miles of desert to El Hanka. They started at six

June 6.

o'clock in the evening of the 6th of June with an allowance of three pints of water for each man, and after traversing twenty-six miles, halted at seven

June 7.

o'clock on the morning of the 7th. But at ten o'clock, the thermometer then standing at one hundred and nine degrees, they were urged forward by the guides, who declared that the camels would require water if they rested longer in the sun. They resumed the march accordingly, but the men began to fall down fast ; and after three hours the officers, at the Colonel's example, cut their baggage from the backs

[1] Hook's *Life of Sir David Baird*, i. 289-386.

of the camels, and set the men upon them in its place. 1801.
An hour later the hot south wind began to blow ; the June 7.
temperature rose to one hundred and sixteen degrees ;
and at four o'clock in the afternoon the Colonel was
obliged to call a halt.   The water-skins had been
cracked by the sun and the water had become thick,
but the officers divided their little stock of Madeira
with the men, and so refreshed them.   At seven in
the evening the wind and extreme heat abated, and
the column pushed on, leaving behind it seventeen
men, who were unable to travel, with camels to carry
them.   At eleven o'clock at night the detachment
again halted in pitchy darkness, and instantly every
officer and man dropped asleep from exhaustion.   At
four o'clock in the morning of the 8th they fell into June 8.
their ranks, drenched with dew and benumbed with
cold, and struggled on.   At two o'clock in the afternoon the hot wind again blew fiercely, but the men
found it less trying than before, and between four and five
o'clock they reached the springs of El Hanka, having
traversed the seventy miles in less than forty-eight
hours.   Not a man had tasted food since leaving Suez,
lest he should aggravate his thirst.   In the course of
the next three hours the stragglers all came in, and
on the next day eight of the seventeen men who had June 9.
been left behind rode in on their camels, the remaining
nine having died.   Such a feat of courage and endurance is not unworthy of record.[1]

Meanwhile, after the embarkation of Belliard's army,
Hutchinson assembled his whole force, about sixteen
thousand strong, at the old position occupied by Coote
on the peninsula of Aboukir ; and on the 15th of August Aug. 15.
he arrived there in person to direct the siege of Alexandria.   Lake Mareotis having by this time assumed
the dimensions of an inland sea, the Guards', Ludlow's,
and Finch's Brigades, nearly five thousand strong, were
embarked under the command of Major-general Coote
on the evening of the 16th, so as to effect a landing to the Aug. 16.

[1] Cannon's *Records of the Eighty-sixth Foot.*

1801.　west of Alexandria, and to invest the city from both sides.[1]

Aug. 17.　On the following morning a small detachment of the enemy, which had been brought to the shore to hinder a disembarkation, was held in check by a feint of Finch's Brigade, while the remainder of the force landed about seven miles to the westward of the city; Hutchinson favouring the whole movement by a false attack from the east. Coote's first business was the reduction of Fort Marabout, on an island off the north shore over against his landing-place. With great difficulty heavy guns were dragged up within

Aug. 21.　range of the fort, which surrendered on the 21st. While this operation was going forward his main body had advanced two miles nearer to Alexandria, and within three thousand yards of a French detachment which had been thrown out by Menou upon that side. The enemy's force was well posted on advantageous ground with batteries and gunboats upon each flank; but with the help of the cannon of the fleet on the sea,

Aug. 22.　and of the gunboats on the lake, Coote drove the French from this position with little difficulty or loss on the 22nd, capturing seven of their guns.

Aug. 23.　　On the following day Hutchinson reinforced Coote

---

[1] The force was on the 9th of August newly brigaded as follows :—

　Guards' Brigade.—Coldstream and Third Guards—Major-general Lord Cavan.

　1st Brigade.—25th, 44th, 1/27th, 2/27th — Major-general Ludlow.

　2nd Brigade.—24th, 26th, 1/54th, 2/54th — Major-general Finch.

　3rd Brigade.—Stuart, de Roll, Dillon, Watteville—Brigadier-general John Stuart.

　4th Brigade.—8th, 18th, 79th, 90th—Brigadier-general Hope.

　5th Brigade.—30th, 50th, 89th, 92nd—Brigadier-general Doyle.

　6th Brigade.—1st, 1/20th, 2/20th, Irish Fencibles—Brigadier-general Blake.

　Reserve.—2nd, 23rd, 28th, 40th, 42nd, Grenadier Companies, and 4 Light Companies, Löwenstein's Rifles, Chasseurs Britanniques, Corsican Rangers—Major-general Moore, Brigadier-general Oakes.

with Blake's Brigade, having decided to carry out his 1801.
principal attack upon Alexandria from that side. Menou,
indeed, while making his works on the eastern front
most formidable, had entirely neglected those on the west.
Accordingly, on the 25th, Coote opened fire from two Aug. 25.
batteries against an advanced redoubt of the French,
and on the same night drove back their picquets with
the loss of a hundred men, capturing a position suitable
for the erection of a second battery within close range.
On the 26th four batteries opened upon the enemy's Aug. 26.
entrenched camp on the eastern front, and on the
same evening Menou asked for a suspension of arms
with a view to capitulation. His first demands were
inadmissible, but on the 2nd of September an agree- Sept. 2.
ment was signed under which he and his men, like
the rest of the French army, were to be shipped
in English transports to the havens of France. Two
days earlier Baird arrived at Rosetta, having dragged Aug. 31.
his unfortunate troops through the desert and hurried
them down the valley of the Nile, only to arrive,
through no fault of his own, too late.

Thus the Egyptian campaign ended with brilliant
and unexpected success to the British arms, owing
principally to the incredible mismanagement of the
French Commander-in-chief. The numbers of the
French are variously stated, by themselves at twenty-
five thousand men, by moderate Englishmen at
twenty-seven thousand, by others at over thirty
thousand. Yet the whole of these were beaten in
detail by a force which never exceeded seventeen
thousand British, simply because Menou played the
Austrian and dispersed his force. Five thousand
men and a dozen more guns at Aboukir would have
prevented the disembarkation, and Menou could
perfectly well have spared ten or fifteen thousand.
Again, even after the British had landed, he could
still have met them with superior forces before
Alexandria and forced them to fight an action on
disadvantageous terms, which, whether won or lost,

1801. would probably have weakened the British army so much as to compel them to re-embark. With such divisions and quarrels as existed in the French army, any General worth the name would have seen that a serious reverse must be fatal, whereas an initial success would banish all evil. The French, in spite of all drawbacks and disadvantages, fought most gallantly until after the 21st of March. They were old and skilful soldiers; they had superiority in cavalry and artillery; and they might hope that a great victory would hasten their release from the country which they had learned to abominate. But when they found that the British were not easily beaten, they would try no more; and hence the very discreditable capitulation of Belliard's greatly superior force at Cairo.

The whole story is a bitter commentary upon Bonaparte's original expedition, which cost France a far greater price than is usually admitted. Apart from the fleet destroyed by Nelson at the battle of the Nile, several transports and small vessels of war were captured on their way to Alexandria, and a final effort of the joint squadrons of France and Spain to effect the relief of the Egyptian army was defeated by Sir James Saumarez on the 12th of July 1801 with the loss of two Spanish ships blown up and one French ship taken. Add to this the constant strain which the bare thought of this unhappy force must have thrown upon the naval and military administration of France, the spasmodic and hazardous efforts to relieve it by such abortive cruises as those of Ganteaume, and finally the waste of French soldiers who fell, died, or deserted in Egypt, and it is easy to see that Bonaparte's venture, despite his triumphs over undisciplined Mamelukes and Turks, was most disastrous to his country. He was already projecting another as insane expedition which shall be noticed in due time; but this of Egypt was a sufficient indication of the gambling spirit which was to be his ruin.

Equally culpable with Bonaparte's proceedings in

Egypt were those of Henry Dundas.   It may truly be 1801.
said that without the help of Menou even gallant old
Abercromby would have failed to save him.   The more
the matter is examined, the more shameful appears the
careless neglect with which the two forces from the
Mediterranean and from India were hurried to Egypt.
The Minister had taken as little pains to ascertain the
strength of the French force as to instruct himself concerning the navigation of the Red Sea ; and he had
actually set the armies in motion with a vague idea that
the one was to kindle insurrection in Upper Egypt and
the other to take Alexandria.   Baird, after a most
dangerous and protracted voyage against the prevailing
winds, found himself at anchor in an insecure and unhealthy port of the Red Sea, with orders to cross the
desert, but without a word of information as to what resistance he was likely to meet with or what he was to do
when he reached the Nile.   An able man in Menou's
place would have forced the armies both from India
and from the Mediterranean to retire with precipitation
and possibly with disaster ; and indeed but for Hutchinson's bold advance to Cairo, a small detachment
might well have destroyed the fragments of Baird's
army in succession as fast as they reached Keneh.   The
nerve shown by both of these commanders in their
extremely difficult situations does high honour to them
both ; but their success was due to themselves and not
in any sense to the Secretary of State for War.   Dundas,
true to his nature, ordered the troops upon an errand
which, according to all human calculation, should have
ended certainly in failure and possibly in disgrace.   Let
not, therefore, the Egyptian expedition be taken as in
the slightest degree atoning for his previous faults, for
it was dictated by precisely the same ignorance, folly,
and presumption as had inspired all his previous enterprises.   Its success probably saved him at the time
from impeachment, but cannot redeem him now from
condemnation.

Though the terms granted to Menou's army were

1801. practically the same as those conceded twenty months before to Kleber at El Arish, yet the effect of the victorious campaign was great in Europe, still greater in England, and greatest of all in the British Army. The three actions at Aboukir had proved that in fair fight British soldiers could still beat even French veterans of the army of Italy. Unfortunately the new Ministry had not the wisdom nor the courage to take due advantage of this revival of strength and hope. Hawkesbury, Addington's Foreign Secretary, made secret overtures for peace to Bonaparte in March, before anything had been heard of the success or failure of the Egyptian expedition, and before time had been allowed for the execution of the measures prepared against the Armed Neutrality. Within a fortnight the whole situation was changed. The action of the 21st of March decided the fate of Egypt; between the 22nd and the 29th General Trigge, with a small force from Antigua, captured with little trouble or loss the Danish and Swedish Islands of St. Bartholomew, St. Martin, St. John, St. Thomas, and St. Croix, in the West Indies;[1] and on the 1st of April Nelson won the battle of Copenhagen. A little less precipitation—it would be juster to say a little more common sense—would have saved the Cabinet from betraying to Bonaparte its want of confidence in itself and in its armed forces; but there can be little doubt that in thus grasping eagerly at peace it felt assured of the support of Pitt. The late Prime Minister was extremely alarmed at the financial condition of the country. Though beyond doubt of great ability in fiscal matters, he had not, strangely enough, grasped the fact that a loan of a hundred pounds at three per cent, floated at seventy-five, was practically an inconvertible loan raised at four and a half per cent. A man who had raised scores of millions upon such terms and had squandered them upon useless allies and foolish

---

[1] The troops engaged were 1/1st, Buffs, 11th, 64th, and the 2nd and 8th W.I.R.

and unprofitable expeditions, might well have felt mis- 1801.
givings.   Flattering adorers might call him the pilot
who weathered the storm, but the title cannot abolish
the fact that war was to him an unknown sea, and that
he was too arrogant to take counsel of those that
had learned to navigate it.

Bonaparte of course preyed upon the fears of Addington's ministry by ostentatious preparations for an
invasion of Britain from Boulogne and other ports
upon the French coast.   These were but a feint,[1] but
they sufficed to cause anxiety at the Admiralty and in
the country at large.   The Ministry, however, threw
the whole burden of defence upon the Navy, and with
a hardihood which is still the astonishment of French
officers,[2] stripped the three kingdoms of almost every
trained man in order to pursue their success in Egypt.
Had Bonaparte converted his feint into a real attack
with no more than fifty thousand or, in Ireland, even
twenty thousand men, he could hardly have failed of
success.   "God send that we may have no occasion to
decide the matter on shore," wrote Cornwallis, who at
this time held the Eastern command, "where I have
too much reason to apprehend that the contest must
terminate in the disgrace of the General and the destruction of the country."[3]   Events, however, proved
that the Ministers were justified in their action ; and
though probably they were prompted less by real
audacity than by a blind reliance on Volunteers, which,
for the most part existed only on paper, they are
entitled to praise for their spirit and courage.   Strangely
enough the French Admiral Latouche Tréville was far
more ardent for an attempt upon England, particularly
after the failure of Nelson's attack upon the flotilla at
Boulogne, than Bonaparte himself.   The man who

[1] Conclusive evidence of this appears in *Projets et Tentatives de
Débarquement aux Îles Britanniques* (published by the Historical
Section of the French General Staff), ii. 291-418, and in particular
pp. 295, 302, 305, 314, 321.
[2] *Projets et Tentatives*, ii. 400.
[3] *Cornwallis Corres.* iii. 381.

1801. really shrank from the struggle was the dreaded First Consul.

In truth matters had not gone well for Bonaparte in 1801, and in great measure through his own fault. By too overbearing a tone he alienated the new Tsar Alexander, and the British Government did not neglect the opportunity of seeking reconciliation with Russia. Alexander's renunciation of the Grand Mastership of the Knights of Malta made the way easy ; and in July England and Russia concluded a treaty which put an end to all differences between them as to the maritime rights of neutral powers. In the Iberian Peninsula also Bonaparte's design had failed. Pursuant to treaty, the Spanish army, with an auxiliary force of French May. troops, invaded Portugal in May, and by the end of the month was in possession of the province of Alemtejo. The First Consul counted greatly upon this stroke to compel the British Government to renounce all of England's conquests ; but it proved to be a mere flourish in the air. Portugal agreed to purchase the evacuation of her territory by engaging to close her ports to British vessels, to cede Olivenza to Spain, and to pay an indemnity to France. The King of Spain, anxious to remove French troops as soon as possible from Spanish soil, ratified the treaty at once ; and Lucien Bonaparte likewise accepted it on his brother's behalf. Napoleon, furious with rage, talked loudly of a fresh invasion of Portugal ; and, since negotiations June. for peace had been reopened, he instructed his emissary to make exorbitant demands upon England. But the moment for bluster was past, for every week brought news of further successes of the British on the Nile ; and it was very evident that, in the game of diplomacy, Egypt was a card which would shortly pass from Bonaparte's to Hawkesbury's hand. Finally, the news of the fall of Alexandria caused the First Consul to hasten the presentation of his final terms before the news should reach England ; and the preliminaries of peace, drawn up on the assumption that Menou still held his

own, were signed in London on the 1st of October. 1801.
On the very next day arrived Hutchinson's despatch Oct. 2.
reporting the total expulsion of the French from
Egypt.

It is really impossible to imagine why the Ministry
should have been so hasty in concluding this treaty.
In July they had prematurely reckoned that Egypt
was actually theirs; and in August Hutchinson had
written that the fall of Alexandria was certain and its
garrison in the worst possible condition.[1]   Yet, without
waiting to hear again from him, they set their hands to
these preliminaries, and actually congratulated themselves that all should have been settled before the fate
of Egypt was known.   They yielded all of England's
conquests except Trinidad and Ceylon, and evacuated
Porto Ferrajo in the island of Elba, where a British
officer, Colonel Airey, with a small body of foreign
troops had for five months defied all the strength of
France.   In return they obtained the integrity of
Portugal, Naples, and the Ottoman Empire, leaving
France in actual or disguised possession of Holland,
Switzerland, the left bank of the Rhine, and Northern
Italy.

In such a peace wise and far-seeing men, like
Grenville and Windham, could see nothing but the
prospect of military establishments maintained per-
petually upon a footing for war without the satisfaction
of hostilities.   The enormous preponderance of power
gained by France could not but be a perpetual menace,
and for this reason they wished to fight on until some
better terms could be won.   Beyond all doubt they
were right.   England was indeed weary of the war,
but France was wearier still, and Napoleon had pledged
himself to give her peace and honourable peace.   Moreover, despite the enormous increase of her debt, the
military and economic condition of England had improved since 1793, whereas there had yet been no time

[1] Hobart to Hutchinson, 22nd July; Hutchinson to Hobart,
16th and 19th August 1801.

1801. to restore financial equilibrium in France. But the Ministers, for the sake of a little cheap popularity, chose to try the experiment whether the French nation would be content, on obtaining peace, to devote itself to internal improvement. They forgot that they had to do not with the nation but with Bonaparte, who had already a score of schemes of ambition and aggrandisement seething in his brain, and who never allowed even the most solemn engagements to interfere with his good pleasure. Moreover, with touching simplicity they left several most important positions unsettled in the preliminary treaty, and then, with singular infelicity of choice, selected Cornwallis as their diplomatic agent to conduct the final negotiations. He was hopelessly outwitted by Napoleon Bonaparte and his brother Joseph ; and, long before his business was concluded, the Government realised that its experiment was already a failure. The peace of Amiens was signed on the 25th of March 1802, but it would be of no profit to specify its conditions. It was no more than a suspension of arms ; and on the next occasion when England was to conclude a treaty with France it was to be on terms of her own dictation.

AUTHORITIES.—For the Egyptian campaign the printed authorities are numerous and good—Walsh's *Campaign in Egypt*, Wilson's *Expedition to Egypt*, Anderson's *Journal of the Forces under Sir Ralph Abercromby*, Bunbury's *Great War with France*, *Life of Sir Ralph Abercromby*, *Diary of Sir John Moore*, *Narrative of a Private Soldier in the Ninety-second Foot*, Reynier's *State of Egypt after the Battle of Heliopolis*. The French official account, edited by M. de Jonquière, has not yet reached the period of the British invasion of Egypt. The official despatches are in *W.O. Orig. Corres.*, 190-196.

CHAPTER XXX

IT now remains for me to review, according to the practice pursued throughout this work, the changes and improvements in administration, training, and equipment, which were introduced into the Army during the first period of the war of the French Revolution. It has already been necessary for the right understanding of the narrative to dwell at some length upon many of them ; but it will, I think, be both convenient and instructive briefly to recapitulate every one of them in order, and to weave them, together with new matter, into a single coherent summary. For this decade of 1793 to 1803 was more fruitful in reform than any equal term of years in the history of the Army.

In the highest branches of administration the most important changes were the appointment of a Secretary of State for War, the reconstitution of the Commander-in-chief's office, and the abolition of the Irish Establishment upon the union of the three Kingdoms in 1800. To each of these three matters a few words must be devoted in succession.

At the opening of the war the arrangements at the War Office and Horse Guards were much the same as they had been in 1756. There was no Commander-in-chief, and Lord Amherst was appointed to perform the duties of that post with the title of General on the Staff. But Pitt, instead of allowing Grenville to direct the campaign in Flanders, and Dundas to control the operations in the West Indies, according to precedent, threw the conduct of the war in every quarter into the hands of a single Minister ; and set the seal upon this novelty in 1794 by making this Minister Secretary of State for War.   In principle the measure was right and sound, and should be remembered to Pitt's honour.   In 1798 the administration of the Colonies was added to this office, and from that time for more than fifty years the Minister who held it was known as the Secretary for War and Colonies.   Nor was the blending of the two departments at the time either unwise or unreasonable.   Our Colonies at the time were reduced practically to the West Indies only, many of them recently conquered from the enemy, and all of them, with one or two exceptions, recently the scene of active military operations.   To place Army and Colonies under a single head was therefore in principle wise, and in practice a means of easing much friction in the Cabinet.

The creation of a Secretary of State for War did not in theory affect the position of that rather mysterious functionary the Secretary at War.   Sir George Yonge, who occupied the latter post in 1793, was not a man who was likely greatly to trouble himself with administrative niceties.   He went Governor to the Cape in 1799, and was recalled in 1801 for having granted to certain men of ascertained bad character the monopoly of supplying meat to the garrison, contrary to the Commissary-general's advice, and for having shared in their profits himself.[1]   It may therefore be assumed that he was content to limit himself at the War Office to such duties as afforded opportunity for jobbery and pilfering, without aspiration to any higher sphere of usefulness.   But the case was very different with his successor, William Windham, a man of original ideas and very great ability.   He stood between the new Secretary of State on the one side and the new Commander-in-chief on the other, nominally charged with

[1] *R.O. Col. Corres., Cape of Good Hope*, Hobart to Gen. Dundas, 2nd May 1801.

financial responsibility for the expenditure of both, and yet vested with little or no control over the actions of either. His predecessors in years of peace had been practically commanders-in-chief; he found himself theoretically reduced to the status of a financial clerk. Moreover, since there was a Parliamentary Under-Secretary of State for War, there was encroachment even upon these humble functions. In fact he was a superfluity, though by no means inclined to consider himself as such; and in consequence the archives of the War Office at this period reveal some curious features, well worthy of notice, in our military administration.

After the junction of the Duke of Portland's following with Pitt in 1794, the ministry was of course formed out of a coalition, a name which is synonymous in our history with weak government. Windham represented Portland's party in the military councils of the nation; Dundas represented Pitt's; and Huskisson, the Under-Secretary of State, appears to have been the mouthpiece of all parties, not excluding the Opposition. Windham, as has been seen, was a very warm advocate for making the French Royalists in general, and those upon the Atlantic coast in particular, the centre of the British attack upon the Revolution; or, in other words, he would fain from the first have turned Brittany and La Vendée into the principal spheres of operations against France. Herein, no doubt, he showed sagacity and wisdom. Dundas, on the contrary, while quite ready to ally himself with the worthless self-seekers who dishonoured the name of Royalist in the West Indies, shrank from giving to the Vendean chiefs the whole-hearted support which would have carried them to Paris. But Windham, with all the influence of Portland at his back, was not lightly to be ignored; wherefore Dundas, in order to silence his importunity, dealt him out occasional doles of men and money, which were sufficient to encourage Charette and his brave companions to commit themselves irrevocably, but inadequate to afford them the support which would have ensured their success. No Englishman can recall without shame the fate of these gallant Frenchmen, the only band of united Royalists who fought for their cause with unselfish devotion ; but the secret of the tragedy lies in the inherent vices of a coalition-ministry. Dundas was unwilling heartily to help them ; Windham was as unwilling to desert them ; and Pitt fell back upon a compromise which ruined them completely, and very seriously injured his own country. His position was undoubtedly difficult, and yet a way was to be found for escape from it. A council of skilled military men, judging the question upon purely military grounds, could have decided it aright ; and where political opinions were evenly balanced upon a matter of military policy, it would have been reasonable to have allowed the weight of the sword to turn the scale. But unfortunately this was the very last thing that would ever have occurred to Pitt.

The position of Huskisson appears to have been even stranger than Windham's. Officers like Charles Grey, who had quarrelled with Dundas, or like Moira, who would have nothing to do with him, addressed Huskisson with perfect freedom and confidence, and used him as the instrument for impressing their views upon Dundas, and so upon the Cabinet. The expedition for the destruction of the sluices at Ostend was managed from beginning to end by Huskisson, just as the disastrous embarkation of the Royalists at Quiberon was wholly the work of Windham. Home Popham contrived to gain Charles Grey to the raid upon Ostend ; Grey in turn (mistakenly, as I think) commended it to Huskisson ; and thereupon the matter was set in train, despite the strenuous opposition of the Admiralty. In fact Dundas's "turn for facilitating business," which Pitt so greatly admired, appears to have consisted in allowing eager subordinates to carry out their own designs from time to time, upon condition that they should leave him free in turn to pursue his own devices. Thus it came about that there were three several civilians at the War Office, nominally working together to promote a common military policy, yet each at the same time contending for particular attention to some extraneous operation which exclusively interested himself. Practically, therefore, there were three Ministers of War, instead of one, and there would have been a fourth but for Grenville's firm refusal to be saddled with the military direction of the Royalists in France, which Dundas endeavoured by stealth to foist upon him.

It may be urged that this lamentable state of things arose accidentally, from the peculiar circumstances of the time and the peculiar characters of the men concerned, and from no inherent defect in administrative principle. There is some truth in this ; and yet it must be recorded that the appointment of the first Secretary of State for War was a great administrative failure.   There was not the unity of command which Pitt had a right to expect from the creation of the office ; and the chief reason was that the true functions of the new Minister had never been properly considered.   Pitt doubtless counted upon Dundas for the efficient organisation of the new department, and the fact is a grave reproach to his judgment of men ; but it is probable that he was quite unconscious, when the warrant was drafted for the third Secretary of State, that he was initiating a new departure in administration.   Had Dundas been as capable as Pitt conceived him to be, he could have established new traditions for the conduct of war which would have earned for him the enduring gratitude of posterity.   He missed a great opportunity, and it must be confessed that Pitt missed it also.   A man so deeply versed in the history of English parties must have known that the admission of Windham to the War Office would raise up a rival to Dundas.   He might have guessed that, by attaching to his confidant a council of military advisers and thus arming him with the weapon of expert military opinion, he would have enabled him to bear down all opposition.   But he did nothing of the kind ; and the result was that Windham and Huskisson could claim, with perfectly good reason, that they were as well qualified to direct military operations as Dundas himself.

Thus Pitt gave full play to all the defects of a coalition-ministry, an evil against which a great statesman would have been upon his guard. It is only natural that the conduct of our great wars should commonly fall upon coalitions. In times of great national peril the spirit of patriotism leads men to sink minor differences and to league themselves with former political opponents for their country's sake ; yet, owing to the peculiar properties of government by party, this apparent unity gives no corresponding increase of strength. It is written in our history beyond all denial that in the absence of a strong and efficient Opposition the ablest ministry must rapidly deteriorate, and that a weak and insignificant opposition declines rapidly into disreputability, and even into sedition. And thus is reached the paradoxical but distressing conclusion that the efficiency of the Government varies inversely as the unanimity of the nation. The absolute exclusion of military men from the councils of the Ministry intensified these evils under the rule of Pitt ; and hence it was not even a well-ordered but a distracted imbecility which governed the conduct of the war in all its branches.

The new Commander-in-chief,[1] on the other hand, proved himself to be far more capable in the organisation of his department. The scope of his duties was totally undefined ; and with invasions impending and practically no real army in existence, the Duke of York naturally imagined at first that the complete and absolute control over every part of the military service was vested

[1] The Duke of York was appointed Field-Marshal on the Staff, 10th February 1795 ; Commander-in-chief in Great Britain, 3rd April 1798 ; Captain-general of the forces in Great Britain and all forces employed in the Continent of Europe, 4th September 1799 ; Commander-in-chief of the forces in Great Britain and Ireland, 9th June 1801.

in him. This not unreasonably was resented by the Secretary at War, who by statute of 1783 was responsible to Parliament for all military expenditure. The existence of this statute was unfortunate, since it closed the way to an important reform. It is too generally forgotten that commanders, whether of detachments or large armies in the field, are charged as much with administrative as purely military functions, and are answerable for the expenditure of considerable—it may be enormous—sums of money. To master the difficult duties thus thrust upon them in time of war, they require training in time of peace ; and no training can be better than to entrust them with the outlay of the funds voted for their departments at all times. A strict audit should of course be enforced, and every security provided for the protection of the civil Minister, who under the Constitution is responsible to Parliament for the moneys allocated to the military service at large. But the essential thing is that officers should be familiarised with the handling of large sums and with the expenditure of the same to the best advantage, that they may the better be able to fulfil those duties when on active service. Fraud and misconduct are perhaps even less to be apprehended from military than from civil officers, since the former are amenable not only to civil penalties but to the summary process of military law. Sir George Yonge, convicted as Governor of the Cape of a conspiracy to swindle the King's troops, escaped with a recall and the loss of his appointment. An officer guilty of the same crime would have been liable to trial by court-martial and to dismissal from the service, with public record of his disgrace in the Gazette.

But though the Duke failed to obtain the control over expenditure which he had desired, the importance of the Secretary at War began none the less to dwindle from the day of his appointment as Commander-in-chief. Later on, as shall be told in a future volume, the Duke was anxious that his Military Secretary should have a seat in the House of Commons to assist the civilian

Secretary in the exposition of military matters ; but before 1802 there was apparently no thought of this. It remained for him therefore only to confine the powers of the Secretary at War within due limits, which was not finally accomplished until 1799, when it was laid down that all correspondence relating to discipline and military regulations should pass through the Adjutant-general, all concerning quarters and marches through the Quartermaster-general, and purely financial matters only through the Secretary at War. The mere re-modelling of the administration upon the principle that military authority should be supreme in military affairs sufficed to extend the Duke's powers enormously ; and it was high time, for discipline had fallen utterly to decay owing to the encroachments of the civil head of the War Office upon the province of the Commander-in-chief.

Before 1795 the Adjutant-general's correspond-ence had been confined to the discipline of the army in Great Britain and of the forces in the field. That officer now became the centre of information and authority upon all matters affecting numbers and efficiency. The Duke initiated a system of returns, as also of confidential reports concerning every officer in the service, all of which came up to the Adjutant-general and gave him the power that springs from knowledge. More significant still was the appoint-ment of a Military Secretary as the channel of com-munication between all ranks of the army and the Commander-in-chief. This was an absolute novelty in the service and exceedingly valuable, since, by removing all shadow of excuse for correspondence between officers and the Secretary at War, it put an end to the inter-ference of politicians and other civilians with matters of discipline. By appropriating also to his office all pro-motions and all appointments excepting the very highest, which necessarily remained in the hands of the Cabinet, the Duke drew the army still closer to its military head ; and by establishing a regular chain of communication downwards from the Commander-in-chief through

Generals commanding districts and Colonels commanding regiments, he preserved his touch with all ranks
of the army, and held them from highest to lowest in
subordination.

Nevertheless, his powers continued to be in many
respects greatly circumscribed.   In the first place,
neither he nor his staff were consulted upon any
military enterprise that was under consideration of
the Cabinet.   He was simply asked whether he could
furnish so many men at such a time, to fulfil the plans
of the Ministry ; and with his aye or no his part in
the matter was ended.   In other words, his functions
were purely executive.   So far as regarded the actual
operations of war, the Cabinet was right in making
them so, for no one man could have found time at
once to plan campaigns and to train an army.   The
real blemish was that Ministers assigned to themselves no military advisers, in thorough co-operation
and sympathy with the Commander-in-chief, to guide
them in the conduct of war.   Nor does it appear that
his advice was sought or taken upon the disposal of the
troops at home, otherwise the army that returned from
the Helder might have been kept together for exercise
and instruction, as Abercromby had recommended.
One probable reason for this was that the Government
possessed no police except the armed forces of the
Crown, and, mistaught by long tradition, thought it
more important to disperse them as constables than to
concentrate them as soldiers.   In such matters the
Commander-in-chief was absolutely powerless, for he
could not legally order a corporal's guard to march
from London to Windsor without a route from
the Secretary at War.   Abroad, the transfer of troops
from country to country appears to have lain in the
province of the Secretary of State for War, who gave
general orders for the purpose but left all further
detail to the direction of the Commander-in-chief.   In
fact the limits in the jurisdiction of the various
functionaries who aspired to command the army were

often exceedingly obscure, the Secretary for War, as
has been already told, frequently competing in a most
bewildering fashion with the Secretary for the Colonies,
until the two offices were amalgamated.   However, the
absolute removal from the civilians of all authority
concerning promotion and discipline was a gain of
unspeakable value ; and it shall presently be seen that
the Duke's reforms in the Army at large bore worthy
comparison with those effected at the Horse Guards.

Less satisfactory at this period was the condition of
the Board of Ordnance, though Cornwallis became
Master-general at about the same time when the
Duke of York became Commander-in-chief.   What
was amiss in the office it is not quite easy to say ; but
it is certain that it was in constant disrepute for
dilatoriness and inefficiency, and that the Regiment of
Artillery was never in so bad a state as between 1783
and 1803.   Moore in Egypt declared that it had
failed both there and at the Helder from want of
intelligence and military spirit in the officers.   " There
is certainly something wrong about our artillery," he
wrote ; " it was formerly our best corps, it is now far
from it."   Adding to this testimony the Duke of
York's complaints of his waggons and harness in 1793,
the delay in providing the siege-train for Dunkirk, the
detention of Abercromby's expedition in 1795, the
rotten gun-carriages furnished to Stuart for Minorca in
1798, and the miserable character of the ammunition-
waggons despatched to the Helder in 1799, I am forced
to the conclusion not only that the Ordnance was in a
thoroughly unsatisfactory state, but that Cornwallis
did nothing to improve it.   It may well be that the
multiplicity of duties thrust upon him allowed him no
time to attend to his duties as Master-general ; but in
this case he should have been careful to enjoin the
greater zeal upon his subordinates.   The truth seems
to be that there was considerable friction between the
Ordnance and the War Office ; and Cornwallis wrote
so sneeringly of the Duke of York's appointment as

Commander-in-chief that, quite possibly, he sympathised unconsciously with his own department in thwarting the Duke's attempts at reform.

Be that as it may, it is certain that the Ordnance Office showed itself so disobliging to the War Office and Horse Guards in the matter of providing detachments of Military Artificers for active service, that the Duke formed a corps of the same kind, called the Staff Corps, which should stand on the same footing as the cavalry and infantry towards the Commander-in-chief. Beginning with an establishment of one company of Pioneers, this Staff Corps was in 1800 augmented to five companies, which did useful service under Abercromby in Egypt ; but this does not disguise the fact that it was set up by the War Office in rivalry with a similar body already subject to the Ordnance Office, and that consequently the country was put to the expense of two corps when one should have sufficed. It is noteworthy also that the Ordnance made no effort to place their Artificers under the command of the officers of the Engineers, a reform obviously desirable at once for economy and efficiency. Altogether, it seems to me that Cornwallis and his subordinates were found wanting at this time. It would indeed have been a great advantage if the Duke of York had been appointed Master-general of the Ordnance as well as Captain-general of the Army after the precedent of Marlborough ; but Ministers should not be blamed because he was not. They could not know by instinct how successful the Duke was to approve himself as an administrator.[1]

I pass now to the Treasury, the third office concerned with the general administration of the Army, through its control not only of the business of pay but of the services of transport and supply. Upon this department the War Office and Horse Guards made an encroachment by the formation, first of the Royal

---

[1] *S. C. L. B.* 31st July 1799 ; 14th January 1800. Conolly, *History of the Royal Sappers and Miners,* i. 119.

Waggoners in 1794 and secondly of the Royal
Waggon Train in 1799, whereby transport was transferred in part from civil to military hands and organised
upon a military system.   Since, however, the train
possessed few vehicles or animals of its own, the
necessary consequence followed that its officers, if sent
forward to purchase or hire transport for a projected
campaign, were still subjected to the Commissaries of
the Treasury.   The department of the Commissariat
consisted of a Commissary - general of Stores, six
Deputy-commissaries, and seven assistants; but it was
still inefficient, generally speaking, for work in the
field, though there were one or two of its officers who
received high commendation both from Abercromby
and Charles Stuart.   In fact, though this particular
branch of the service had advanced somewhat, it was
still backward; nor was it destined to improve until
Arthur Wellesley, taught by much experience with the
bullocks of Mysore, finally brought it to real efficiency
in the Peninsula.

Regarding transport by sea, which was in the hands
of a Board consisting of five naval captains and a
secretary, no very flattering account can be given.   There
can be no doubt that, through the enormous increase of
Britain's commerce during the war and her practical
monopoly of the carrying trade by sea, tonnage was
often most difficult to procure; but in embarkation
after embarkation there were just complaints of insufficient accommodation and unseaworthy vessels.
Worst of all were the arrangements for transferring
recruits from Ireland to the depot at Chatham, when
men suffering from infectious fevers were hurried
aboard bad and crowded vessels to carry disease and
death to their unfortunate comrades.   The mortality
on these short passages was consequently appalling.
The men, only just enlisted, were subject to no
discipline; they were provided neither with medical
officers nor medical stores; and since they refused
from superstitious scruples to commit the corpses of

their comrades to the sea, they came into port, the living with the dead, in unspeakable filth and corruption.[1] It is true that the blame for this state of things by no means rested wholly, perhaps not even chiefly, with the Board of Transport; but that body seems to have been out of touch with all other departments, and to have treated ships merely as ships and not as floating abodes for soldiers. Consequently healthy men were often embarked for long voyages upon infected vessels, wherein they perished by the score and even by the hundred.

In truth it is difficult in these days to realise the perils and discomforts patiently endured by officers and men in leaky transports, when frequently they could not sleep dry for weeks together. Not the least of the dangers was the drunkenness and incompetence of the masters and mates, which on at least one occasion compelled a captain of infantry to take command and navigate a ship from the West Indies to England. Marvellous to say, he brought her safely into Cork, though his observations had led him to believe that he was in the Downs when in reality he was off the mouth of the Mersey; but it was to his credit that his error was no greater.[2] Towards the end of the war, as has been mentioned, old ships of fifty-four and sixty guns were used for troopships, with the cannon removed from the lower-decks; but this, being an ill-organised service, resulted in constant friction between Army and Navy. In fact the only ships on which the troops were healthy and comfortable were those of the East India

[1] *S.P. Ireland*, Sir Jerome Fitzpatrick to Major-gen. Fox, 1st April 1798.

[2] *Autobiography of Sir J. M'Grigor*, p. 78. My old chief, the late Lieutenant-general Sir William Jervois, told me that in 1841, being then a subaltern of Engineers, he sailed to the Cape in a hired transport. The master and mate came to blows a few days out, and the only sextant on the ship went overboard in the struggle. Fortunately, he himself happened to possess a quadrant, by the help of which the navigation of the vessel was carried on. The voyage to Capetown lasted 140 days.

Company, which, as is testified by the reports from the General at the Cape during 1798 and 1799, were beyond reproach. Nor must it be supposed that the troops were under different regulations on board the East Indiamen, for the rules for the entire service were made uniform in 1795, and were remarkably good and sound. The difference was due simply and solely to the size, quality, and internal fittings of the ships themselves. So far, therefore, as the Admiralty and Treasury were concerned with the Army, it cannot be said that they covered themselves with credit; and it is no extreme statement to assert that their duties would have been better performed if transferred to the military authorities.

The fourth department concerned with the administration of the armed forces was the Home Office, which reigned supreme over the Fencibles, Militia, and Volunteers, including Yeomanry Cavalry. Here, however, once again circumstances compelled the War Office and Horse Guards to trespass upon a province which had hitherto been closed to them. The reduction of Fencible regiments in order to drive their men into the Regular Army first brought the Home Office and War Office into closer contact. This contact was turned into collision by the first Act for the enlistment of recruits from the Militia into the Line, for the Lords-Lieutenant discountenanced the measure and made its execution a failure.[1] Finally, the arrangements for the defence of the Kingdom against invasion turned collision for a time into friction. The Militia occupied at that time a peculiar position in the country. It was supported from the proceeds of the land-tax, which, being the principal contribution of the land-owners to the general revenue, led the country gentlemen to claim a kind of proprietary interest in the force. For this reason they felt a pride in furnishing it with officers; and indeed the Militia lists of that period are simply a catalogue of the names of the leading county-families, the greater

---

[1] *Dropmore Papers*, iv. 224.

magnates holding the higher, and the lesser the lower ranks. Over all presided the Lord-Lieutenant, who not only as a rule was actually a colonel of Militia, but was charged with the distribution of commissions and with the more serious duty of keeping the peace within his county.   Hence his office was of the greatest importance and, if he were really competent to execute it, of singular weight and authority.

Many of the Lords-Lieutenant were gentlemen of the highest character, great ability, and strong public spirit, with a standard of conduct, a courtesy to high and low, and a simple though noble dignity of bearing which gained for their every word and deed an unquestioning obedience and respect within their jurisdiction.   Others, though unendowed with great personal qualities, possessed none the less great weight and influence through their wealth, their rank, their ownership of pocket-boroughs and their powers of patronage generally.   In fact they were great magnates whose path in life was hung with blue and red ribands, and led at the very least to a gorgeous funeral in the ancestral vault. But all alike were to some extent petty Sovereigns, with the Militia for their army. They were attached to the force, frequently spent very large sums upon it, and easily grew to regard it as their own.   Their officers shared their views, and hence in many cases a regiment of Militia became a very exclusive county-club, with a just pride in itself which was of not a little value.

It was therefore a rude shock to many corps when in 1798 the Generals of their districts demanded of them their flank-companies to be formed into distinct battalions under officers of the regular Army. Some of the more pompous Colonels denounced the entire proposal as unconstitutional, and threatened to carry the matter before the courts of law.   The Militia, they urged, was not the Army ; it was not subject to the Commander-in-chief ; it had nothing to do with War Office or Horse Guards ; and no part of it could legally be torn away from its own officers to be trained according to a false German system. Foremost among the champions of this opinion was Lord Buckingham, a self-important busybody of conceit so amazing as to make even his very genuine and generous patriotism seem ridiculous. Puffed up with his dignity as Lord-Lieutenant and Colonel, he plagued the whole Cabinet with arguments upon the constitutional aspect of the question, and was hardly to be silenced even by the adverse opinion of the legal officers of the Crown. As a matter of common sense it was difficult to meet the contention of the Generals that, if they were responsible for the defence of the country, they must be permitted to handle their troops in their own way. The controversy was therefore decided in favour of the Commander-in-chief, and this was the first step towards the uniting of all the land-forces of the Crown under a single department; though many years were still to pass before the country was to perceive the folly of dividing them between a Minister of Offence and a Minister of Defence.[1]

The Union of Ireland with Great Britain contributed enormously towards the simplification of our military affairs at large. Until 1800, all the cumbrous machinery which hampered the progress of the Army at home had been duplicated in the sister kingdom. Ireland had her own sovereign, the Lord-Lieutenant, her own Commander-in-chief, her own War Office, her own Paymaster-general, her own Board of Ordnance, her own artillery, her own establishment for the strength of regiments and her own rates of pay. For years this arrangement had been the distraction of administrators, as it still is of historians, giving rise to endless jobbery and incredible financial confusion. The transfer even of a single officer from the British to the Irish Establishment signified a troublesome adjustment of differences of pay; and the transfer of a regiment meant not only change of emoluments and position

---

[1] *Dropmore Papers*, iv. 169, 177, 179, 207.   *Grey MSS.*

but the choice of a new Agent and subjection to new and extremely capricious patronage. Every Lord-Lieutenant was bound to submit to the King his periodical lists of promotions and vacancies, on which George the Third would write minutes in his own hand, occasionally exposing and checking some flagrant job. Nothing is more remarkable, amid the many evidences of the old King's indefatigable industry, than the care with which he perused all military papers from Ireland.

From the administrative departments I turn now to the Regular Army itself. Its nominal strength, according to the annual establishments in these years, may be found upon another page,[1] but its effective numbers in rank and file, that is to say exclusive of officers and sergeants, did not reach one hundred thousand men until 1795, varied from that figure to one hundred and twenty thousand from 1795 to 1799, and only in 1800 attained to one hundred and forty thousand. Since the foreign troops enlisted in the British service are included in these totals, the figures may be taken to represent, roughly speaking, the effective strength of all ranks of the truly British forces. The number of recruits enlisted in the three kingdoms from 1793 to 1800 was almost exactly two hundred and ten thousand, of which over forty thousand were obtained in 1795 and about the same number in 1799. The various experiments in recruiting have already been enumerated in the course of my narrative, but may now be briefly recapitulated. In 1793 the ordinary methods were followed, the bounty offered being ten guineas, but was shortly superseded by General Cunyngham's ingenious scheme for making new levies pay for themselves. Then in 1794 was adopted the scandalous and extravagant resource of allowing an unlimited number of officers to raise men for rank, which was followed at the close of the same year by the infamous system of contracting with certain individuals to supply recruits at twenty guineas

[1] Appendices C, D.

a head.   In 1796 an Act was passed for the levying of recruits from parish to parish for both Army and Navy, which proved to be an absolute failure.   By the end of 1797 the whole of these expedients had been found wanting, and in November six regiments were ordered to enlist boys under eighteen years of age with a bounty of a guinea and a half.[1]   Finally, in January 1798, was passed the first Act for tempting ten thousand militiamen to join the Army by a bounty of ten pounds, which failed, as has been told, owing to the opposition of the Lords-Lieutenant.   The same principle was successfully extended by a second Act of July 1799 ; and in October of the same year a second Act empowered the King to enlist an unlimited number of militiamen in whole companies and battalions.   It must, however, be borne in mind that the men thus drawn from the old constitutional force were engaged for service in Europe only, and that they fought in Egypt simply as a favour to their country.   The difficulty in procuring men for general service was still great ; and even in July 1800 a certain Ensign Nugent accepted a contract to furnish fifteen hundred men and five hundred boys at prices varying from fifteen guineas to twenty-four pounds a head.[2]

As to the Militia itself, its average strength in England from 1794 to 1798 was about forty-two thousand men, but in the latter year it was increased by the establishment of the Supplementary Militia to a nominal total of one hundred thousand. This, however, lasted for but one year, for the withdrawal of recruits

---

[1] The regiments were the 9th, 16th, 22nd, 34th, 55th, and 65th. The 32nd and 45th were also ordered to recruit boys in 1800. *S.C.L.B.*, 2nd Dec. 1797 ; 10th Feb., 6th July 1800.   The three regiments which first tried this experiment were the 22nd, 34th, and 55th. *Memoirs of John Shipp*, p. 14.

[2] *S.C.L.B.*, 1st July 1800.   The amount paid for each man enlisted in Ireland was £24, in England £21 ; for each boy enlisted in Ireland £18 : 15s., in England £15 : 15s.; this seems to have covered all expenses, including the provisions of the men with necessaries.

for the Regular Army soon lowered the figures very greatly ; and in 1801 the united strength of the Militia and Fencibles in the three kingdoms was set down as only one hundred and four thousand men.   The most interesting points in the history of the force during this period are the formation in 1793 of the Irish Militia, at first sixteen thousand and later twenty-one thousand men, and of the Scottish Militia, six thousand men, in 1797 ; the draining of the Militia of England to supply seamen and gunners in 1795, and of the Militia of all three kingdoms to furnish recruits after 1798 ; and finally the passage of the British and the Irish Militia in opposite directions over St. George's Channel, to do duty in each other's kingdoms.

I pass next to the Fencibles, though by right they should have taken the precedence of the Militia, which was assigned to them by lot in 1795.[1]   These, to repeat my former definition, were regular troops enlisted for service at home and for the duration of the war only, and were designed to liberate the Regular Army from the United Kingdom for service abroad.   It is extremely difficult to arrive at their actual strength, for their establishment was frequently reduced (in the hope of forcing the discharged men to enter the regiments of the Line) and as frequently reaugmented.   Most of the Fencible corps were created either in 1794 or 1798, and to judge by the old Monthly Army Lists[2] of 1799, the greatest number of them in existence at one time in Great Britain was thirty-one regiments of cavalry and forty-five battalions of infantry.   But by March 1800 the greater part of the cavalry had been disembodied, so

[1] *C.C.L.B.*, 6th April 1795.

[2] I cannot say when these unofficial monthly Army Lists came into being, nor, indeed, have I ever seen more than two or three specimens, which I bought at a second-hand bookstall for a few pence.   They are minute quartos of sixty pages, in very small type, and I do not know where any complete collection of them is to be found.   The official list of Auxiliary Forces in 1800 shows thirteen regiments of Fencible Cavalry, and forty-six battalions of Fencible Infantry.

that it would not be wise to reckon the Fencibles as exceeding, at their highest figure, twenty to twenty-five thousand men.   It has already been mentioned that several of the Fencible regiments volunteered for service abroad and that the Ancient Irish found their way to Egypt.   Most, if not all, of the Fencible Infantry was disbanded in May 1801, before the signature of the preliminaries of peace ;[1] but one relic of these forgotten corps still lives a distinguished life among us.   In April 1799 Colonel Wemyss of the Sutherland Fencibles received a letter of service to raise a regular regiment from that corps and county, the bounty being ten guineas for fencible men and fifteen for new recruits ; and so came into being the Ninety-third Highlanders.[2]

But this principle of creating corps for duty in garrison only—for such was the true nature of the Fencibles—was not confined to the United Kingdom. In 1795 Skinner's regiment of Fencible Infantry was recruited for service in Newfoundland and North America only.   In the same year such soldiers of the Line as were fit for light work but unequal to a campaign were drafted into a Garrison Regiment, which, though intended for Gibraltar, was employed chiefly in England. Again, in August 1800, Fraser's corps of two companies, apparently augmented from a single company which had been enlisted for African service in 1794, was created for duty at Goree.[3]   These were of course only imitations of the small bodies of trained men which had been organised by Simcoe for Canada and Grose for New South Wales shortly after the close of the American War.   What their value may have been

[1] S.C.L.B., 3rd to 13th May 1801.
[2] S.C.L.B., 16th April 1799.   Stewart (*Highland Clans*, ii. 280) says that the Sutherland Fencibles were disbanded in 1798 (a most unlikely date), and the Ninety-third formed in May 1800.   I have not found the order for disbandment, while the letter of service bears the date that I have assigned to it.
[3] S.C.L.B., 25th April, 1st September 1795; 25th June 1794; 27th to 29th August 1800.

it is extremely difficult to say, but it is tolerably safe to conjecture that the Garrison Regiment consisted of all the useless old soldiers (with their wives and children) of whom the colonels of the Line desired to be rid, and that Fraser's was composed of convicts and incorrigible offenders who preferred even the West Coast of Africa to the misery of the hulks.   In the same category of local troops, but of far greater value, must be reckoned the West India Regiments, which in November 1798 had reached their full number of twelve battalions. The formation of these native levies for the garrison of our tropical possessions is one of the most important facts in the military history of this period.   The principle has since been indefinitely extended, though it is still subject to temporary limitations owing to the reluctance of white settlers to put arms in the hands of the coloured races.

Next after the Fencibles, the Provisional Cavalry and Volunteers demand consideration.   The Provisional Cavalry, as the reader will remember, was called into existence when the alarm of invasion was at its greatest, in November 1796.   A part of it, for the counties of Berkshire, Kent, Somerset, Suffolk, Northumberland and Worcester, was embodied in 1797, and disembodied at the same time with the Fencible Cavalry in the spring of 1800.   I have been unable to discover what degree of efficiency it may have originally possessed, or with what description of officer it was provided ; but if there was any merit either in the higher or the lower ranks, this force after three years' training should have been of considerable value.   It must, however, be remarked that the Government shrank from the unpopularity of using its powers of compulsion in respect of the Provisional Cavalry, readily abdicating them in favour of doubtful promises of voluntary service.   Before the Act for its creation had been for many weeks in force, an amending enactment was passed, providing that if any town or county should raise volunteers equal to three-fourths of the number required under the original Act, then the Lord-Lieutenant should have power to dispense with Provisional Cavalry and to raise Yeomanry, or, in other words, Volunteer Cavalry. This was of a piece with Pitt's military policy at large. He never passed an Act for National Defence without an amendment to substitute "You may serve" for "You must serve." No doubt he could have adduced many arguments in favour of this course, based ultimately upon the proposition, which he regarded as an axiom, that his withdrawal from office would mean the ruin of England. None the less the principle was surely unsound. An Act to compel men to voluntary service, which (absurd as it may seem) was the purport of this and other of his measures, is an Act to enable men to evade service.

Meanwhile it is significant of the inefficiency of the civil administration of the War Office that information concerning the Volunteers in these years is both scanty and untrustworthy. By the time when hostilities were renewed in 1803 the orderly and methodical rule of the Duke of York had established a system of returns and statistics full of minute information ; but being fully occupied with the task of remodelling the discipline of the Army amid all the pressure and distraction of the war, he had not succeeded in reducing this particular district of chaos to order by 1801. From such information as I can glean from the records of the War Office, the Yeomanry Cavalry in Great Britain in 1798 counted a total of one hundred and sixty-three troops ;[1] but the entries are certainly incomplete, for the official list for 1800 shows a total of two hundred and one corps, with an aggregate of four hundred troops, for Great Britain alone. According to

[1] Raised in 1794 . . . . . 81 troops.
       " 1795 . . . . . 14 "
       " 1796 . . . . . 4 "
       " 1797 . . . . . 46 "
       " 1798 . . . . . 18 "

                        163 troops.

a return of January 1801 [1] the nominal strength of the Yeomanry or Volunteer Cavalry in the three kingdoms was close upon twenty-four thousand men, exclusive of officers ; but it is added that at least one-third should be deducted from this total, which would reduce it to sixteen thousand, and it may be doubted whether in actual practice the force could have produced above twelve thousand fit for service.   Besides these there were local Associations of Cavalry numbering sixty-nine corps in all, of which the great majority consisted of a single troop only.

Of the Volunteer Infantry and Artillery (for in some of the towns on the coast the companies were formed, one-third of infantry and two-thirds of artillery) it is equally difficult to speak with certainty.   From all that I can gather there were from fourteen hundred to fourteen hundred and fifty companies of Volunteers in Great Britain and about seventy-five in Ireland, the greatest part of them having been formed in 1794, 1797, and 1798.[2]   The return above referred to gives their nominal strength at just below one hundred and twenty-three thousand non-commissioned officers and men, or, after deduction of one-third, perhaps eighty thousand effective.   But over and above these there were the Voluntary Associations for Defence, counting in all seventy-eight distinct corps with over five

[1] Printed in *Projets et Tentatives de Débarquement aux Îles Britanniques*, ii. 396.

[2] In a lecture delivered at the Staff College, before I had discovered this return, I gave the number of the volunteers as 26,000 only.   The companies actually enumerated in the books of the Secretary at War do not exceed 450, and hence my miscalculation. The official list of 1800 shows 619 Volunteer Infantry corps, numbering apparently 1432 companies ; but it is not always easy to reckon the number of companies in a corps.   Nothing can exceed the disorder and want of system in the records of that department of the War Office.   In collecting material for this chapter, I have frequently found subjects of exactly similar nature recorded indifferently in one or other of three series of entry-books, with occasional excursions into a fourth and a fifth.   On the other hand, I have found important orders printed in contemporary handbooks, but not recorded in the entry books at all.

hundred companies. The military authorities seem to have taken no account of these, probably with perfect justice ; and it is extremely doubtful whether all the Volunteers could have put above sixty thousand men into the field.

It should be mentioned that the Yeomanry supplied their own belts and swords, receiving an allowance for the same, and that both they and the Volunteers were subject to the same rules in respect of pay. The Government supplied both alike with clothing, and paid regular wages to one sergeant in each troop and company, in order to make good as far as possible its inability to furnish non-commissioned officers from the regular Army. The officers received two days' pay, according to their rank, and the men two shillings weekly, on attending exercise for two days in the seven ; the principle being that until called out for permanent duty they should be paid for each day upon which they were present at drill.[1] The blot upon the organisation of the Volunteer Infantry, as I have remarked elsewhere, was the departure from the old principle of affiliating it to the Militia, a blunder which has been fruitful in waste and extravagance. But it is only necessary to glance at this confusion of regular regiments for general service, regular regiments for European service, regular regiments for home service, invalid companies and other corps for garrisons at home and abroad, Militia, provisional Cavalry, Yeomanry, Volunteers, Associations of Cavalry, and Associations of Infantry, to be satisfied that the Ministry had never really grappled with the problem of national defence. Such a multiplicity of denominations might be construed to indicate activity, but its true significance is poverty of thought and of power in organisation. Setting aside coloured levies, I

---

[1] *S.C.L.B.*, 17th May 1794, 19th February 1796. The North Devon Yeomanry refused the assistance of Government in the matter of clothing and appointments. *Ibid*, 15th May 1798. I cannot suppose this to be an unique case of patriotism among the Yeomanry and Volunteers.

think it extremely doubtful whether in any one year from 1793 to 1802 the effective strength of the Regular Army and Auxiliary forces exceeded, even if it attained, the figure of two hundred thousand men.

A word must now be given to foreign troops, by which is meant not those merely hired from foreign countries, like the Hanoverians, but those regularly enlisted into the British service. The confusion in the records makes this subject also exceedingly obscure. Letters of service to foreigners, chiefly Emigrants, to raise regiments of all kinds are to be found in abundance, but whether many of these corps ever existed except on paper it is difficult to say. Sometimes it may be confidently asserted that they were still-born; sometimes, as for instance Stuart's foreign regiments at Lisbon, they appear suddenly after years of silence as full grown; occasionally, as in the case of the *Chasseurs Britanniques*, they drop as though from the skies into the middle of a British army in the field, and it is fortunate if by chance some unofficial record of their origin is preserved. The one thing certain is that from the moment when a letter of service for a foreign corps was issued, the Secretary of State for War treated the levy as ready to his hand, and laid his plans accordingly. Thus in July 1800 the Prince of Orange engaged himself to raise a large body of Dutch soldiers. Dundas promptly wrote to Abercromby that these were five thousand strong, and should be employed in Portugal; a month later he announced that they would be required for service in Ireland; and finally it appeared that they were not forthcoming at all.[1] This makes one great difficulty in tracing the history of foreign corps. Another is that the majority of them were called by their Colonel's names, which were sometimes changed, sometimes duplicated, and occasionally abolished altogether in favour of some florid title more or less connected with the Royal Family of England. The death of these corps is often

[1] *S.C.L.B.*, 11th July 1800. *W.O. Orig. Corres.*, Dundas to Abercromby, 13th October; to Pulteney, 17th November 1800.

as mysterious as their birth. To all appearances they
have been buried in the West Indies or swallowed up
by the Sixtieth, when the historian is startled by their
sudden appearance, either through resurrection or re-
generation, in the heart of Europe. On the other hand,
some which seemed to be full of vigorous life vanish
abruptly into space, leaving not a wrack behind. As
to the regiments formed or ordained for St. Domingo,
any attempt to fathom the secret of their being or their
failure to be is hopeless. There is but one safe guide,
the name of Charmilli, for it may be regarded as
synonymous with fraud ; but unfortunately it is not
easy to determine how many of his colleagues were of
like guile with himself, nor even whether their legions,
real or imaginary, were composed of black men or of
white.

The truth would appear to be that every Agent of
the British Government on the Continent of Europe
was on the watch to gather in recruits of any nation.
Thus it came about that there were in the direct pay of
Britain isolated regiments of French, Germans, Dutch,
Swiss, Corsicans, Minorquins, and Maltese, with an
occasional infusion of Austrians, Italians, and Greeks.
There was even an attempt to raise two battalions of
Albanians, which, however, was only partially successful.[1]
Some few of the foreign corps, easily to be distinguished
in the course of my narrative, were good and valuable
troops ; others would desert even in such inhospitable
localities as St. Lucia and Marmorice Bay ; others
again were absolutely worthless. For how many such
corps Pitt may have paid is a question which he would
most probably have been unable and certainly have
been unwilling to answer ; but it may be doubted
whether, taking one year with another, they supplied
him at any one time with more than five thousand or at
most seven thousand effective men. In fact the system
of competing with foreign crimps for the refuse of the

---

[1] *S.C.L.B.*, 25th May 1799, 24th June 1801 ; Abercromby to
Dundas, 5th May 1800.

recruits of the Continent was a blunder, and a very costly and ignoble blunder ; yet it was of a piece with Pitt's former policy of paying a retaining fee to the Landgrave of Hesse for the first claim to his mercenaries, instead of spending the money upon the amelioration of the British Army.   Never was ostensible economy so false, so short-sighted, so unworthy of a great statesman.

From the numbers and organisation of our armed forces I pass to their pay, clothing, and lodging.   In respect of pay it must be mentioned first that the scarcity of food compelled the Ministers in 1795 to grant a temporary increase to the men, which was effected by consolidating several allowances into a lump sum; with an addition proportionate to the enhanced price of bread.   This favour was conceded by Royal Warrant without previous consultation of Parliament, whereupon the Opposition at once raised the cry that it was calculated to teach the Army to rely upon the generosity of the King rather than of Parliament, and to attach it to the Crown rather than to the nation.   This, of course, was mere factious mischief, for the question at issue was not whether constitutional niceties should be respected, but whether the Army should be converted by starvation into a dangerous mob.   As a matter of fact there was, as has been mentioned, a formidable riot near Seaford in Sussex, when the Oxfordshire Militia broke out of barracks, seized all the wheat and flour in the town, impressed waggons to carry it off, and sold it at fifteen shillings the sack.   The outbreak was quelled, and three of the ringleaders, after trial, were shot.   In the face of this rising the only wonder is that Pitt did not earlier yield to the soldiers this most necessary relief.   But he was generally slow to regard the wants both of Army and Navy.[1]   The real and solid increase of wages to the men was made, it will be remembered,

---

[1] *C.C.L.B.*, 1st September 1795 ; Clode, i. 99.   Clode's habit of taking all Parliamentary speeches seriously, without regard to circumstances or the character of the speakers, is a blot upon an otherwise valuable book.

in 1797, in consequence of the mutiny in the Fleet.[1] It was accompanied, marvellous to say, by an augmentation of pay to the subaltern officers. The deductions for poundage, hospitals, and agency were remitted, an additional shilling a day was granted, and it was ordained that they should receive their pay in full as it fell due, without subjection to vexatious delays and belated refunding of arrears, as had been the rule in the past.[2] This was a great concession. It is true that the subalterns were starving, and that the fact had been represented to Ministers some years before both by the Adjutant-general from the Horse Guards, and by the Duke of York from Flanders ; but this was a trifle to which the Cabinet paid no attention, until the seamen of the Royal Navy showed that starving men were dangerous.

There remains to be considered an important administrative change in the matter of pay. Hitherto the only intermediary between the public and the regiments which composed the Army had been the regimental Agent, holding the Colonel's power of attorney. The Paymaster-general made over all issues of money to this Agent ; he in turn transferred them to the regimental paymaster, who was simply one of the officers selected by the Colonel to perform this in addition to his ordinary duties ; and finally, the regimental paymaster made his issues to the captains for their troops and companies. Each captain then accounted with the regimental paymaster, the paymaster with the Agent and the Agent with the Secretary at War, on whose certificate the final account between the Paymaster-general and the Agent was closed. In 1797, however, an additional officer was allotted to each regiment as paymaster, who was still appointed by the Colonel on the old theory of the latter's pecuniary responsibility for all regimental matters. But the Secretary at War then proceeded to open direct

[1] For the details of the increase see Appendix B.
[2] S.C.L.B., 27th June 1797.

correspondence with the regimental paymasters on all financial business, thereby initiating an extraordinary complication of anomalies which remained unaltered until the abolition of purchase. In theory the paymaster, as the Colonel's nominee and subordinate, was bound to obey him at his peril, according to the terms of the Mutiny Act ; but in practice he was accountable also to a civil court as a civil servant ; so that it was open to him to plead the Colonel's commands in evasion of those of the Secretary at War, and those of the Secretary at War in defiance of his Colonel. The actual result was that the financial position of the Colonel and the Agent towards the regiment and the Treasury became entirely fictitious, which indeed would have been no evil if the clothing of the men had been taken out of the Colonel's hands and the principle of purchase abolished. But the retention of these two ancient institutions made the maintenance of agency imperative, and consequently forbade the reduction of its cost to the public. Hitherto the Agents, in return for that cost, had done most of the detailed work of accountance for the Army ; but now that it had pleased the Secretary at War to take that duty upon himself, it inevitably followed that the country was saddled with the charge of providing him with a large staff of clerks. The Agents were, of course, well content to see their work diminished while their emoluments remained unchanged ; but to the nation the only result of increased expenditure was the establishment of a system alike vicious and unsound. But indeed the ignorance of the civil heads of departments respecting the administrative machinery of their own offices seems to have been deplorable.[1]

From the foregoing the reader will have gathered that the old methods of clothing the soldier remained unaltered, notwithstanding that in almost every campaign there had been complaints of its wastefulness and inefficiency. Thousands of men must have perished

[1] *Clode*, i. 298-301.

in Flanders and Holland in 1793, 1794, and 1799 from insufficient protection against the cold ; while equally in the West Indies the nakedness of the men, particularly in respect of shoes,[1] exposed them to the attacks of insects and so to malignant ulcers, which disabled hundreds from service. The helplessness of the authorities in face of these evils was amazing. In 1793 subscriptions were collected in several towns to provide the troops in Flanders with flannel shirts, and a depôt was formed in Soho Square for the storing of these and similar comforts ; but the Secretary at War appealed to the public rather to expend its money on shoes, of which, as he gravely stated, "the consumption often exceeds the present funds providing them."[2] It seems never to have occurred to him that the " present funds " might have been increased. A very short step towards amendment of the existing practice was taken in 1795, when the expenses of horse-clothing in the cavalry and of alterations to raiment in the infantry were transferred from regimental to public funds, the annual allowance being fixed for the former at twenty pence and for the latter at thirty pence a man.[3] But the motive for this measure was rather the deliverance of starving soldiers from a stoppage of pay than any wish for an advance on the road to true reform.

In 1798, however, serious criticisms were passed by the Finance Committee of the House of Commons upon the whole system of clothing the Army. While admitting that Colonelcies were bestowed upon deserving officers, this Committee with good reason disapproved the principle that officers should make profit from the clothing of their men, and recommended that for the future a Board of General

---

[1] Readers who have lived in the tropics hardly need to be reminded of chigoes, vulgarly called "jiggers." These insects burrow under the toe-nails to lay their eggs, which in course of incubation set up dangerous inflammation. Tens of thousands of men have lost one or more joints of their toes in this way.

[2] S.C.L.B., 14th November 1793.

[3] C.C.L.B., 1st September 1795.

Officers should make contracts for the clothing of the whole of the forces, whether Regulars, Fencibles, or Militia, the loss to the Colonels of the Regulars being made good to them by compensation.   Beyond all doubt there was very much to be said in favour of some plan of this kind; and the Colonels themselves would have welcomed the exchange of a certain for an uncertain reward.   But the cost interposed a fatal objection.   It must be remembered that at this period General Officers received no pay as such except when employed in some definite position on active service, when a special allowance was voted for them by Parliament. At other times unless they held command of a district, the Governorship of a fortress or a Colony, or the Colonelcy of a regiment they received nothing beyond the pay, or half-pay, of their regimental rank.   Practically, therefore, a Colonelcy, through the emolument derived from clothing, was the only recompense that could be given to a General in time of peace, no matter how long or distinguished his service.[1]   This practice was of course in accordance with the principle upon which the Army had been built up, namely, that it should pay for itself; and any attempt to tamper with that principle might bring the whole structure to the ground.   The cost of indemnifying all Colonels of regiments, added to that of the newly-suggested system of clothing, would have caused a storm in Parliament. It was urged also, not without force, that a contract on so gigantic a scale as for the clothing of the whole army would be a dangerous experiment, and that Colonels and Quartermasters, having no longer a personal interest in the matter, would be less zealous for economy than heretofore, while their love of

[1] Thus when Major-general Irving succeeded Lieutenant-general Vaughan on the death of the latter in the West Indies he could draw none of his allowances, and received in fact nothing but his pay as Lieutenant-colonel.   The result was that in a few weeks he found himself £1000 in debt owing to the expenses of his new position.   *W.O. Orig. Corres.*, Irving to Dundas, 10th August 1795.

smartness at the same time would not tend to keep down expense to the public. Finally it was pointed out that the gains of Colonels were really extremely hazardous, since an augmentation of their regiments might bring them either large profits or heavy losses according as it was ordered immediately before or immediately after the annual assignment of off-reckonings. While, therefore, they asked for deliverance from conditions so inequitable, they would naturally expect no trifling compensation.

In the face of these considerations the Finance Committee was unable to persist in its proposals for reform ; and accordingly the amended regulations for clothing, dated the 23rd of April 1801, accepted the old system with some few changes of detail only. New rules were made to reduce the fluctuations in the Colonel's emoluments as far as possible ; and then the far more important question of the soldier's raiment was cautiously approached. The difficulty as to shoes was overcome by the issue to every private of two pair of shoes, in lieu of his half-mounting,[1] and to every sergeant of three shillings in addition. Great-coats also were supplied for the first time to the whole of the troops, the nation generously providing the first batch of them and leaving it to the Colonels to maintain them out of the allowance granted for watch-coats. This allowance amounted to one shilling for every man annually, but was increased after 1798 by the abolition of lapels, whereby twenty pence was saved on the price of a soldier's coat and liberated for application to the purpose aforesaid. The extreme cunning of the Treasury in shielding the nation from additional expense on account of shoes and great-coats is very characteristic. Every soldier enlisted since 1793 had cost the country at least twenty pounds before he embarked on active service, but in tens of thousands of cases this money—to say nothing of a man's life—was

---

[1] Half-mounting consisted of a neck cloth (changed in 1795 to a black stock), shirt, one pair of shoes and stockings.

sacrificed through the miserable grudging of the few shillings that would have saved him from death by exposure.   It has needed many years to drive from the heads of British statesmen the idea that it is not sound economy to pay a heavy price for a man on one day and to kill him within a month in order to save a few shillings.[1]

I come now to the matter of lodging, wherein at this time was accomplished not only a change but a revolution.   The old system, which provided for the quartering of troops in ale-houses upon the terms laid down in the Mutiny Act, had always been deficient and had at last become ridiculous.[2]   There were indeed barracks in forty-three different garrisons and fortresses, with nominal accommodation for twenty-one thousand infantry and artillery ; but, even if the space had sufficed for twice the number, the troops could not, owing to the demand for their services as police, have been distributed into so few centres.   Moreover, the need for small bodies of soldiers in many towns had been increased by the rapid growth of manufacturing industries and by the activity of revolutionary agitators among the artisans.   In fact it may be said outright that it was the want of an efficient constabulary that drove Pitt to cover the country with new barracks. To this end he in June 1792 summoned Colonel Oliver Delancey, then a Deputy-adjutant-general at head-quarters, and asked him to undertake the duty of constructing buildings to house the troops, with the title of Barrackmaster-general.   After first stipulating that he should not become a public accountant, Delancey accepted the appointment ; and his office was established by warrant in the following year.   Pitt took no vote from Parliament for the proposed work,

[1] *Misc. Orders,* 9th April 1800, 23rd April, 20th May 1801. *Entry Books, Board of General Officers,* 20th February 1798. *Treatise on Military Finance,* 1795.
   [2] It must be remembered that this applied to Great Britain only. There had long been barracks in Ireland.

allowing the cost to be defrayed out of the vague charge which went by the name of " Extraordinaries of the Army." The advantage of this arrangement was that nothing concerning it came before the House of Commons until a considerable sum of money had been spent on account. Fox in 1793 and General Smith in 1796 spoke in condemnation of the general policy of the measure, but Windham pledged himself for the economy and good management of the new department ; and there could be no question, to any reasonable man, that the need for barracks was urgent. The matter therefore was allowed to go quietly forward ; and through the peculiar nature of his appointment Delancey was empowered to purchase or hire plots of land, to contract for the erection of buildings, the supply of bedding, and so forth, and in fact to conduct financial operations on an enormous scale without the slightest supervision or control. His duties demanded a man of exceptional training, experience and ability in business, with a staff of assistants expert in surveying and building. Military advice was required only for the settlement of general principles in the construction of barracks and the selection of sites, though the choice even of these latter was dictated by considerations of police rather than of strategy. Beyond this the functions of the Barrackmaster-general were purely commercial. He was simply a large trader in the particular markets with which military men were least conversant because least concerned.

No doubt there were a few officers in the Army who possessed the qualifications to wield the powers thus entrusted to the newly-created department. Delancey was not one of them. He made the most extravagant bargains both for land and buildings, and actually entrusted the contract for the fittings of barracks to a single individual, upon the easiest and most insecure of agreements. The Secretary at War, after a slight struggle to exert some kind of control over the expenditure, seems to have abandoned the attempt with perfect equanimity and to have connived with ready helplessness at all irregularities. The Commissioners of Audit were ignored and the authority of the Treasury set aside on the most ridiculous pretexts; and when enquiry was at last made in 1804, it was found that over nine million pounds of public money had been issued to the Barrackmaster-general's department, and that no accurate account could be produced either of the public or private expenditure of the same. The part played by Delancey himself appears to have been most disgraceful. He not only appropriated large sums to himself under the guise of personal expenses, but appointed a vast number of subordinate barrack-masters, even in places where there were no barracks, all of whom, of course, were paid with public money. Indeed it should seem that officers commanding regiments were likewise appointed agents to superintend the construction of barracks, with power to incur debts to the amount of thousands of pounds and with little or no financial responsibility. Thus not only facility but absolute temptation towards extravagance, if not towards corrupt dealing, was thrown in the way of the entire military service.

Yet it is humiliating to record that Delancey not only escaped unscathed but received a pension of six pounds a day on retiring from his office in 1804, which reward he enjoyed, together with the Colonelcy of the Seventeenth Light Dragoons, until his death in 1822. No doubt he owed his immunity from disgrace to the fact that the Ministers were obliged to shield him. The constitution of his office was absolutely indefensible; and indeed it is impossible to understand how any public servant, military or civil, could have been permitted to dispose of millions of public treasure without the slightest financial check. Yet the Ministers alone appear to have been responsible for this carelessness, for the principal persons present, when the establishment of the Barrackmastership was broached to Delancey, were Pitt, Dundas, and Sir George Yonge. When

Delancey was ultimately called to account, his defiance of the Commissioners of Audit was excused on the flimsy plea that his accounts were exempt from examination, by special agreement between himself and the King ; but it was never pretended that his appointment was a royal job. Nor is it possible to contend that the whole transaction originated in some corrupt design of the military authorities, for, in the first place, barracks had lain in the province of the Ordnance before the creation of the new department, and, in the second place, the supreme military control was vested in 1792 in Sir George Yonge, the Secretary at War. Most astonishing of all is the fact that Windham, though apprised in 1795 of the laxity of the Barrackmaster-general's methods, took no step whatever to scrutinise or correct them. That he should knowingly have involved himself in any nefarious practice is absolutely incredible ; yet, since his particular function was to watch all expenditure of the nation's money on military objects, it is difficult to acquit him of neglect of duty. There can be no doubt that Delancey was guilty of a shameful breach of trust towards the Ministers, and they as guilty of a breach of trust towards the nation.

The explanation of the whole matter seems to be that Pitt, in despair of obtaining the assent of Parliament to a great scheme for constructing barracks,—or, in other words, to a great revolution in the military system of Great Britain,—resolved to compass his ends by stealth no matter at what cost. It is impossible not to admire his courage, for patriotism can have been his only motive ; and it is perhaps hardly too much to say that, if he had fallen in 1797, this transaction of the barracks might have cost him his life. But he who does evil that good may come should be careful that the least possible harm shall ensue on the evil and the greatest possible benefit proceed from the good ; and herein Pitt failed, apparently not a little from that unhappy ignorance of the world which made him so poor a judge of men. Delancey should never have been selected as Barrackmaster-general, nor Yonge as Secretary at War, nor Dundas as Secretary of State for War. However, over two hundred barracks were ultimately built for one hundred and forty-six thousand infantry and seventeen thousand cavalry ; and it is significant that of forty-eight constructed for the cavalry, two only were calculated to contain as many as six troops. In fact they were not military barracks, but police-stations for the maintenance of internal order ; and from this cause they were far less beneficial than they should have been to the Army. Their original cost was extravagantly wasteful, and after a century they are almost worse than valueless ; but for this last Pitt cannot be blamed, since in his time a true constabulary was still undreamed of. However, the fact remains that in a few short years the British Army was imperceptibly transferred from quarters in ale-houses to quarters in barracks.[1]

The different arms of the service now claim our attention, and first of all the Cavalry. Its history during this period combines a strange mixture of glory and disgrace, with the brilliant actions of Villiers-en-Cauchies, Beaumont, and Willems on one side, and on the other the mutiny of the Fifth Dragoons and the race of Castlebar. Speaking generally, the condition of the Cavalry at the opening of the war seems to have been bad, partly owing to the extreme dispersion of regiments and the under-payment of subalterns, which were causes beyond its control, partly from general idleness and neglect. The Duke of York therefore took the mounted troops early in hand ; and having first circulated Dundas's book of drill to commanding officers and enjoined its use for all regiments, he in March 1796 appointed a board of General Officers to enquire as to the clothing, saddlery, and equipment of the men. On the 18th of May these Generals produced their report. As to clothing they recommended the

[1] Clode, i. 240, *sq.*; *S.C.L.B.*, 25th Feb. 1796.

abolition of the old long coat in favour of one with short skirts, the substitution for epaulettes of wings strong enough to turn a sword cut, breeches of plush with woollen lining instead of leather, and boots well hollowed at the back to be the more easily drawn on and off. In the matter of saddlery they produced a new pattern of saddle, and recommended the abolition of housings, the showy and ponderous drapery which served for an ornament to the horse and for a coverlet to the man. The arms and equipment they left un-altered, desiring only that the bayonet should be issued to light as well as to heavy dragoons; which suggestion was rejected. As to horses they pointed out that the breed of black horses formerly ridden by all heavy cavalry was either extinct or completely transformed, the animals in the market being suitable only for draught and unfit to carry a soldier. But at the same time they reported that a new type of horse, bred chiefly for gentlemen's carriages, had been introduced, which was well adapted to take the place of the blacks for work in the ranks. Finally, they urged that a veterinary surgeon, a saddler, and an armourer should be attached to every regiment of cavalry in the service.[1]

Practically the whole of these recommendations were adopted, and some of the new regulations probably afforded great relief to the officers. The price of chargers had risen, as was natural, considering the in-crease of Regular, Fencible, and Yeomanry Cavalry; and the fact had apparently been made by some officers an excuse for not providing themselves with an animal of any kind. To remedy this an order was issued, shortly before the signing of the report above named that if any officer neglected to buy himself a charger, his Colonel should buy one for him at a cost not ex-ceeding fifty pounds, and stop the amount from his pay. But at the same time permission was granted for officers to ride nag-tailed horses, not under fifteen

[1] C.C.L.B., 10th July 1795, 3rd March, 18th May 1796.

hands in height, from which it is to be inferred that
the price of black chargers with tails undocked had
become prohibitive. A month later the Third, Fifth,
and Sixth Dragoon Guards, and the Fourth and Sixth
Dragoons were named in orders as allowed to ride
brown, bay, or chestnut horses ; and this was a greater
reform than at first sight appears, for display had been
so highly valued in the Cavalry that any change which
might depreciate it was welcome.

The introduction of veterinary surgeons also anticipated the issue of the report, the order for appointing one
to each regiment bearing date the 15th of April 1796.
The pay assigned to them was ninety-five pounds a year ;
and since apparently the supply of veterinary surgeons
was unequal to the demand, it was arranged that regiments which were unable to obtain one should receive
one-half of that sum towards the support of a student
at the Veterinary College. It should seem that the
intention had been for commanding officers to send
some of their farriers (to whom hitherto the medical
charge of troop-horses had been entrusted) to receive
instruction at the College ; but this scheme proved to
be impracticable. In September 1796, therefore, it
was laid down that Veterinary Surgeons should receive
the King's commission ; their pay was raised to seven
shillings a day ; and a Principal Veterinary Surgeon
to the Army was appointed with salary of ten shillings
a day. Thus the new department was finally established, and with trained horse-doctors, saddlers,
armourers, and armourer-sergeants, which last were
added in 1802, the efficiency of the Cavalry bade fair
to show substantial improvement.[1]

Nevertheless the training of the mounted troops
still remained very imperfect. The new drill, with its
novelty of executing manœuvres by threes, was indeed
made obligatory in 1795, and a code of signals for the
trumpet was drawn up and made uniform for all regi-

[1] *C.C.L.B.*, 3rd June 1796, 1st July 1802 ; *S.C.L.B.*, 15th
April, 21st September 1796.

ments in 1798. In 1796 also regulations for sword-exercise, drawn up by the fencing-master, Angelo, were published by authority, and schools of instruction therein were opened at several centres both for the Regular and the Auxiliary Cavalry. But still nothing was officially required of the dragoons, light or heavy, beyond excellence in performing showy evolutions; the more difficult duties of scouting, reconnaissance, and dismounted work being entirely neglected. Of the many new regiments raised, both regular and auxiliary, nearly all were nominally light dragoons, yet not one had the slightest knowledge of the special functions of that arm.

A certain General Money, who had entered the French service as volunteer in 1792 and had held high command in the field until the entry of England into the war compelled him to resign it, protested strongly in published pamphlets against this false and mistaken system. He pointed out that in England, the most strongly enclosed country in the world, there were forty thousand cavalry, of which not a single troop was properly armed or trained for dismounted duty; and it is a positive fact that only twelve carbines were issued to each troop of Fencibles.[1] "Is there," asked Money, "between London and Ipswich any ground on which three squadrons of horse can form without being in reach of musketeers from the hedgerows in their front and flank? Of what use then, in God's name, is cavalry when they cannot form to charge? for if they cannot form they cannot charge." He quoted the success and efficiency of the French mounted chasseurs in Italy and in other campaigns, and pleaded with great eloquence and force for the introduction of similar corps in England; but he was not sanguine of success. "Till this new system of horse-chasseurs be adopted by Austria and Prussia, whom we copy in most things, and have copied for a century past, nothing will be done." Such was his prediction, and it was perfectly

[1] S.C.L.B., 25th June 1974.

correct. Although the corps of Simcoe and Tarleton had furnished perfect models of light horse—as much at home in the saddle as heavy dragoons, as much at home on foot as riflemen—not the slightest effort was made to imitate them.   Yet the very difficult and trying campaign against the Maroons had shown how easily a good regiment of light dragoons could be converted on occasion into the best of light infantry.   In fact the omission to form and to instruct corps of dismountable dragoons can only be regarded as a grave reproach upon the officers who were responsible for the efficiency of the British Cavalry ; and it must be ascribed, in Money's pungent phrase, chiefly to mere "jack-boot prejudice."[1]

At the same time it must be said, in defence of the Board of Generals who reported on the Cavalry, that they refrained from offering recommendations respecting the Light Dragoons owing to the expense lately thrown upon the Colonels by the alteration of the uniform in 1784. It should seem, therefore, that reform was in some measure checked by the original sin of the clothing system ; but even so the delinquencies of regimental officers are not wholly excused, for they did not prepare their men well even for work in the saddle.   The swords, it is true, were of an abominable pattern, long and straight for the heavy dragoons, shorter and much curved for their lighter brothers, but in neither case possessing any guard except a single bar ; and for this they were not responsible.   But it was greatly to their discredit that their regiments, though taught to charge, were never taught to rally.   In short, apart from the addition of the few expert officers already named, and the introduction of uniformity in drill, the attempt to improve the cavalry appears to have ended in the substitution of grey for blue in the uniform of Light Dragoons in India, and the dressing of the hair of all ranks in a queue measuring ten inches in length below the collar.   Such

[1] Money, *Letter to the Right Hon. W. Windham*, 1799.

trivialities have too often been preferred to solid and well-considered reform.[1]

The Artillery, as has been already hinted, was not at its best at this period, owing partly to the disorder in the office of Ordnance, partly to the growth, for some reason, of a bad spirit in the corps. Nevertheless it made progress in several directions towards the efficiency which it ultimately attained in the Peninsula. The first brigade of Horse Artillery, it will be remembered, came into existence in January 1793 with two companies, each counting one hundred men of all ranks and two hundred and eighteen horses. In September of the same year the establishment of these companies was raised to three hundred of all ranks with four hundred horses. In July 1794 the brigade was transformed into four troops, with nearly eight hundred of all ranks and over a thousand horses ; in September of the same year it rose to nearly twelve hundred of all ranks with close upon sixteen hundred horses ; and finally in September and October 1801 it was augmented first to seven and then to ten troops, each counting one hundred and eighty of all ranks with nearly six hundred horses. We have seen the Horse Artillery on active service at the Helder in 1799 ; but General John Moore saw one troop at drill two years earlier in 1797, and pronounced that he could conceive of nothing in higher order. The armament of each troop consisted of four six-pounders, two twelve-pounders, and two light howitzers.[2]

The Field Artillery (if I may use a term which did not then exist) likewise underwent a rapid series of augmentations, the existing supply of gunners having been exhausted in the first year of the war. In the spring of 1793 the corps consisted of four battalions with a total establishment of thirty-seven hundred men ; in

---

[1] *C.C.L.B.*, 21st June and 4th July 1796.

[2] *Warrant Books*, 11th September 1793 ; 12th July and September 1794 ; 1st September and 12th October 1801. *Diary of Sir John Moore*, i. 263.

September there were added to it five hundred gunners and four hundred drivers, of which the latter appear to have existed chiefly on paper, for the Duke of York was always complaining of the dearth of them in Flanders. However in 1794 there was formed a new corps of Captains-commissaries and Drivers for the parks of Artillery serving in England, which was organised in divisions, each consisting of thirty drivers and nine non - commissioned officers and artificers. Twenty - eight of these divisions were assigned to the four parks in England and eighteen to those in the Netherlands, with a Captain-commissary and Lieutenant-commissary in charge of each park. The full strength of the corps was rather over two thousand of all ranks, with three thousand five hundred horses; and apparently there was affiliated to it an establishment of bat-horses for eighty-four regiments, numbering in all three hundred and thirty - six men and over seventeen hundred horses. This last was presumably formed to carry the reserve of ammunition for the infantry, otherwise it could hardly have been under the control of the Board of Ordnance. It is easy to understand that when military organisation had been given to the drivers of artillery, there should have been eagerness in all other branches of the service to take advantage of the precedent.

Meanwhile in August 1794 a fifth battalion was added to the British gunners; in November four companies of French Emigrant Artillery, complete with drivers, was taken into British pay; in July 1799 followed a sixth battalion; and in February 1801 a seventh was formed by the incorporation of the Irish Artillery. Moreover in 1793 a company of invalid gunners had been formed for Bermuda, and by 1801 there was a whole battalion of these veterans, nearly one thousand strong. Altogether, when the preliminaries of peace were signed, the Artillery had risen to the strength of between nine and ten thousand men, exclusive of all drivers but those of the Horse

Artillery. It was the peculiar distinction of the Horse Artillery that its drivers formed part and parcel of each troop ; and it is difficult to say why the like organisation was not adopted for the Field Artillery. However, some approach to it was made in September 1801 by replacing the corps of Captains-commissaries with a corps of gunner-drivers, distributed into seven companies, evidently to meet the wants of the seven battalions. Each of these new companies included three officers and three hundred and fifty non-commissioned officers, artificers, and drivers, making a total of nearly thirty-two hundred men with five thousand eight hundred horses. It is difficult for us to realise, at this distance of time, what an enormous advance in efficiency is indicated by these apparently primitive arrangements.[1]

Turning to the work of the Artillery in the field, one notable point is the constant employment of heavy ordnance in the general actions during the campaigns of the Netherlands in 1793 and 1794, when twenty-four pounders were as freely used as field-pieces. The explanation seems to lie in the practice of fortifying very extensive positions to enormous strength, which was employed first by the French in order to shield their raw levies, and later by the Allies to make good their inferiority of numbers. In the days of Saxe when two armies sat down opposite each other entrenched to the teeth, it was invariably dearth of forage or supplies that compelled one or other of them to move away ; but through the improvement of roads it seems to have become the habit, for a time, of armies to keep heavy guns always at hand so as to confront positions which were practically fortresses with ordnance suitable for a siege. Like causes produce like effects, and after a long period of disuse the custom has been revived for campaigns of entrenched positions (if the expression may be allowed) in the twentieth century.

[1] *Warrant Books*, 11th September 1793 ; 4th August, 9th September, 1st November 1794 ; 27th February 1796 ; 16th July 1799 ; 16th February and 1st September 1801.

Another important matter was the gradual tendency to take from the infantry their battalion-guns and to use cannon in larger tactical units, so as to turn to full advantage their long range for missile action, instead of employing them simply to eke our musketry with grape-shot.   Abercromby, it will be remembered, introduced this novelty in Holland in 1799, when for the first time a British army took the field with a special officer in command of the whole of its artillery.   There was still to be a slight reaction in favour of the older system, but it is noteworthy that in 1798 and 1801 orders were issued for an officer and eighteen men of each regiment of cavalry and thirty-four men of each regiment of infantry to be trained to serve the galloping-guns and battalion-guns, evidently with the idea of liberating all true artillerymen for their own cannon.   It will be seen in due time that the galloping-guns of the light dragoons, though now forgotten, played a considerable part in more than one great action in India.[1]

Of the Engineers there is comparatively little to be said except that their officers were constantly employed in the highest and most difficult duties of the Staff in the field.   After the evacuation of the Low Countries there was little scope for their talent in the siege of regular fortifications, and Abercromby complained that those who conducted the operations against Morne Fortuné were ignorant of their business.   In 1801 their establishment was raised to two battalions, each of fifty-six officers ; and in April 1802 the appointment of an Inspector-general of Fortifications showed that the defences of the United Kingdom were to receive greater attention.   The private soldiers of this branch of the service were not under the direct command of the officers of Engineers, and still bore the name of Royal Military Artificers.   Of these four new companies were formed in 1793, two for Flanders, one for Canada, and one for the West Indies ; and by the end of that

[1] *C.C.L.B.*, 19th April 1798, 23rd September 1801.

year their establishment appears to have included altogether ten companies, numbering in all a thousand men. In small detachments these Artificers bore their part in every campaign of the war, though their services became less conspicuous after the creation, which has been already recorded, of the Staff Corps by the Commander-in-chief.

I come now to the principal arm of all, the Infantry, the actual progress of which during the war must be described on the whole as somewhat disappointing. Nevertheless it was on the eve of two great improvements, the one of abolition, the other of creation, which demand particular notice. In the first place, the practice of massing together the companies of Light Infantry and Grenadiers, though we shall meet with it to the eve of the Peninsular War, began to show signs of dying out ; and indeed there can be no doubt that in the British Army it was extremely pernicious. The flank-companies were always the choicest of a battalion, and the detachment of them for formation into a separate corps signified practically that the remaining companies were ruined for their benefit. A very flagrant instance was that of the twenty-eight flank-companies sent with Sir Charles Grey to the West Indies, which indeed made up between them a superb little body of troops, but practically destroyed for some years the efficiency of the battalions from which they had been drawn. Generals, of course, favoured the system because it gave them a body of picked men ; and it was particularly dear to officers of the old school, such as Amherst, Howe, and Grey. Dundas, indeed, complained that Amherst had done irreparable mischief in this way during his short tenure of the chief command ; and the reproach was not wholly unmerited, though the consequences would have been far less serious if the battalions had not been reduced to such miserable weakness before the outbreak of the war.[1]

[1] Dundas to Grenville, 21st July 1798. *Dropmore Papers*, iv. 263-264.

But another grave objection to the practice was that it concealed the real point at issue, namely, the need for Light Infantry properly armed, trained, and equipped as such ; which the massed Light Companies of the Army failed utterly to satisfy.   Lord Howe had created such infantry in 1757 ; Tarleton and Simcoe had copied him in the American War of Independence ; besides which, as has already been told, every battalion had organised for itself a company of riflemen.   Grey, with American reminiscences strong upon him, had given his light-companies a special course of instruction at Barbados in 1794 ; but Murray and Craig had been obliged to resort to foreign levies under the different denominations of rangers, chasseurs, and jäger.   In fact the only soldier untaught in the work of light infantry was the British.   In 1795 a beginning was indeed made by forming two companies of marksmen in the North Riding Militia of York, which were the first regular British riflemen ever seen in the country ; but though they were dressed in green they were neither selected, trained, nor properly accoutred for their work.   In fact they were a mere parody on true light infantry and might just as well have been dressed in scarlet and armed with a musket.[1]   It seems, indeed, that the authorities were positively afraid to enjoin novel and peculiar instruction upon any but a new corps.   In vain General Money urged that one-fifth of the British Infantry of the Line and half of the Supplementary Militia should be at once converted into genuine riflemen : no heed was paid to him.   In campaign after campaign the French tactics threw the need for such soldiers into stronger relief ; but, as the foreign corps in the British service gradually perished from want of recruits, the British Generals found themselves more and more at a loss to supply the want. The fragments of some of these corps were indeed swept together in 1798 to form a Fifth battalion of the

---

[1] *Militia Letter Books*, 24th July 1795. James's *Regimental Companion*, ii. 393-394.

Sixtieth, which was at once constituted into a rifle-battalion with a peculiar dress of green jacket, white waistcoat and blue pantaloons ; but though this introduced the thin end of the wedge into the British Army it did not affect soldiers of British nationality.[1]   Then came the campaign of the Helder, wherein a few companies of riflemen might more than once have turned the scale, especially during the advance of Moore's brigade upon Egmont op Zee ; but none were to hand, and for want of them England failed of success and very nearly lost the best officer in her Army.

At last, however, in January 1800, the Duke of York ordered a detachment of three officers and thirty-four men to be furnished by each of fifteen regiments of the Line[2] to Colonel Coote Manningham, for instruction in the use of the rifle and in the exercise of true light infantry.   Manningham had commanded several light companies under Grey in the West Indies, and was therefore well qualified for the work ; but the response to the Duke of York's order was not very cordial.   Six of the selected regiments seized the opportunity to send to him all their unserviceable men, and one in particular supplied no fewer than twenty-two out of thirty who were of this description. None the less these detachments were assembled in March at Horsham, from which they marched to Windsor Forest, there to be trained by Lieutenant-colonel William Stewart, an excellent officer of broad ideas.   It had never been intended that the men should

[1] *S.C.L.B.* 12th January ; *C.C.L.B.* 19th January 1798.

[2] The 2/1st, 21st, 23rd, 25th, 27th, 29th, 49th, 55th, 69th, 71st, 72nd, 79th, 85th, 92nd. Cope's *History of the Rifle Brigade*, pp. 1-2.   I may add that the first letters of the Adj.-gen. to Manningham mention only six of these regiments (*C.C.L.B.* 7th January, 8th February 1800), while Cope gives a list of fourteen on his first page and fifteen on his second.   It appears that the Duke of York consulted Cornwallis as to the formation of this corps, and that Cornwallis, while advising that all the men should be trained as light infantry, would have armed only one-tenth of them with rifles, quoting the experience of a Colonel of Hessian Jäger in America.   *Cornwallis Corres.* iii. 177.

be permanently kept together, the design being presently to send them back to their own battalions to diffuse knowledge of the rifle in the Army; for, according to the official view, it was impossible from the nature of the case that Manningham's corps should be a permanent one. However, at Stewart's request, the whole of it was embarked in July for the expedition to Ferrol, and was not broken up until some weeks later at Malta. What then happened to it is something of a mystery; but the corps appears to have been recreated in the course of the autumn with a new establishment of ten companies under its former officers, but with men chiefly drawn from the disembodied Irish Fencibles. The patterns of its clothing and accoutrements were settled in December, and on the 31st of March 1801 a letter of service was granted, apparently as an afterthought, for the formation of Manningham's Rifle Corps. Possibly there was some doubt even to the last whether the companies should be kept together or again dispersed to preach the gospel of the rifle in the Army; but the wiser counsel prevailed, and thus was born the regiment which still marches to the tune of Ninety-five, but is not less famous under its later name of the Rifle Brigade.[1]

The zeal for the multiplication of riflemen did not at once exhaust itself, for in September 1801 a rifle company was added to the Second Battalion of the Sixtieth; and in July it was decreed that all descriptions of riflemen should be dressed alike, without distinction except of buttons and facings.[2] The uniform consisted of a short green jacket and close-fitting pantaloons,

---

[1] *British Military Library*, ii. 564 *sq.* *S.C.L.B.*, 1st December 1800, 12th March 1801; *C.C.L.B.*, 29th September, 18th December 1800. Cope's *History of the Rifle Brigade*. The *B.M. Library* above quoted speaks of a letter of service of 25th August 1800. This, the date of the landing at Ferrol, was taken for the commissions of the officers, but I can find no record of the letter. The regiment received the number Ninety-five on 18th January 1803. *S.C.L.B. sub. dat.*

[2] *S.C.L.B.*, 24th September 1801; *C.C.L.B.*, 13th July 1802.

with a plain leather cap for the men and a light dragoon's helmet for the officers. The sergeants carried a whistle, which alone marked their difference from the privates. The officers wore a black shoulder-belt with silver ornaments and a whistle, besides the crimson sash which was worn round the waist by all who held the King's commission ; while a curved sword, together with heavy black lace on the jacket, helped to assimilate their dress to that of light dragoons. The weapon of the men was a rifle, called the Baker rifle, which though a clumsy weapon was reputed to be extremely accurate up to three hundred yards' range ; their side-arm was a sword which could be fixed as a bayonet. Cartridges were not used as a rule, but every man carried a powder-horn and bag of bullets to enable him to load his rifle with what was called "running ball," which was the method preferred for this particular arm. The buttons of the dress were dull ; all ornaments of bright metal were discarded ; and the barrel of the rifle was brown, so as to make the men as little conspicuous as possible. Finally, all movements were carried out by signal of bugle-horn, the calls for which had been lately revised ; and a treatise upon light troops by M. de Jarry was recommended for general guidance and instruction.

Manningham and Stewart needed little teaching, for they were men who could think for themselves. In the year 1801 the Standing Orders of the regiment were drawn up, containing novelties positively startling to the old school of martinets. Therein provision was made not only for bestowing on the soldiers medals for good conduct and for bravery in the field, but also for careful and systematic training in musketry, for classifying men according to their skill at the target, for distinction of the best as marksmen, for the formation of a regimental school with periodic examinations, for the delivery of lectures upon military subjects, and even for the encouragement of athletic exercises. It needed only the finishing touches of Moore in the camp at

Shorncliffe for the new Rifle Corps to begin life with a regimental system that would defy the wear of a century. It is no exaggeration to say that the foundation of the Rifle Brigade marks a new era in the history of the British infantry.

A few small details must be mentioned before the infantry is finally dismissed. Its clothing and equipment remained unaltered except for the abolition of lapels and the introduction of a felt or leathern cap, seemingly the forerunner of the chaco, in place of the cocked hat.[1] Officers also were required to wear when on duty a red and gold band round their hats, with a rosette of the same material, and a gorget tied with ribbons of the colour of the regimental facings.[2] The plumes of officers were also definitely appointed to be white for grenadier-companies, green for light-companies, and red and white for battalion-companies.[3] Hair powder was generally abolished in the Army in 1795, but the order required to be repeated before Colonels would obey it.[4] The queue, however, was still retained, except in the case of Grenadiers and Light Infantry, who were required to turn their hair up under their hats.[5] The drill, being new, remained unchanged; but inspecting officers had liberty to permit regiments to be drawn up in two instead of three ranks even for review.[6] The Duke of York raised the whole standard of manœuvre in the field by the orders which he issued in 1795 for the exercise of the troops in camp. Mondays and Fridays were given up to battalion-drill, Tuesdays and Saturdays to brigade-drill, Wednesdays to a field-day of all the troops, and

---

[1] *S.C.L.B.*, 28th January 1796, 11th December 1799. To judge from contemporary pictures the new cap, in some of its forms, greatly resembled a chimney-pot hat.

[2] *C.C.L.B.*, 3rd May 1796. Possibly the gold band passed away with the cocked hat.

[3] *Ibid.* 13th September 1797.

[4] *Ibid.* 19th July 1795, 8th September 1797.

[5] *Ibid.* 6th June 1799.

[6] *Ibid.* 24th September 1801.

Thursdays, as in the Navy, were a day of rest.[1] Regiments of Militia were also formed into brigades for the first time in 1797, no doubt with good results.[2] Discipline in general was greatly improved by the Duke's very proper severity towards officers who were remiss in joining their regiments or in the performance of their duty ; but there was still much room for improvement in this respect. As regards the men, flogging was as frequent as ever, though a soldier could generally commute a very heavy sentence by consenting to serve in the Sixtieth or in the East and West Indies ; and the instances of men who accepted this alternative are innumerable. Taking the general condition of the infantry, however, in 1802, there can be no doubt that it was immensely improved since 1793.

Having already spoken of Transport and Supply under the head of the Treasury, I pass now to the Medical Service. After the scandalous revelations of the hospitals in Holland in 1793 and 1794 some reform in this branch of the Army was imperative ; but for the better understanding of the subject, which is exceedingly obscure, a brief sketch must be given of the early constitution of the Medical Department. The Surgeon and his assistant were essentially regimental officers, being by origin servants of the Colonel according to the old regimental system. As such they purchased their situations and received an allowance, which had originally been levied by stoppage from the men's pay, but was later made good by the Captains from the funds of their companies. In the matter of medicines they were nominally subject to a royal warrant of 1747, whereby a certain individual was appointed Apothecary-general with the monopoly, for himself and his heirs, of providing drugs for the Army ; but in 1793 the surgeon received a sum proportioned to the strength of his corps on the understanding that he should furnish all necessary medicines.

[1] C.C.L.B., 16th May 1795.
[2] Ibid. 17th February 1797.

As to general administration, there was an Apothecary-general, and there had been a Physician-general and a Surgeon-general ever since the days of Charles the Second.   There had also been Inspectors of Hospitals since 1758, but their supervision appears to have been of the most perfunctory.   In 1794 a Medical Board was appointed to direct the Medical service of the Army, and in 1796[1] it was ordained that surgeons were to be regularly paid, that all their perquisites were to be abolished, that medicines and hospitals were to be paid for by Government, and that they themselves were to rank with captains when choosing quarters and to be entitled to a retiring allowance.   At the same time surgeons' mates were promoted to the dignity of commissioned officers.

In 1798, however, the Medical Board was abolished and its duties divided between the Physician-general, Surgeon-general, and Inspector of Hospitals, in so injudicious a fashion as to set these three departments fighting desperately for patronage and importance.   However, some compensation for this blunder was found in the new regulations that every physician must possess a medical diploma or degree, and that surgeons' mates were to pass a medical examination before receiving a commission.   But at the same time the new organisation was so imperfect that regimental surgeons, though their pay had been increased, were once more so far entrusted with their former powers that they became at once medical officers, contractors for supplies, and directors of expenditure, whereby they were exposed to temptations very difficult for a poor man to resist.   It is amusing to note that three years later the office of Ordnance set up a Medical Department of its own, since apparently its jealousy of the War Office forbade it to save the country the expense of forming two separate establishments.   For the rest the improved position of the doctors was assured by assigning to

[1] *S.C.L.B.*, 16th April 1796

them a uniform of plain scarlet in the Army at large, and of blue in the Light Dragoons. It was a pity that other difficulties could not have been as easily settled as this.[1]

Nevertheless the appalling losses in the West Indies did awake the authorities very seriously to the importance of preserving the health of the soldiers; and the result was a decided improvement in the condition of the four great military hospitals at Deal, Portsmouth, Plymouth, and Gosport, and of the York Hospital at Chelsea. It is interesting to remark that the Coldstream Guards and the Eighty-fifth were inoculated against smallpox "in the mode adopted by Dr. Jenner" in the course of 1799, and that the War Office did not grudge one hundred guineas to Jenner for his trouble.[2] Much thought was given also to the care of men in the tropics, and a table of very sound and sensible regulations was produced which, if faithfully observed, would have saved many lives. But the enforcement of these rules depended necessarily on the zeal not of doctors only, but of each and every officer; and this, owing to laziness and ignorance, was too rarely to be depended on. Even so elementary a principle as that the men should not, if possible, be exposed to the tropical sun, was often neglected; and it is probable that hundreds of men were sacrificed by being compelled to stand as guards, or for other useless purposes, in the full blaze of noon. Unpardonable though this was, the officers must not be too hardly judged. They have seldom been encouraged in the British service to think for themselves, and they may well have shrunk from the responsibility of breaking all English rules, and from the difficulty of adjusting military duty to strange climatic conditions without injury to discipline. To this day all young Englishmen need severe though

---

[1] *C.C.L.B.*, 20th September 1797, 21st July 1798; *Warrant Books*, 1st September 1801. *Autobiography of Sir J. M'Grigor*, pp. xvii.-xxi.

[2] *Ibid.* 15th and 22nd April 1799, 27th August 1800.

sympathetic restraint to prevent them from taking liberties with a tropical climate ; and in those days sanitary science was still in its infancy.

Finally I come to the department of the Chaplain-general. Hitherto chaplains, like surgeons, had been purely regimental officers, holding commissions from the King but being none the less appointed by the Colonels, who in the early days of the Army frequently made arrangements for dispensing the reverend gentlemen from their duty and putting their pay into their own pockets.[1] By royal warrant of 1796 regimental chaplains were abolished, and it was arranged that general chaplains, with pay of ten shillings a day, should be appointed for troops in foreign garrisons and in the field ; while the clergy in the neighbourhood of the barracks should perform divine service at home, receiving an allowance of twenty-five pounds a year. A retiring allowance of four shillings a day was offered to all regimental chaplains who chose to resign ; but it was made clear to them that if they remained in the Army they must be subject to a Chaplain-general, who was appointed to control them and their brethren. It is remarkable that the consideration accorded to the clergy by the Army under William the Third and Anne should have vanished so completely by the end of the eighteenth century. Auvergne, Story, and Hare, all of them chaplains, were the principal chroniclers of the campaigns between 1689 and 1714 ; but after their disappearance no such men seem to have come forward to take their place, though a Naval Chaplain on H.M.S. *Boyne* did indeed write the history of Grey's and Jervis's expedition to the West Indies. In my own researches I have found little or nothing to indicate that chaplains even existed in the Army ; and no man, except John Wesley, gave the slightest pastoral care to the soldier.[2] No doubt this was

[1] Walton, *History of the British Standing Army*, p. 760.
[2] For a brief but excellent account of Wesley's relations with British soldiers see Sir George Trevelyan's *American Revolution*, vol. ii. part ii. 296-304.

due to the torpor in which at that time the Church of England was sunk ; yet it is strange that in these ten years of war the name of not a single chaplain should ·have come down to us.   In no respect do modern days present a greater contrast to ancient than in the attitude of the Church towards the British soldier.

Altogether therefore the Army was on the road to amendment, for though its standards might not always be high they were none the less rising in every department.   The praise of this steady improvement belongs chiefly to the Duke of York ; but all his efforts would have been of little avail but for his strenuous pursuit of one principal object, the restoration of discipline among the officers.   And herein perhaps the most powerful influence of all was the Duke's own sense of justice. He made himself easily accessible to every officer in the Army ; and though there might well be some who nursed just grievances, there was not one who could complain that he had been turned away unheard by the Commander-in-chief.   Apart from all rules and regulations for correspondence and so forth, he forwarded his general scheme of keeping officers in subordination by certain distinctions of dress for General and Staff Officers [1]—a small matter which is mentioned only to show how thorough was his work in this matter ; for side by side with it he was working at a far greater project for the instruction of officers in their profession. This took shape in March 1799 in the opening of a school at High Wycombe by M. de Jarry, who having been a professor at the Military School of Berlin was well qualified to found such an institution.   The number of pupils was limited to thirty, each of whom was nominated by the Commander-in-chief, and was required to bring to his studies a certain knowledge of his profession, of French, and of geometry.   This school a few years later came to be known as the Staff College.

[1] *C.C.L.B.*, 3rd May 1796, 31st January 1799.

But the Duke in 1800 went a step further, and summoned a Board of Generals to advise as to the establishment of a second College for the education of aspirants to the military calling ; and thus came into being the Royal Military College, first opened in 1802 in a hired house at Great Marlow.   Its members were at first limited to one hundred gentlemen cadets, divided into three classes.   Of these thirty, being sons of officers who had perished on active service, were entitled to free education, board, and clothing ; twenty more, being sons of officers still in the service, were entitled to the like privilege for forty pounds a year ; and fifty more, sons of civilians, paid the full fee of ninety pounds a year.   Students were allowed to enter the College at thirteen and to remain there four years, after which, on passing a satisfactory examination, they received a commission.   Such was the origin of the institution now identified with the name of Sandhurst ; and its establishment signified very much, for it imperceptibly introduced education as a rival to hard cash for the key to entrance and advancement in the Army.   If the foundation of these two Colleges had been the only service done by the Duke for his country, he would have deserved well of the nation.

But he by no means confined his measures to the improvement of officers only.   From the time of his accession to command there are signs of a movement through the service towards a different treatment of the soldier, and towards the ruling of him by appeal to his higher nature and his self-respect as well as to his fears. I do not say that this was general in the Army any more than in the Navy, for the cat-o'-nine-tails was far too busy ; but at least it existed.   There is no military officer, so far as I know, who can be held up as an exact parallel to Collingwood, who was charged with the taming of all the most dangerous seamen at a most dangerous time, and accomplished it practically without the use of the lash—a marvellous achievement which is partially explained by the fact that, under his rules of discipline, officers were obliged to address the men with civility. Probably Charles Stuart and Abercromby were the soldiers who approached most nearly to him in this respect, Stuart being also the man who drew closest to Nelson in the adoration which he commanded from his men. One of the most noble features in our great naval commanders at that greatest period of our naval history was the anxious care with which they looked to the health of their men. St. Vincent, the iron disciplinarian; Nelson, the inspired and inspiring leader; Collingwood, the unselfish and patriotic gentleman, all alike were nearly as proud of an empty sick-bay as of a victory. Herein, it can happily be recorded, they found worthy rivals in the Army. Charles Grey, Ralph Abercromby, Charles Stuart, John Moore, and Thomas Maitland, stern disciplinarians one and all, possessed that peculiar thoughtfulness for the soldier's comfort which loses no opportunity of staving off from him avoidable hardship and privation. It is not by fair words or affable condescension, but by ever watchful attention to their health and their wants that the hearts of men are won by a commander in the field.[1] It is a reproach to us that the story of Ralph Abercromby and the soldier's blanket in Egypt is not as familiar to every schoolboy as that of Philip Sidney and the cup of water at Zutphen.

From such leaders as these regimental officers could not but take their example; and, to judge by a few small indications, the spirit of kindness and respect towards the men was nowhere stronger than at headquarters. Hitherto soldiers in the field had been treated in the War Office as mere ciphers. After an action a return of killed and wounded was indeed sent in, but it

---

[1] "His steady observance of discipline, his ever-watchful attention to the health and wants of his troops, the persevering and unconquerable spirit which marked his military career, the splendour of his actions in the field and the heroism of his death are worth the imitation of all who desire, like him, a life of honour and a death of glory."—*G.O. of the Duke of York on the death of Sir Ralph Abercromby.*

contained only the number, not the names, of the fallen. In 1799, however, four Colonels who had ventured to furnish so bald a statement were sharply rebuked by the Commander-in-chief for their neglect; and the names of the dead were required of them for the sake of the widows and orphans.[1]   Three months later an order was issued that all inquiries as to the death or existence of private soldiers and non-commissioned officers could be made free of charge ; and at about the same time the postage of all letters addressed to any men, then serving in Holland, below the rank of commissioned officer was reduced to one penny.[2]   In short it was recognised that soldiers were not machines but men, to whom their countrymen owed encouragement, sympathy, and help, alike for themselves and for those whom their death might leave destitute behind them. And the soldiers had established their claim to such recognition.   At least nine regiments of the Line and one of the Militia contributed regularly a voluntary subscription to the funds for prosecuting the war, and only ceased in 1799 when, in consequence of the imposition of the income-tax, the Ministers with many expressions of gratitude declined any longer to receive it.[3]   We have not yet seen the last of the benefits which the Duke of York was yet to confer upon the soldier, and which was to complete the good work which he had so well begun.   For the present it must suffice that in 1795 he took over a number of undisciplined and disorganised regiments, filled for the most part with the worst stamp of man and officer, and that in less than seven years he converted these unpromising elements into an Army.

[1] *C.C.L.B.*, 1st March 1799.
[2] James, *Regimental Companion*, ii. 386.
[3] Circular to 1st L.G., 1st D.G., 14th L.D., 15th, 16th, 24th, 26th, 33rd Foot, and Leicester Militia. *C.C.L.B.*, 20th August 1799.

APPENDIX A

TABLE OF REGULAR REGIMENTS RAISED, 1793-1802

Note.—The numbers in brackets are those by which the regiments were designated upon formation. The regiments marked ? appear never to have been formed. Those marked R were recruiting regiments, formed only to be drafted into existing regiments.

CAVALRY

	Date
Gardner's Light Dragoons . . .	20th January 1793
Beaumont's Light Dragoons (21st) . .	10th March 1794
Fielding's Light Dragoons (22nd) . .	10th ,, ,,
Fullarton's Light Dragoons (23rd) . .	10th ,, ,,
Gwyn's Light Dragoons (25th) . . .	10th ,, ,,
Loftus's Light Dragoons (24th) . . .	20th ,, ,,
Manners's Light Dragoons (26th) . .	30th ,, 1795
Blathwayt's Light Dragoons (27th) . .	30th ,, ,,
Lawrie's Light Dragoons (28th) . .	30th ,, ,,
Heathfield's Light Dragoons (29th) . .	30th ,, ,,
Carden's[1] Light Dragoons (30th) . .	27th June ,,
St. Leger's Light Dragoons (31st) . .	27th ,, ,,
Blake's Light Dragoons (32nd) . .	27th ,, ,,
Blackwood's Light Dragoons (33rd) . .	27th ,, ,,

FOOT

	Date
SEVENTY-EIGHTH Highlanders (Humberstone Mackenzie's)	7th March 1793
SEVENTY-NINTH (Alan Cameron's) . .	17th August 1793
EIGHTIETH (Lord Paget's) . . .	12th September 1793
EIGHTY-SEVENTH (Doyle's) . . .	18th ,, ,,
EIGHTY-FIRST (Bertie's) . . .	23rd ,, ,,
EIGHTY-EIGHTH (De Burgh's) . .	25th ,, ,,
Scots Brigade (94th) Cunningham's, Halkett's, Ferrier's . . .	26th ,, ,,
EIGHTY-SECOND (Leigh's) . . .	27th ,, ,,

[1] These four regiments (30th to 33rd) were drafted out and reduced 26th February 1796.

	Date
John Murray's (96th)	1st November 1793
EIGHTY-FOURTH (Bernard's) . . .	2nd ,, ,,
Fletcher Campbell's (91st) . . .	12th ,, ,,
EIGHTY-SIXTH (Cuyler's)	12th ,, ,,
Edmeston's (95th)	12th ,, ,,
Balfour's (93rd)	12th ,, ,,
EIGHTY-FIFTH (Nugent's) . . .	18th ,, ,,
EIGHTY-THIRD (Fitch's) . . .	18th December ,,
Trench's (102nd)	18th ,, ,,
Argyll's ?	10th February 1794
NINETIETH (Thomas Graham's) . .	10th ,, ,,
Stuart Douglas's ?	10th ,, ,,
NINETY-FIRST (98th), Duncan Campbell's or Breadalbane's	10th ,, ,,
EIGHTY-NINTH (Crosbie's)	? ,,
NINETY-SECOND (100th), Marquis of Huntly's	10th ,, ,,
James Grant's (97th) . . .	10th ,, ,,
2nd Batt. SEVENTY-EIGHTH . . .	10th ,, ,,
Fullarton's (101st)	10th March ,,
2nd Batts. to EIGHTY-FIRST, EIGHTY-SECOND, and NINETIETH	12th ,, ,,
L'Hoste's (104th), raised by town of Manchester	1st April ,,
Alex. Hay's (109th), raised by city of Aberdeen	1st ,, ,,
Bulwer's (106th), raised by city of Norwich	1st ,, ,,
Somerset's (103rd), raised by city of Bristol	1st ,, ,,
Forbes's (105th) (Borough of Leeds) . .	18th ,, ,,
Roberts's (11th) (Town of Birmingham) .	18th ,, ,,
Macdonnell's (113th)	18th ,, ,,
Pigot's (130th)	18th ,, ,,
Prince William's (115th)	2nd May ,,
2nd Batt. EIGHTY-FOURTH . . .	29th July ,,
Sutherland's (City of Lincoln) ? . .	22nd August ,,
St. John's (117th)	22nd ,, ,,
Simon Fraser's (133rd) . . .	22nd ,, ,,
Williams's (120th)	27th ,, ,,
D. J. Cameron's (Loyal Sheffield) .	27th ,, ,,
Podmore's (City of Chester) . .	28th ,, ,,
Pringle's (Jedburgh Burghs) . .	28th ,, ,,
Stribling's (City of Exeter) ? . .	28th ,, ,,
Montgomerie's (Glasgow) . . .	28th ,, ,,
Treen's (Stamford) (125th) . .	28th ,, ,,
Troughton (Gentlemen of Coventry) (129th)	28th ,, ,,
D. Cameron's (Wakefield) (132nd) .	11th September ,,
Howe's	25th ,, ,,

The following twenty-two regiments were also raised in 1794, though the dates of the letters of service are not recorded. The dates here given are from the Army List :—

	Date	
Stratford's (122nd)	25th July	1794
Lewis's (134th)	2nd November	„
Hewitt's (92nd)	1st October	„
Hutchinson's (94th)	1st „	„
A. Campbell's (116th) . . .	10th February	„
Donoughmore's (112th) . . .	21st July	„
Macnamara's (121st) . . .	20th June	„
Leatherband's (123rd) . . .	22nd August	„
Beresford's (124th)	11th „	„
Trigge's (99th)	10th February	„
Keating's (107th) . . .	8th April	„
Ward's	7th August	„
Llandaff's (114th) . . .	9th April	„
Granard's (108th) . . .	17th May	„
O'Donnell's (110th) . . .	6th June	„
Talbot's (118th) . . .	22nd July	„
Rochford's (119th) . . .	29th May	„
Mountnorris's (126th) . . .	26th April	„
Cradock's (127th) . . .	16th „	„
Ogle's (128th)	4th October	„
Conningham's	25th August	„
C. Macdonnell's	27th November	„
Blair's (Liverpool)	20th February	1795
2nd Batt. EIGHTY-THIRD . .	16th March	„
2nd Batt. SEVENTH . . .	8th April	„
Robert Wood's. R . . .	8th May	„
Pennington's (131st) . . .	23rd June	„
Macdonald's	23rd July	„
Lewis's Garrison Battalion . .	1st September	„
Grant's Highlanders. R . . .	33rd „	„
Vere Hunt's (135th). R . .	4th February	1796
Steele's. R	12th „	„
French's. R	9th March	„
Plunkett's. R	2nd May	„
Macdonald's. R . . .	6th „	„
James Campbell's. R . .	12th „	„
Macdonnell's. R . . .	28th „	„
Shaw's. R	11th June	„
O'Connor's. R . . .	31st August	„
James Murray's. R . .	5th October	„
Hauger's. R . . .	6th „	„
Bradshaw's. R . . .	17th May	1797
5th Batt. of SIXTIETH . . .	12th January	1798

	Date	
Bissett's. R	16th March	1798
Ogle's. R	28th April	,,
Armstrong's. R	10th July	,,
Kingstone's. R	2nd August	,,
Nugent's. R.	17th October	,,
NINETY-THIRD HIGHLANDERS (Wemyss's) .	16th April	1799
6th Batt. of SIXTIETH	30th July	,,
RIFLE BRIGADE (95th, Manningham's) .	21st February	1800
Nugent's. R.	1st July	,,

CORPS FOR COLONIAL GARRISONS

Skinner's Fencibles (Newfoundland). .	29th April 1795
Fraser's two Companies for Goree . .	27th August 1800

TRANSPORT AND ARTIFICERS' CORPS

Poole's Corps of Waggoners . . .	7th March 1794
Hamilton's Corps of Waggoners . .	12th August and 21st September 1799
Corps of Pioneers (Staff Corps) . .	31st July 1799, 14th January 1800

ARTILLERY DRIVERS

Corps of Captains-commissaries and Drivers (35 divisions)	9th September 1794
Corps of Gunner Drivers (7 companies, 3180 men, 5676 horses) . . .	1st ,, 1801

APPENDIX B

PAY OF THE ARMY

THE proclamation for raising the pay of the Army is dated 25th May 1797, and runs to the following effect :—

Over and above all other allowances the private has hitherto received 6d. a day pay, and lately 2¼d. more in commutation of certain abolished allowances. From this day his pay shall be 1s. daily, from which he is to pay the extra price of bread and meat, amounting to 1¾d. a day, so that the net increase is 2d. a day.

From this 1s. a day a sum not exceeding 4s. a week shall be applied to his messing ; a sum not exceeding 1s. 6d. a week shall be stopped for necessaries, and the remainder, 1s. 6d. a week, shall be paid to the soldier subject to the usual deduction for washing and articles for cleaning his appointments.

Thus, pay of a private

	Infantry.	Dragoons.
	7s. 0d. a week	8s. 9d. a week
Stoppages as above	5s. 6d. ,,	7s. 1½d. ,,
Remains	1s. 6d. a week	1s. 7½d. a week

In camp he shall receive 5¼d. per week, being the difference between bread and beer allowance in camp and in quarters.

If meat exceed 6d. per lb. and bread 1½d. per lb., such extra price shall be paid by the public to the amount of ¾ lb. of meat and 1 lb. of bread daily.

The daily pay of the foot and invalids now stands as follows [1] :—

	Foot.	Invalids.
Private	1s. 0d.	0s. 11½d.
Drummer	1s. 1¾d.	1s. 1¼d.
Corporal	1s. 2¼d.	1s. 1¾d.
Sergeant	1s. 6¾d.	1s. 6¼d.

[The pay of subalterns of cavalry was augmented by an order of 27th June 1797 to the following effect.]

The pay of subalterns of cavalry will in future be issued in full, without delay for arrears, and without deduction for poundage, hospital, and agency. Also an allowance of 1s. a day additional shall be made to them, which, however, shall bring with it no increase of half-pay.[2]

[1] *C.C.L.B.*, 25th May 1797.   [2] *S.C.L.B.*, 27th June 1797.

PAY OF THE ARMY

DAILY RATES OF THE SUBSISTENCE OR PAY AND ALLOWANCE OF THE OFFICERS AND MEN OF THE CAVALRY

LIFE GUARDS

	Subsistence per diem.
Colonel	£1 7 0
Lieut.-colonel	1 3 3
Major	0 19 6
Second Major	0 19 6
Captain	0 12 0
Lieutenant	0 8 3
Lieutenant and Adjutant	0 8 3
Cornet	0 7 3
Surgeon	0 9 0
Veterinary Surgeon	0 8 0
Quartermaster	0 4 9
Corporal	0 3 9¼
Trumpeter	0 3 9
Kettle Drummer	0 3 9
Private	0 3 2¼

N.B.—The above rates of pay for the corporals and privates include in each case 1s. 3d. a day for the subsistence of a horse. Marshal for both regiments, £25 per annum.

ROYAL REGIMENT OF HORSE GUARDS

	Subsistence per diem.
Colonel, as Colonel[1]	£2 7 0
First Lieut.-colonel, as Lieut.-colonel	
Lieut.-colonel	1 2 6
Second Lieut.-colonel	1 2 6
First Major	1 1 6
Second Major	1 1 6
Captain	0 16 6
Lieutenant	0 11 6
Cornet	0 11 0
Adjutant	0 10 0
Surgeon	0 9 0
Assistant Surgeon	0 8 6
Veterinary Surgeon	0 8 0
Quartermaster	0 6 6
Corporal	0 3 0¼
Trumpeter	0 2 5¼
Kettle Drummer	0 3 0¼
Private	0 2 5¼

N.B.—The above rates of pay for the non-commissioned officers and privates include in each case 9d. a day for the subsistence of a horse.

DRAGOON GUARDS AND DRAGOONS.[2]

	Pay and allowance per diem.
Colonel	£1 12 10
Lieut.-colonel	1 3 0
Major	0 19 3
Captain	0 14 7
Lieutenant	0 9 0
Cornet	0 8 0
Paymaster	0 15 0
Adjutant	0 10 0
Surgeon	0 11 4
Assistant Surgeon[3]	0 7 6
Veterinary Surgeon	0 8 0
Paymaster-sergeant	0 2 11
Sergeant	0 2 11
Corporal	0 2 4⅜
Trumpeter	0 2 4
Private	0 2 0

[1] This includes eight Warrant Men at 2s. per diem each.

[2] In addition to the rate of pay above specified for Dragoon Guards and Dragoons, the Colonel or Commandant of a Corps has an allowance for each Troop of which the same may consist, of 1s. 2d. a day in lieu of the pay of one Warrant Man, and 1s. 6d. a day in lieu of the pay of one Hautbois.

[3] By His Majesty's Warrant of 22nd May 1804, the Assistant Surgeon is allowed 1s. per diem for a horse in addition to the above pay.

DAILY RATES OF THE SUBSISTENCE OR PAY AND ALLOWANCE OF THE OFFICERS AND MEN OF THE INFANTRY

FOOT GUARDS.

	Subsistence per diem.		
	£	s.	d.
Colonel[1]	£1	10	6
Lieut.-colonel	1	1	6
Major	0	18	6
Captain	0	12	6
Lieutenant	0	6	0
Ensign	0	4	6
Adjutant	0	10	0
Quartermaster. Pay, 4s. 8d., allowance 1s.	0	5	8
Battalion Surgeon	0	10	0
Assistant Surgeon	0	7	6
Solicitor	0	3	0
Sergeant	0	1	10¾
Corporal	0	1	4¾
Drum-major	0	1	0
Drummer	0	1	2¼
Deputy-marshal	0	0	9
Hautbois	0	1	6
Private	0	1	1

INFANTRY OF THE LINE AND MILITIA.[2]

	Pay and allowance per diem.		
	£	s.	d.
Colonel	£1	2	6
Lieut.-colonel	0	15	11
Major	0	14	1
Captain	0	9	5
Lieutenant, with additional allowance	0	5	8
Second Lieutenant or Ensign, with additional allowance	0	4	8
Paymaster	0	15	0
Adjutant	0	8	0
Quartermaster, with additional allowance	0	5	8
Surgeon of the Line and Militia	0	9	5
Assistant Surgeon	0	7	6
Surgeon's Mate in Militia[3]	0	4	6
Sergeant-major or Quartermaster-sergeant	0	2	0¾
Paymaster-sergeant	0	1	6¾
Sergeant	0	1	6¾
Corporal	0	1	2¼
Drummer	0	1	1¾
Fifer	0	1	1¾
Private	0	1	0

INDEPENDENT COMPANIES OF INVALIDS.

	Pay and allowance per diem.		
	£	s.	d.
Captain	£0	9	5
Lieutenant	0	5	8
Ensign	0	4	8
Sergeant	0	1	6¼
Corporal	0	1	1¾
Drummer	0	1	1¼
Private	0	0	11¼

[1] In addition to the above the Colonel receives with his subsistence an allowance of the pay of one Warrant Man per company, viz. in the 1st Foot Guards 32 Warrant Men at 6s. 7d. each per day, and in the 2nd and 3rd Foot Guards for 20 Warrant Men at the same rate.

[2] In addition to the rate of pay above specified for Infantry of the Line and Militia, the Colonel or Commandant of a Corps has an allowance for each company of which the same may consist, of 6d. a day in lieu of the pay of a Warrant Man. Each Lieutenant and Ensign in the Militia, not holding another Commission, has an allowance of 1s. a day in addition to the above-mentioned rate of pay. In the Militia, where the Paymaster must necessarily hold a Commission in the Corps, his pay is made up to 15s. a day, and an allowance of 1s. 6¾d. a day is made for the Paymaster's Clerk, who is not borne in addition to the numbers of Corps.

[3] By a regulation dated 27th June 1803, Surgeon's Mates of the Militia are to receive the same pay as Assistant Surgeons of the Line; but if they hold another Commission they receive 3s. 6d. with the pay, if Lieutenant, of 4s. 8d., if an Ensign, of 3s. 8d.

APPENDIX C

BRITISH AND IRISH MILITARY ESTABLISHMENTS, 1793-1802

(From the Estimates in the Journals of the British and Irish
Houses of Commons.)

British Establishment.	1793.	1794.	1795.	1796.	1797.
Home	17,344	60,244	119,380	49,219	60,765
Plantations	18,194	41,490	40,261	82,182	64,227
India .	10,700	10,700	10,700	10,718	12,390
Artillery .	3,730	6,415	7,084	7,664	7,664
Embodied Militia (and Fencibles)	17,602	42,803	62,791	65,662	66,096
Foreign troops .	...	33,754	35,820	20,288	12,000
Total .	67,570	195,406	276,036	235,733	223,000
Irish Establishment.					
Army (including Regulars and Fencibles)	12,000 [1]	12,000	20,246	19,012	37,667
Militia .	17,500 ?	17,500	21,369	22,698	22,698 [2]
Total .	29,500	29,500	41,615	41,710	60,365
Total British and Irish Establishments	97,070	124,906	317,651	277,443	283,365

[1] The Irish Establishment, as fixed by Act of Parliament, was 15,000 men, but of these 3000 were quartered abroad, and are here included in the British Establishment, though their cost was borne by the Irish Exchequer.

[2] A vote was taken also for Yeomanry, both horse and foot.

APPENDIX C—*Continued*

British Establishment.	1798.	1799.	1800.	1801.	1802.
Home . . .	48,609	52,051	80,275	75,619	70,299
Plantations . .	34,320	31,445	41,719	72,829	25,494
India . . .	22,174	24,972	23,752	26,219	26,219
Artillery . .	7,664	7,358	9,126	9,500	10,296
Embodied Militia and Fencibles	62,202	134,786	56,522	104,619	...
Embodied Militia and additional	75,000	...	...	...	...
Foreign troops . .	4,807	4,323	14,754	...	...
Total . .	254,776	257,137	226,148	288,786	132,308 [1]
Irish Establishment.				Merged in the British Estab- lishment upon the Union.	
Army . . .	39,620	32,268	45,831		
Militia . . .	26,634	26,890	27,112		
(Yeomanry) .	(37,539)	...	...		
Total . .	103,793	59,158	72,943		
Total British and Irish Establishments	291,030	316,295	299,091	288,786	132,308

[1] Peace estimates.

APPENDIX D

EFFECTIVE STRENGTH OF THE REGULAR ARMY (EXCLUSIVE OF ARTILLERY), 1793-1801, WITH THE NUMBER OF RECRUITS RAISED IN EACH YEAR

Year.	Number of Recruits raised.	Cavalry.	Foot Guards.	Infantry.	Total.
1793	17,033	4,681	2,885	31,379	38,945
1794	38,563	14,527	6,103	64,467	85,097
1795	40,463	28,810	6,081	94,371	124,262
1796	16,336	19,899	5,390	86,707	111,996
1797	16,096	21,601	5,480	77,781	104,862
1798	21,457	23,236	5,797	73,530	102,563
1799	41,316	26,135	8,307	80,810	115,252
1800	17,829	29,583	7,927	103,288	140,798
1801	No return	23,178	8,734	117,953	149,865

Note.—The numbers include foreign troops, but privates and corporals only of all regiments. To arrive at the full strength, including sergeants and commissioned officers, add ⅛.

APPENDIX E

List of Fencible Regiments for the Formation of which Letters of Service were Issued, 1793-1802

CAVALRY

Date.	No. of Troops.	Colonel or Commander.	Description.
1794			
March 14	6	J. C. Villiers	First Regiment
„ „	6	Sir Watkin Wynn	Ancient British
„ „	6	Tho. Peter Legh	Lancashire
„ 25	6	G. N. Edwards	Rutland
„ 31	1	Sir G. Thomas	Sussex
„ „	2	Cholmely Dering	New Romney (Duke of York's Own)
„ „	1	R. J. Adeane	Cambridgeshire
„ „	6	St. Leger	? Never formed
„ „	6	Earl of Poulett	Somersetshire
„ „	6	Montague Burgoyne	Loyal Essex
April 4	4	Lord Falmouth	Cornwall (increased to 6 troops, 14th April 1795)
„ „	2	Lord Ancrum	Midlothian
„ 7	2	Duke of Buccleuch	? Amalgamated with Ancrum's
„ 10	6	Hon. W. A. Harbord	Norfolk
„ 12	2	Sir Alex. Don	Berwickshire (increased to 4 troops, 17th April 1795)
„ 19	4	Earl of Darlington	Princess of Wales's
„ 30	6	Lord Onslow	Surrey
„ „	6	Jenkinson (Lord Hawkesbury)	Cinque Ports
„ „	6	Charles Rooke	Windsor Foresters
May 1	2	T. C. Everitt	Hampshire
„ 12	2	Sir J. Scott	Roxburgh and Selkirk (increased to 4 troops, 21st April 1795)

941

CAVALRY—*continued*

Date.	No. of Troops.	Colonel or Commander.	Description.
1794 May 12	2	Dunlop	Ayr (increased to 6 troops, 12th Jan. 1796)
,, ,,	2	Maxwell	Dumfries (increased to 4 troops, 20th June 1794)
,, ,,	1	C. Hamilton	Dumbarton (increased to 2 troops, 20th June 1794 ; amalgamated with Lanark)
,, ,,	2	John Anstruther Thompson	Fife (increased to 4 troops, 3rd August 1795)
,, ,,	2	J. Hamilton	East and West Lothian
,, ,,	2	W. Hamilton	Lanark (increased to 4 troops, 7th July 1794 ; amalgamated with Dumbarton)
,, ,,	1	Sir A. Levingston	Linlithgow
,, ,,	2	Sir J. Scott	Roxburgh
,, ,,	3	Charles Moray	Perth (increased to 6 troops, 28th May 1795)
,, ,,	1	H. Davis	Pembrokeshire (increased to 3 troops, 17th April 1795)
,, ,,	2	Hon. T. Parker	Oxfordshire
,, 20	6	Earl of Warwick	Warwickshire
1795 May 1	4	Andrew M'Dowall	Princess Royal's Own

The Regiments that survived until 1799 were :—

Ayr	Lothian Mid
Berwickshire	Norfolk
Ancient British	Oxfordshire
Cambridgeshire	Pembrokeshire
Cinque Ports	Perthshire
Cornwall	Princess of Wales's
Dumfriesshire	Princess Royal's Own
Loyal Essex	New Romney
Fifeshire	Roxburgh and Selkirk
First Regiment	Rutland
Hampshire	Somersetshire
Lanark and Dumbarton	Surrey, Sussex
Lancashire	Warwickshire
Lothian (E. and W.)	Windsor Foresters

Irish Fencible Cavalry—

Lord Roden's, 18th July 1795 | Lord Stentworth's, 18th July 1795

INFANTRY

Date.	No. of Coys.	Colonel or Commander.	Description.
1793 Feb. 20	3	Duke of Athol *	Royal Manx
March 2	8	Earl of Breadalbane	Breadalbane (1st Batt.)
„ „	8	Marquis of Lorne	Argyllshire
„ „	8	Earl of Eglinton	Lowland (West)
„ „	8	Earl of Hopetoun	Southern
„ „	8	Earl Gower (William Wemyss)	Sutherland
„ „	8	Sir James Grant	Strathspey
„ „	8	Duke of Gordon	Northern
„ 8	8	Earl of Breadalbane	Breadalbane (2nd Batt.)
April 20	3	Thomas Balfour	Orkney
1794 March 7	8	Thomas Sinclair *	Rothesay and Caithness (1st Batt.)
August 14	10	Alex. M'Donnell *	Glengarry
„ „	10	Colin Campbell *	Dumbartonshire
Sept. 27	2	John Fraser	Angus Volunteers
Oct. 16	10	Lord Grey de Wilton*	Royal Lancashire Volunteers
„ 20	10	James Durham *	Fifeshire
„ „	10	Archibald Douglas *	Angusshire
„ „	10	William Robertson	Perthshire
„ „	10	James Leith *	Princess of Wales (Aberdeen Highlanders)
„ „	10	H. M. Clavering *	Argyllshire (2nd Batt.)
„ „	10	M. H. Baillie *	Reay
„ „	10	Lieut.-Col. Morison	? Never formed
„ „	10	John Manners Ker *	Northampton
„ „	10	J. E. Urquhart *	Loyal Essex
„ „	10	James O'Connor *	Loyal Nottingham
;, „	10	Sir Robert Stewart	Loyal British
„ „	10	John Robinson *	Suffolk
„ „	10	Alex. Mall *	? Robert Anstruther's (Loyal Tay)
„ „	10	W. F. Forster *	Loyal Somerset
„ „	10	Hon. G. A. C. Stapylton *	York
Nov. 15	10	Robert Hall *	Devon and Cornwall
„ „	10	Thomas Balfour *	Lowland North
„ „	10	Sir Ben. Dunbar	Caithness Legion
„ „	10	David Hunter	? Never formed
„ „	?	Major Parkyns *	Prince of Wales's Leicester
„ „		Handcock	Loyal Irish
„ 17		C. Courtenay *	Cheshire

* The Regiments marked thus endured until 1801.

INFANTRY—*continued*

Date.	No. of Coys.	Colonel or Commander.	Description.
1794 Nov. 19	10	Sinclair	Rothesay and Caithness (2nd Batt.)
„ 20	2	Mackenzie	Ross-shire
„ 21		John Baillie *	Loyal Inverness
„ 28		Earl of Elgin *	Lord Elgin's
„ 29	2	James Fraser *	Fraser Regiment
Dec. 1	?	Robert Wood	? A false entry, Wood having raised a regular regiment
„ 9		Earl of Breadalbane *	Breadalbane (3rd Batt.)
„ 15	10	Handcock	Loyal Irish
1795 Feb. 26	10	Barrington Price *	Loyal Durham
„ 28	10	Francis Blake *	Northumberland
April 7	10	Duke of Athol *	Royal Manx (2nd Batt.)
„ 25	10	Skinner *	Newfoundland
1796 April 19	1	Gudgeon *	Scilly
1798 Feb. 8	2	Malcolmson	Shetland
May 29	10	Lord Macdonald *	None
June 15	10	Cameron *	Lochaber
„ „	10	Macleod *	Princess Charlotte of Wales's (Loyal Macleod)
„ „	10	Dunbar	? Never formed
„ „	10	Sir W. Johnstone *	Prince of Wales's Own
„ „	10	Arch. M'Neill *	3rd Argyll
„ „	10	Sir Vere Hunt	Loyal Limerick
July 20	10	Dunlop	? Never formed
„ 26	10	Hay *	Duke of York's Own Banffshire
„ 27	10	Sir E. Leslie *	Loyal Tarbert
„ 31	10	Alex. M'Grigor	? Never formed
Aug. 8	10	Louis Mackenzie *	Ross and Cromarty
„ „	10	Edwards *	Cambrian Rangers
„ 10	10	Tyndale	? Never formed
Sept. 21	10	M'Gregor Murray *	Clanalpine
Nov. 26	10	Pollen	None
Dec. 1	10	James Kann	? Never formed
1799 June 4	10	T. J. Fitzgerald *	Ancient Irish

* The Regiments marked thus endured until 1801.

INDEX

74 ; agrees to give British protection
to St. Domingo, 79 ; sends orders to
Barbadoes for the capture of Tobago,
79 ; commits himself to the protection of the French West Indies, 79 ;
sends emissary to Jamaica, 82 ; his
plans for future campaign in the
Mediterranean, 1794, 117 ; appointed first Secretary for War,
208 ; the creation of the office an
administrative failure, 875 ; his conduct of the campaigns in the Netherlands, 113, 125-126, 141, 145-146,
149-150, 301-303 ; his conduct of the
operations at Toulon, 141, 168, 175-
178 ; his conduct of the war in the
Leeward West Indies, 331, 343, 347,
469, 472, 475, 550-551 ; Windward
West Indies, 351, 367-368, 375-378,
426-427, 430-433, 451-452, 459,
477-482, 537, 543-544 ; against the
Dutch Colonies, 393, 401-405, 507 ;
raids on the French coast, 153-156,
412 sq., 416-423, 775-779 ; raids on
the Dutch coast, 520, 587 ; his
design for an expedition to South
America, 527 ; his conduct of the
war in the Mediterranean, 604-606,
620-621, 775-780, 782, 786, 788,
795-796, 798 ; his conduct of the expedition to North Holland, 645-650,
708 ; his conduct of the war in the
East Indies, 720 ; his conduct of the
expedition to Egypt, 800-807, 809,
845-847, 865 ; his measures for recruiting the army, 211-215, 407,
522, 639-642

Dundas, Ralph, General, 107

Dundas, Thomas, General, 354, 368 ;
his service in the West Indies, 352,
354-359, 364-367 ; his death, 367

Dunkirk, to be claimed as Great Britain's
indemnity for war, 85 ; siege of, 102,
103, 112, 118, 120, 122, 124-127,
129, 131, 132 ; cost to the allies of
the siege of, 132

Dutch Netherlands, or United Provinces,
England's treaty obligations to, 56 ;
apathy of the people in national
defence, 64 ; Dumouriez's invasion
of, 62-65 ; British troops sent for
protection of, 65 ; expulsion of the
French forces, 69 ; the army of,
95 ; misbehaviour of its troops in
1794, 308, 310, 313 ; the provinces
occupied by the French, 323 ; the
Stadtholder driven to take refuge
in England, 387 ; Dutch Republic
formed in alliance with France, 391 ;
British attacks on the Dutch

Colonies, 394-404 ; effort of the
Dutch to recapture the Cape of Good
Hope, 506 sq. ; British raids on the
Dutch coast, 520 ; Dutch expedition
for the invasion of Ireland, 569 ;
persecution of the Dutch Republic
by Bonaparte, 581 ; British expedition to North Holland, 1799, 641
sq.

Duval, Mons., 331

Dyle (river), 287-288

East Indies, the capture of Pondicherry,
402 ; the first menace of trouble in,
605 ; the conquest of Mysore, 711-
745 ; pacification of Southern India,
746-748 ; dangers from French
officers in, 714-715

Eden, Sir Morton, British Ambassador at
Vienna, 87, 523 ; suggests that
Austria should be bribed to retain
Belgium, 84 ; completely deceived
by Thugut, 137

Eenigenburg, 663

Egmont-aan-Zee, 691-692 ; battle of, 683
sq.

Egmont Binnen, 695

Egypt, Bonaparte's expedition to, 582-585,
607, 637-638 ; British expedition to,
800-863

Einhoven, 304

El Aft (Egypt), 850

El Arish, Convention of, 774, 802

Elba, captured by the British, 510-512

El Hamed, 851

Elliot, Sir Gilbert (afterwards Earl of
Minto), sent Commissioner to
Toulon, 168 ; at Corsica, 180-181,
188, 199, 575

Elphinstone, Captain (R.N., later Admiral Lord Keith), his service at
Toulon, 158 ; his service in the
expedition to the Cape, 394-402 ;
compels the Dutch fleet in Saldanha
Bay to surrender, 507-509 ; his
service in the Mediterranean, 773,
780, 784-786 ; his difference with
Abercromby at Cadiz, 793-794 ; in
the Egyptian expedition, 817

Emigrants, French, at Coblentz, 28, 31 ;
responsible for Brunswick's mani-
festo, 45-46 ; Emigrant regiments in
the Netherlands campaign, 311,
322 ; Emigrant regiments in West
Indies, 341-342

Emmerick, 309

Erskine, General Sir James, his difference
with Nelson, 634-635

Essen, General (Russian), 675, 677, 683,
690, 691, 694, 695

between Great Britain and, 116 ; compelled to neutrality by Napoleon, 506 ; Austria seeks alliance with (1798), 582, 610 ; Nelson's return to Naples after the battle of the Nile, 610 ; the King and Queen of Naples and Lady Hamilton, 614 ; the King takes the offensive by Nelson's order, 615 ; conquest of the country by the French, and conversion into Parthenopean Republic, 615 ; recovery of the Neapolitan dominions by Nelson and Cardinal Ruffo, 631

Napoleon Bonaparte, a spectator of the attack on the Tuileries, 40 ; appointed by Carnot to take command of the artillery at Toulon, 162, 163 ; his plan of attack, 167 ; saved from ruin by Carnot, 203 ; the 13th of Vendémiaire, 501 ; sent to Italy by Carnot, 504 ; Sardinia delivered into the hands of the Republic, 505 ; Lodi, 505 ; his supremacy in Italy, 505 ; presses the siege of Mantua, 506 ; organises a body of Corsican refugees at Leghorn, 509 ; Lonato and Castiglione, 510 ; Bassano, 511 ; Caldiero and Arcola, 523 ; Rivoli, 526 ; he advances into Austria, 533 ; concludes the Treaty of Leoben, 533 ; conditions of Treaty, 534 ; seizes Corfu, 534 ; his aggression on all sides, 581, 582 ; his Egyptian expedition, 582-585, 607-608, 637-638 ; his failure at Acre, 637 ; he lands in France, 636, 638 ; he becomes First Consul after the 18th Brumaire, 769 ; his great political sagacity, 770, 771 ; his pacific overtures, 770 ; his Italian campaign of 1800, 783, 785 ; his renewed overtures to the Emperor Francis, 788 ; his diplomatic activity after Marengo, 806, 848 ; his anxiety to have his army in Egypt, 812-813 ; he alienates the Czar from England, 868 ; his schemes upset in the Iberian Peninsula 868 ; Peace of Amiens, 869-870

National or Constituent Assembly of France and the Army, 16, 17, 22, 32, 39, 40, 75

National Guard of France, 13-15, 18, 34-36 ; its uniform, 15 ; uniform of, adopted for the whole Army, 127

Navy, the British, its demands upon the Army, 82, 116 n., 277 ; its perfect harmony with the Army under Jervis, 383 ; its quarrels with the Army under Hood, 195-196 ; its devotion saves the Army at Isle d'Yeu, 421 ; the mutinies at Spithead and the Nore, 529, 530 ; its outcry against the Army after Ferrol, 791-792 ; Nelson's criticisms of the Army, 797 ; and see Duckworth, Hood, Jervis, Nelson

Necker, Mons., 13

Neerwinden, battle of, 68

Nelson, Captain and Admiral Horatio, his service in Corsica, 189 n., 192-193, 197 ; his chase of Bonaparte, 1798, 607 ; battle of the Nile, 607 ; his return to Naples, 608, 611 ; his anxiety to follow up his successes, 614 ; escorts the Court of Naples to Palermo, 615 ; begs Stuart to send a battalion to Sicily, 623 ; his success in the recovery of the Neapolitan dominions, 631 ; his jealousy of the Russians in the Mediterranean, 634 ; his extravagant scheme for recovery of the Roman States, 634 ; he leaves Naples for Vienna, 786 ; his harsh strictures on British generals, 797-798 ; his victory at Copenhagen, 866

Nice invaded by the French, 1792, 5

Nicolls, Brigadier, his service in the West Indies, 438, 483

Nieuport, 226, 284-286 ; surrender of, 286

Nimeguen, 63, 301, 309, 311, 312, 315

Nivelles, 287

Nomain, 103

Nouvion, 234

Novarese, Austria's greed for the, 139

Nugent, Colonel, raises the Eighty-fifth Foot, 210

Oakes, Brigadier-general, his service in Egypt, 819 n., 822

O'Hara, General, Sir Charles, his service at Toulon, 167, 168, 170

Onnaing, 103

Ooi, 312

Orange, the Prince of (Stadtholder), his preternatural dulness and apathy, 64 ; takes refuge in England, 387

Orange, the Hereditary Prince of, his part in the Netherlands campaign of 1793, 110, 111, 120 ; of 1794, 300-302 ; his part in the North Holland campaign of 1799, 668

Orchies, 103, 226, 279, 281

Osnabrück, 323

Ostend, 112, 113, 148-150, 279-282, 284

Osterhout, 301

Lightning Source UK Ltd.
Milton Keynes UK
18 August 2010
158577UK00001B/31/P